About Chekhov

THE UNFINISHED SYMPHONY

Ivan Bunin

Edited and translated from the Russian
by Thomas Gaiton Marullo

NORTHWESTERN UNIVERSITY PRESS / EVANSTON, ILLINOIS

Northwestern University Press
www.nupress.northwestern.edu

ISBN-13: 978-0-8101-2382-3 (cloth)
ISBN-10: 0-8101-2382-7 (cloth)
ISBN-13: 978-0-8101-2388-5 (paper)
ISBN-10: 0-8101-2388-6 (paper)

Library of Congress Cataloging-in-Publication Data

Bunin, Ivan Alekseevich, 1870–1953.
　　[O Chekhove. English]
　　About Chekhov : the unfinished symphony / Ivan Bunin ; edited and
translated from the Russian by Thomas Gaiton Marullo.
　　　　p. cm.—(Studies in Russian literature and theory)
　　Includes bibliographical references and index.
　　ISBN 978-0-8101-2388-5 (pbk. : alk. paper)—
ISBN 978-0-8101-2382-3 (cloth : alk. paper)
　　1. Chekhov, Anton Pavlovich, 1860–1904. 2. Bunin, Ivan Alekseevich, 1870–
1953—Friends and associates. 3. Authors, Russian—19th century—Biography.
I. Marullo, Thomas Gaiton. II. Title. III. Series.
PG3458.B8413　2007
891.72'3—dc22　　　　　　　　　　　　　　　　　　　　　2006102078

For Angela Cannon, scholar and colleague

Contents

Editor's Preface

On April 27, 1911, seven years after the death of Anton Chekhov, his sister, Maria, wrote to the writer and bibliographer Pyotr Bykov, "You asked for someone who could write a biography of my deceased brother. If you recall, I recommended Iv. Al. Bunin. . . . Now I even ask you to do it. No one writes better than he; he knew and understood my deceased brother very well; he can go about the endeavor objectively. . . . I repeat, I would very much like this biography to correspond to reality and to be written by I. A. Bunin."[1]

Almost fifty years would pass before Maria's dream would be realized. Although Bunin had discussed and written about Chekhov at various intervals throughout his life,[2] it was not until 1947 that he decided to write a full-length work on the writer. The impetus for his decision was a book entitled *Chekhov as Recalled by His Contemporaries*, edited by one Leonid Kotov in Moscow.[3]

At first glance, the work had little to recommend itself. Indeed, its

1. At the same time, Maria had also asked Bunin to write the introduction for an edition of Chekhov's letters she had been editing. Bunin agreed, but the idea for such a piece was scrapped when the work became a series of biographical essays that attended each volume of the edition. See Maria Chekhova, "Iz dalekogo proshlogo," in *Vokrug Chekhova*, ed. E. Sakhorova (Moscow: Pravda, 1990), 363–64. Also see N. Gitovich, "I. A. Bunin: Iz nezakonchennoi knigi o Chekhove," in *Literaturnoe nasledstvo: Anton Chekhov*, vol. 68, ed. N. Vinogradov et al. (Moscow: Akademii Nauk SSSR, 1960), 640.

2. Bunin had previously published his recollections of Chekhov, entitled "Pamiati Chekhova," in *Sbornik tovarishchestva "Znanie" za 1904 god*, bk. 3 (St. Petersburg: Tovarishchestvo, 1905); *Pamiati Chekhova* (Moscow: Obshchesto liubitelei rossisskoi slovesnosti, 1906); "Iz zapisnoi knizhki," in *Sobranie sochinenii v shesti tomakh*, vol. 6 (Moscow: A. F. Marks, 1915); and *Reminiscences of Anton Chekhov by Maxim Gorky, Alexander Kuprin, and I. A. Bunin*, ed. and trans. S. Koteliansky and L. Woolf (New York: B. W. Huebsch, 1921).

Also, on May 29, 1934, Bunin had approached Gleb Struve with a suggestion to translate and publish his memoirs of the writer. See G. Struve, "Iz perepiski s I. A. Buninym," *Annali* 11 (1968): 26.

3. See L. Kotov, ed., *Chekhov v vospominaniiakh sovremennikov* (Moscow: Gosurdarstvennoe izdatel'stvo khudozhesvennoi literatury, 1947).

gray-green cover seemed as lifeless and drab as the bolshevized land from which it had come. When Bunin opened Kotov's *Chekhov*, though, he experienced a bittersweet surprise. Before his eyes were resurrected not only the writer of *The Cherry Orchard* but also the world of prerevolutionary Russia, peopled by individuals he had known only too well. There were members of Chekhov's family: his brother Mikhail and his sister, Maria. There was his wife, the actress Olga Knipper. There were the painter Ilya Repin and the stage directors Konstantin Stanislavsky and Vladimir Nemirovich-Danchenko. Most poignantly, perhaps, there were the writers with whom Bunin had ridden the political and aesthetic waves that had engulfed patriarchal Russia and with whom he had laughed and cried, embraced and fought in the last three or so decades of both its existence and his life there. Some, such as Maxim Gorky, Vladimir Korolenko, and Alexander Kuprin, still held center stage with readers. Others, including Nikolai Teleshov, Vikenty Veresaev, Ignaty Potapenko, Sergei Elpatievsky, and Stepan Skitalets, had faded into oblivion. Finally, Kotov's *Chekhov* included the memoirs of an old friend, Lydia Avilova, who was also a writer and who, much to Bunin's surprise, disclosed that she had been Chekhov's one and only love.

Bunin took grim satisfaction in that of all the contributors to Kotov's *Chekhov as Recalled by His Contemporaries,* only Maria Chekhova, Nikolai Teleshov, and Olga Knipper were still alive. (Chekhova died in 1957, Teleshov in 1957, and Knipper in 1959.) He was distressed, though, by what he saw as a key flaw of the work, namely, that Bunin himself, as a close friend of Chekhov's as well as Russia's first Nobel laureate (1933), had not been included among the writer's "contemporaries."

In truth, Bunin should have not have been surprised by Kotov's omission. Totally opposed to the Bolsheviks, Bunin had left Russia in 1920 to live as an exile in France. From there he had taken every opportunity to condemn both the Bolsheviks and the Soviet state, often with a vehemence that even his fellow exiles found excessive. Even in the conciliatory years between Soviets and émigrés in the years immediately following World War II, Bunin remained adamant in his stance toward the homeland. True, he had cheered the Russian victory over the Germans and had even thought about a return to the country of his birth; but he also knew that the shadows of Lenin and Stalin still loomed large in the minds and hearts of its citizens. Party officials had responded in kind. In 1947, Bunin was still persona non grata, the rat who had left the Soviet ship to live abroad with capitalists and counterrevolutionaries.

As was often the case with Bunin, though, what he experienced as a loss for himself was a gain for the world. The fact that he not been included in Kotov's *Chekhov as Recalled by His Contemporaries* was the impetus for him to realize a long-standing idea: Bunin himself would write the work to explain Chekhov and his art to the world.

Although Bunin died before he finished *About Chekhov*,[4] the work is important for several reasons. Bunin sought to rescue Chekhov from what he saw as three limiting mind-sets that, like a cancer, continued to feed upon the writer's popularity, reputation, and assessments of his work. First, there were the conflicting political, social, and aesthetic views of Westerners, Soviets, and émigrés on Chekhov and his art. Westerners saw Chekhov as a child of the "cherry orchard," who bemoaned the lot of dysfunctional aristocrats in the twilight of patriarchal Russia. The Soviets looked to Chekhov as a budding Bolshevik, that is, as a writer who condemned the rot of his land and who saw the need for "bright futures" as well as for sweeping (read: socialist) change for its citizens. The émigrés regarded Chekhov as a victim of his time and place, a person who, as they did, had withstood dislocation in Russia before the revolution and who, in their view, would surely have joined them into exile after.

The second stereotype Bunin sought to destroy in *About Chekhov* was the deifying cult of the writer—"the Chekhovian hagiography," one scholar wrote[5]—that seems to be the fate of every major literary figure in Russia. Bunin attempted to cast Chekhov instead as an everyman awash in the joys and sorrows, triumphs and tragedies of existence. Further, Bunin wished to

4. Bunin began *About Chekhov* in 1952 and planned to finish the work two years later. Bunin's wife Vera Muromtseva-Bunina recalls that during the many sleepless nights in the last year of his life, Bunin recalled conversations with Chekhov, making notes on scraps of paper, even on cigarette wrappers. She also notes that on the night Bunin died, she had been reading Chekhov's letters to her husband in his study. See Muromtseva-Bunina's introduction to I. Bunin, *O Chekhove* (New York: Izdatel'stvo imeni Chekhova, 1955), 29.

Also see A. Baboreko, "Poslednie gody I. A. Bunina (Novye materialy)," *Voprosy literatury* 3 (1965): 255.

5. For instance, one critic wrote, "Chekhov's star could not be dimmed even in the Russian backwoods." A second noted, "Chekhov [is] . . . the living phenomenon of striking depth, beauty, and complexity." And a third asserted, "Chekhov was a hero—more than that, *the* hero of our time. . . . In fact, when measured by the standards of Christian morality, Chekhov was wholly a saint" (italics in original). See N. Abramovich, "Chelovecheskii put'," *Iubileinyi chekhovskii sbornik* (Moscow: Zaria, 1910), 3; B. Zaitsev, *Chekhov: Literaturnaia biografiia* (New York: Imeni Chekhova, 1954), 160; J. Middletown Murry, "The Humanity of Chekhov," *Athenaeum* 50 (1920): 300.

A key difficulty in the cult of Chekhov was not only that it cast the writer as gentle and bland, diffident and sexless, but that it also regarded Chekhov as the province of a select few who, by education, outlook, and the like, could discern the intricate patterns of his writing. For instance, Edmund Wilson wrote that Chekhov is read "almost exclusively by a specialized literary public, with whom he has sometime been a cult and by whom he has been regarded as the master of so exquisite an art, so far from obvious in its themes and technique, that one can only compare the attitude toward him to the attitude toward Henry James at the time when James had not yet come to figure as a pillar of the national pantheon." E. Wilson, "Seeing Chekhov Plain," *A Window on Russia* (New York: Farrar, Strauss, and Giroux, 1972), 53.

show that the saintly temper and sobriety with which Chekhov purportedly amazed all who knew him concealed a series of painful inner struggles about his life and work. His troubles with both men and women, his doubts about his plays and prose, and his fears of personal and artistic oblivion often cracked the fragile shell of his being, rendering him broken and vulnerable both to the mercy of fate and to the vicissitudes of life.

The final obstacle to what Bunin saw as a proper understanding of Chekhov was the widespread assumption that Chekhov, by both talent and inclination, preferred plays to prose, and that *The Seagull, The Three Sisters, Uncle Vanya,* and *The Cherry Orchard* held sway over *Ward Six,* "A Lady with a Dog," and other fictional masterpieces. Rather, Bunin concurred with Leo Tolstoy to proclaim not only that what Chekhov had written for newspapers, "thick" journals, anthologies, and the like was infinitely superior to what he had penned for the stage but also that his short stories were the true wellsprings of his art, revealing both his talent as an artist and his acumen as a critic of modernity.

For another thing, in *About Chekhov,* Bunin sought—for what would be the final time—to mount an apologia pro vita sua, that is, a stirring defense of his own thoughts and deeds on literature and life. Indeed, Bunin appealed to Chekhov to assure himself and others that what he had been doing for thirty years in Russia and an equal period of time in exile had been worthwhile, that he had risen to the challenge of the last nobleman in literature, and that he had willingly suffered everything that Chekhov had also endured for the sake of the national written expression. In his recollections of Chekhov, therefore, Bunin found peace, knowing that his own examined life had been worth living and that despite war and revolution in both life and art, he had kept both sensibility and sense.

I give *About Chekhov* the subtitle *An Unfinished Symphony* because as Bunin had done both in his fictional works and in such memoir-criticism as his 1937 *The Liberation of Tolstoy (Osvobozhdenie Tolstogo),* he fashioned his memoir as a moving orchestral work on the writer's existence and art. At times, Bunin's *About Chekhov* resounds as a requiem. At other times, it has the air of a pastorale. Still at other times, it harmonizes as a love song or romance. Whatever the musical measure, though, Bunin's goal is the same, namely, to celebrate Chekhov as both an artist and a man and to ensure his rightful place in Russian literary tradition. Indeed, even in its unfinished state, *About Chekhov* stands not only as a stirring testament of one writer's respect and affection for another but also as a living memorial to two highly creative artists.

I also note here that in *About Chekhov,* I have utilized only the salient features of the original memoir, focusing on the relationship between Bunin and Chekhov and omitting well-known biographical facts about Chekhov as well as citations from letters, memoirs, and criticism which either are available in English or do not shed light on the tie between the two men.

Throughout, I have used familiar spellings of proper names in the text and the body of the notes and more precise, scholarly transliterations in the citations. For this reason, many names appear with two spellings, for example, Vishnevsky, Vishnevskii.

Except where noted otherwise, all translations of quotations from Russian sources in the footnotes are mine.

For their invaluable assistance at various stages in the preparation of this work, I wish to acknowledge the members of the Slavic Reference Service of the Slavic Department of the Library of the University of Illinois. This work, along with my previous studies of Bunin, never would have seen the light of day were it not for the assistance of Helen Sullivan, Angela Cannon, Julia Dolinnaya, Maria Cristina Galmarini, and Jan Adamczyk, all of whom unearthed sources, researched footnotes, and answered myriad questions about Bunin, Chekhov, and the times in which the two men lived. Their passion and patience, energy and good cheer sustained me throughout the preparation of this work. These wonderful people also filled me with admiration and awe at their professionalism, expertise, and dedication to me, the realm of scholarship, and the field of Russian studies. Indeed, I would not be where I am personally and professionally were it not for the assistance and encouragement that the members of the Slavic Reference Service at the University of Illinois have extended to me so lovingly and unstintingly in my now thirty-two years as a professor of Russian and Russian literature.

I also owe a profound debt of gratitude to Professor Gary Saul Morson of Northwestern University, who read the initial draft of my translation of *About Chekhov* and who helped to shape the present study; to freelance editor Lori Meek Schuldt and to Sue Betz, Anne Gendler, and Parneshia Jones at Northwestern University Press, who produced this manuscript and who also allowed excerpts of it to be published in *The Paris Review;* to Professor Gregory Sterling, associate dean of the College of Arts and Letters here at Notre Dame, who provided funds for research; to Cheryl Reed, who prepared the manuscript; and to James Stevens, Sheila Dawes, and Steven Atwood, who served as research assistants for this project and who, like the members of the Slavic Reference Service, handled my endless requests with grace, energy, and aplomb.

I also wish to cite my wife, Gloria Gibbs Marullo, whose dire hatred of Bunin is superseded only by her enduring support of me in yet another work on his life and art. Since the start of our time together—we were both studying in Leningrad in 1977–1978—when I told Gloria that I wanted to be a scholar in Russian literature, she has never wavered from being a loyal spouse, colleague, and friend who saw my studies on Bunin and other Russian writers through to successful completion.

Additionally, I thank my cats: Bernadette Marie, Monica Anne, Benedict Joseph, Gonzaga Gaiton, Francis Xavier, and finally, Margaret Mary, who in August 2005 joined her brothers Ignatius Gaiton and Augustine Gaiton in heaven. These people with fur are as tired of Bunin as Gloria is, but in their own wonderful way, they know that they also have a job to do, namely, as Tolstoy once advised Bunin, to teach me not to take life too seriously but to enjoy the moment and all that life has to offer.

Finally, it is with special fondness that I again cite Angela Cannon, now Slavic Reference Librarian at the Library of Congress, who joins the Rublev-like trinity of Helen Sullivan and Julia Gauchman and to whom, as I have done with her colleagues in previous studies of Bunin, I now wish to dedicate *About Chekhov*. Angela's assistance in this study went beyond the possible and expected, normal and sane. Indeed, it seems that not a day went by when I did not receive at least one e-mail from Angela with responses to questions which defied answers and which, in the final analysis, have invested this edition of Bunin with a flair and thoroughness it would not have had otherwise.

From the bottom of my heart, thank you one and all.

T.G.M.

Editor's Introduction: Bunin and Chekhov

Although Ivan Bunin and Anton Chekhov had corresponded since 1891, they did not meet until December 12, 1895. (Bunin was twenty-five, Chekhov was ten years older.) Initial contacts were less than promising. In early January 1891, a cloying if obsequious Bunin had written to Chekhov, "Beginning 'writers' have the habit of plaguing editors, poets, and writers . . . with requests to read their work and to give them an 'objective' opinion of it. . . . I am one of those people; and although I realize that such requests are sometimes tactless and rude . . . I am making it nonetheless. . . . Since you are my favorite contemporary writer, and since I have heard . . . that you are a simple and good man, I have 'chosen' you. If you have time to look at my work, if but only once, I ask that you please do so. For God's sake, tell me if I can send you two or three of my (published) stories, and if you can read them when you have nothing to do, and give me your comments. Forgive my impudence, deeply respected Anton Pavlovich, and look kindly upon my request."[1]

Within the month, Chekhov replied, "I am happy to be of service, but I must warn you that I am a poor critic who always makes mistakes, especially when it comes to . . . beginning writers."[2] Bunin never sent the stories.

A first meeting between Bunin (accompanied by Konstantin Balmont) and Chekhov in December 1895 accomplished little other than for the young writers to present the object of their admiration with copies of their works.[3] A second encounter in April 1899 in Yalta, though, engendered an intense friendship between Bunin and Chekhov that continued until Chekhov's death in 1904.

---

1. A. Baboreko, "Iz perepiski I. A. Bunina," *Novyi mir* 10 (1956): 199.

2. Much of Chekhov's correspondence appears in the collection A. Chekhov, *Polnoe sobranie sochinenii v tridtsati tomakh: Pis'ma v dvenadtsati tomakh,* 30 vols. (Moscow: Nauka, 1974–83), hereafter cited as *Pis'ma* (12 vols.) with volume and page number. For Chekhov's reply to Bunin's initial letter, see Chekhov to Bunin, January 30, 1891, *Pis'ma,* 4:171–72.

3. See N. Bel'chikov et al., eds., *Chekhov i ego sreda. Sbornik* (Leningrad: Akademiia, 1930), 216, 222.

At first glance, Bunin and Chekhov could not have been more different. As regards upbringing, both men were like the class-based characters of
The Cherry Orchard come to life. Bunin was from a gentry family on the
way down. His father, Alexei Nikolaevich Bunin, was a lighthearted ne'er-do-
well who drank, played the guitar, and lost what little resources the family
had. Bunin's upbringing was similarly laissez-faire. He prepared neither for
the university nor for a profession. Rather, as a gentry "hero of his time," he
wandered Russia, responsible only for himself.

By contrast, Chekhov came from peasants on the way up. Only a generation before, his grandfather, Egor Mikhailovich Chekhov, had purchased
freedom for his family. His son and Chekhov's father, Pavel Egorovich
Chekhov, was also a mix of old and new. On the one hand, Pavel was a
samodur or "tyrant" who neither spared the rod nor spoiled the child.
Indeed, any dereliction on the part of Chekhov-*fils* provoked self-righteous
rebuke, cuffing, and strapping from Chekhov-*père*. "I remember that when
I was five years old, my father began to teach me, or to put it more plainly,
whip me," Chekhov wrote autobiographically in his 1895 story *Three Years*
(*Tri goda*). "When I woke up every morning, the first question I asked myself was: 'Will I be whipped today?'"[4] On the other hand, Pavel was not only
attuned to the new opportunities in his land but also determined that Anton
and his siblings would have better lives than he. His dreams became a reality: all six children became educated professionals.[5]

The life of the Chekhov family, though, was often Dickensian: hand-
to-mouth, pillar-to-post.[6] Unlike the wandering and carefree Bunin,
Chekhov knew duty and drudgery, not freedom and fun. When the young
Chekhov was not devoting days and nights to the family store, he was spending his waking hours in church, benumbed by endless ritual and services. "I
have no religion now," Chekhov pronounced summarily to Ivan Leontiev-
Shcheglov in 1892. "When [in church] my two brothers and I sang 'Let My
Prayer Arise' or 'The Archangel's Voice,' everyone . . . was moved. People
envied my parents, but we felt like convicts. . . . For us, childhood was sheer

4. "Despotism . . . so disfigured our childhood that it makes me sick and horrified to think of
it," Chekhov wrote to his brother Alexander on January 2, 1889. "Remember the disgust and
horror we felt every time father made a scene at dinner because there was too much salt in the
soup or called mother a fool." See A. Chekhov, *Polnoe sobranie sochinenii v tridtsati tomakh:
Sochineniia v vosemnadtsati tomakh,* 30 vols. (Moscow: Nauka, 1983–88), 9:39, hereafter cited
as *Sochineniia* (18 vols.) with volume and page numbers; Chekhov to Alexander Chekhov,
January 2, 1889, *Pis'ma,* 3:122.

5. Alexander and Anton were writers. Nikolai became a painter, Mikhail a civil servant, and
Maria and Ivan teachers.

6. For instance, when the Chekhov family arrived in Moscow, they changed lodgings twelve
times in three years.

suffering."[7] Wiggling their toes was the only way the brothers could protest their situation.[8] Indeed, it was not for nothing, Chekhov asserted years later, that "many seminary students become atheists."[9]

Further, from the age of sixteen to his dying day twenty-eight years later, "father Antosha" was fated to be the practical and moral head of his often dysfunctional household. As both a writer and a doctor, he kept the family afloat in the rough seas that surrounded them. "You have a *wife*, who pardons you if you have no money," Chekhov wrote to Leontiev-Shcheglov in 1888. "But I have an entire *regime* that weighs about my neck like a millstone, and that, if I do not earn a certain number of rubles a month, will collapse and crash down upon my shoulders."[10] Self-sacrifice was for Chekhov often the order of the day. Like Gogol's Akaky Akakievich, it once took the writer an entire year to save up the money for an overcoat.[11]

Chekhov also was not averse to reining in members of the family—magisterial sermons to brothers Alexander and Nikolai were key examples—when their drinking, philandering, and the like threatened to destroy themselves and others. The same irresistible urge Chekhov had in himself to move from rags to riches (physical and spiritual) he sought not only for his family but for all he encountered in life. Indeed, it may be seen as more a comment on Chekhov's life than on his fiction when W. H. Auden remarked, "The best Russian writer is Chekhov because he is the only one who has the least bit of common sense."[12]

Bunin and Chekhov were even more unlike in personality and beliefs. Bunin believed that he was the center of the universe. In fact, whenever he felt unfulfilled in his unending wants and needs, he was unbelievably cruel to intimates. Also, the heavy chip Bunin carried on his shoulder cast him as a pessimist who saw himself as a pawn of life: a victim of disaster behind every horizon. He was particularly haunted by death. Throughout his eighty-three

7. Chekhov to Leontiev-Shcheglov, March 9, 1982, *Pis'ma*, 5:20.

8. See the memoirs of Chekhov's aunt, Marfa Chekhova, in B. Lidin, ed., *Chekhov i nash krai* (Rostov-na-Donu: Azovo-Chernomorskoe kraevo, 1935), 26–28.

9. Chekhov to Suvorin, March 17, 1902, *Pis'ma*, 5:25.

10. Chekhov to Leontiev-Shcheglov, April 18, 1888, *Pis'ma*, 2:249. For all his complaining, though, Chekhov enjoyed not only his position as paterfamilias of his clan but also sharing his time between what he saw as the two loves of his life, literature and medicine. As he himself noted cavalierly, literature was his mistress and medicine his wife. "When I grow weary of one," he wrote to Suvorin five months later, "I spend the night with the other. Although this may seem somewhat bizarre, it is not boring, and besides, neither of them loses anything from my infidelity." Chekhov to Suvorin, September 18, 1888, *Pis'ma*, 2:326.

11. Chekhov to Nikolai Leikin, March 7, 1884, in Maria Chekhova, *Pis'ma A. P. Chekhova v shesti tomakh*, vol. 1 (Moscow: Izdatel'stvo M. P. Chekhovoi, 1914), 59.

12. See W. H. Auden, "A Russian with Common Sense," *New Yorker*, no. 28 (September 3, 1973): 62.

years, Bunin believed that he had one foot in the grave, the other on a cabbage peel. All too frequently, he first "left" this world in fevers, fainting, and the like and then recorded, in intimate detail, his terror at self-annihilation and nothingness. Not surprisingly, Bunin was terrified of age and ailing. He panicked at every sniffle; he feared corpses and wakes; he even shunned flowers and furniture if they impressed him as funereal. As a result, it became Bunin's strategy to seek out times and places other than his own. He relished the religions and myths of the Near and Far East, particularly Buddhism.[13] He was also attuned to higher powers, praising God when things went right and damning the Deity when things went wrong.

Unlike Bunin, Chekhov was a consummate gentleman who received people and events with almost pathological reticence and self-effacement. Whereas his younger colleague burst out crying over a moving sunset or song, Chekhov never let tears stream down his face. Further in contrast to Bunin, Chekhov kept his ego in check. For instance, he wrote to Bykov in 1892, "Will you be so kind as to point out to the people in your office [of your journal] that the advertisement in which I am described as 'highly talented' and in which the title of my story is printed in poster-size letters has made a most unpleasant impression on me. It looks like an advertisement of a dentist or a masseur; and besides, it is in bad taste. I know the value of advertisements and I am not against them, but I consider modesty and standards . . . to be the best and most effective advertisement for a literary person."[14] Three years later, he chastised Lydia Avilova: "Why did you call me a 'proud master'? Only turkeys are proud."[15]

Even at the pinnacle of his fame, Chekhov never forgot what he believed were the limits of his talent. He was his own severest critic. He became nervous with any praise of a story or a play, moving his admirers to other topics [16] for fear that fate, the critics,[17] or the "evil eye" would lower

---

13. See T. Marullo, *If You See the Buddha: Studies in the Fiction of Ivan Bunin* (Evanston, Ill: Northwestern University Press, 1998).

14. Chekhov to Bykov, *Pis'ma*, 5:59.

15. As quoted in L. Avilova, "Moi vospominaniia," in *O Chekhove: Vospominaniia i stat'i* (Moscow: Sovremennoe tvorchestvo, 1910), 10.

16. For instance, on May 25, 1928, Bunin told Galina Kuznetsova,

One time a visitor rushed up to Chekhov and said, "Oh, my dear Chekhov, what artistic pleasure your last story gave us."

But Chekhov immediately interrupted, "Tell me, where do you buy your herring? I will tell you where I get mine. At A.'s; he has fat, delicate ones."

Whenever someone talked to Chekhov about his works, he started talking about herring. He did not like to talk about his writings. (G. Kuznetsova, *Grasskii dnevnik* [Washington, D.C: Victor Kamkin, 1967], 62)

17. For instance, Chekhov told Maxim Gorky, "Critics are like gadflies which stop a horse from plowing. The horse strains, muscles tensed like double-bass strings. Meanwhile there's a

the boom on him. "I am too lucky," Chekhov wrote to Alexei Suvorin in 1888. "I begin to cast suspicious glances toward heaven. And I shall hide myself quickly under the table and sit there tamely and quietly, without raising my voice."[18] In fact, regarding his works, Chekhov often feared success more than failure. "When I am not successful," Chekhov wrote to Kazimir Barantsevich in 1889, "I am much braver than when I am. Success turns me into a coward and fills me with a strong desire to hide under the table."[19]

Above all, Chekhov sought to be an everyman in life. In his view, his tragedies and triumphs, weaknesses and strengths made him part of the crowd, not above it. "I have wasted my life in idleness, laughed mindlessly, made a glutton of myself, and indulged in drunkenness and fornication," Chekhov wrote to Leontiev-Shcheglov in 1890. "But . . . as far as morality is concerned, I am distinguished from the ranks neither by pluses or minuses, nor by feats or infamies. I am just like the majority of my race."[20] More positively, he continued to his colleague, "I am simply human. I like nature, literature, beautiful women, and hate routine and despotism."[21] In fact, Chekhov believed that if he had one characteristic that separated him from the rest of society (including Bunin), it was his lack of animosity toward humankind.

What Chekhov expected of himself, he expected of others. He loathed all forms of braggadocio and coarseness, especially from his fellow writers. "Coarse anecdotes never provoked even a smile," Gorky recalled in his memoirs of the writer.[22] Chekhov also mocked the Russian propensity for overblown speeches, toasts, and eulogies. (He once told Nemirovich-Danchenko that he was more afraid of the oration over his grave than of his actual passing.)[23] Further, as much as Chekhov delighted in seeing theater

---

wretched gadfly tickling and buzzing on his cupper, so he has to twitch his skin and flick his tail. But what's all the buzzing about? The gadfly hardly knows. It just feels restless and wants to proclaim its existence while asserting its ability to buzz away on any subject in the world." M. Gor'kii, "A. P. Chekhov," *Polnoe sobranie sochinenii v dvadtsati piati tomakh,* 25 vols. (Moscow: Nauka, 1968–1976), 6:51–52, hereafter cited as *Polnoe sobranie sochinenii* with volume and page numbers.

18. Chekhov to Suvorin, October 10, 1888, *Pis'ma,* 3:23. Cf. Chekhov to Alexander Lazarev-Gruzinsky, October 20, 1888, *Pis'ma,* 3:38: "I am fortune's obscure favorite who has jumped out of the bowels of the humorous papers. . . . I am a *bourgeois-gentilhomme,* and like any in this group, do not hold for very long, like a string that is stretched in a hurry."

19. Chekhov to Barantsevich, February 3, 1889, *Pis'ma,* 3:141.

20. Chekhov to Leontiev-Shcheglov, March 22, 1890, *Pis'ma,* 4:44.

21. I. Leontiev-Shcheglov, "Iz vospominanii ob Antone Chekhove," *Ezhemesiachnye literaturnye i populiarno-nauchnye prilozheniia k zhurnalu "Niva",* no. 7 (July 1905): 416.

22. Consider also Chekhov's embarrassed silence over Tolstoy's coarse bragging over his sexual exploits as a youth. See M. Gor'kii, "Lev Tolstoi," *Polnoe sobranie sochinenii,* 16:270. Also see Gor'kii, "A. P. Chekhov," *Polnoe sobranie sochinenii,* 6:60.

23. V. Nemirovich-Danchenko, "Chekhov," in Kotov, *A. P. Chekhov,* 72 (see preface, n. 3).

resemble life, he despised when life resembled theater. Any kind of unpleasantness and confrontation—such as the disagreements among doctors
as to his treatment or producers as to his plays; or the rancor between his
wife, on one side, and his mother and sister, on the other, for his love, affection, and routine—upset him terribly and exacerbated his already weakened condition. Invariably, Chekhov brought out the best of Bunin or
whomever else he was with. In the writer's presence, Gorky recalled, "everyone involuntarily felt a desire to be simpler, more truthful, more oneself."[24]

Further, whereas Bunin railed against life, Chekhov accepted with
equanimity what he saw as his fate as déclassé,[25] that he had to work harder
than others to succeed both personally and professionally. "What gentry-
born writers have been endowed with by nature," he wrote to Suvorin in
1889, "self-made intellectuals buy at the price of their youth." In fact, when
Chekhov suggested to Suvorin the plotline for a short story, he was telling
the saga of his own tragedy-turned-triumph. "Write a story about a young
man," he continued to his addressee, "the son of a serf, a former shopkeeper,
a choirboy, and a high school and university student. [Write how this indi-
vidual] respects rank, kisses the hands of priests, belongs to a generation
alien to thought, offers thanks for every mouthful of bread, suffers beatings,
goes to school without shoes, engages in street fights, torments animals,
loves dining with rich relatives, and plays the hypocrite before God and society—all without any cause, other than the recognition of his own insignificance. Then tell how this young man presses the toady out of him, drop
by drop, and how, one fine morning, he wakes up to feel his veins flowing
with the blood of a human, not a slave."[26]

Also unlike his younger colleague, Chekhov met life's challenges head-
on, his steadiness and self-assurance insuring success and commanding the
loyalty of all who came his way. He realized many dreams, material and aesthetic. Before Chekhov reached the age of thirty, he had both a steady income and the satisfaction that publishers were competing for his works.
Whereas Bunin never had a home to call his own, Chekhov became a
landowner at the age of thirty-two and later purchased other properties to
fashion as oases to work, relax, and entertain.[27]

24. Gor'kii, "A. P. Chekhov," *Polnoe sobranie sochinenii,* 6:47.

25. "Our existence is not easy," Chekhov wrote to Barantsevich on February 9, 1890 (*Pis'ma,*
4:16), "but you and I were not born into the vale of tears to experience the happiness of horse-
guardsmen or actresses of the French theater. We are lower middle class: we shall remain and
die like them. Such is fate."

26. Chekhov to Suvorin, January 7, 1889, *Pis'ma,* 3:133.

27. In 1899, Nicholas II conferred upon Chekhov the order of Stanislaus third class which,
although being the least distinctive of such awards in imperial Russia, elevated the writer to the
rank of "hereditary nobleman." Revealingly, though, Chekhov never told his relatives or friends
of his new social station.

Chekhov also had a faith in humankind that was strong but sensible. To paraphrase a popular prayer, he had the serenity to accept the things he could not change, the courage to change the things he could, and the wisdom to know the difference. The Deity, though, did not figure prominently in Chekhov's life. Schools of theology and philosophy also earned his scorn. "You cannot make heads or tails of anything in this life," Chekhov wrote to Leontiev-Shcheglov in 1881. "Only fools and charlatans know and understand everything."[28] To Suvorin, he wrote, "It is easy to be pure when you can hate a devil you do not know and love a God whom it never occurs to you to doubt."[29]

It was, rather, the earth beneath Chekhov and what he saw as the natural order of things that were the grounding for his activities and beliefs.[30] "Outside of matter there is no experience or knowledge, and consequently, no truth," Chekhov wrote to Suvorin in 1889. "When a doctor dissects a corpse, even the most inveterate spiritualist must *necessarily* ask where the soul is."[31] In line with such materialism, Chekhov "liked Darwin terribly."[32] He relished sociology, zoology, horticulture, psychiatry, and the philosophy of science. He also championed willpower, education, and science as catalysts for moral and material progress of humankind. "Natural sciences are performing miracles everyday," Chekhov proclaimed to Suvorin in 1894. "Like some invader, they march upon people and conquer it by their grandeur and overwhelming force."[33] In fact, Chekhov was so convinced of

28. Chekhov to Leontiev-Shcheglov, June 9, 1881, *Pis'ma*, 2:283.

29. Chekhov to Suvorin, September 11, 1888, *Pis'ma*, 2:327.

30. This is not to say, however, that Chekhov turned his back on things otherworldly in his life and art. Indeed, such a 1902 story as "The Archbishop" ("Arkhierei") is so imbued with a churchlike aura that it seems the work of a man of faith and prayer, not a confirmed skeptic.

Further, Chekhov believed that if the Deity did exist, the Almighty was belittled by human attempts to understand such a being. Faith, he believed, was the province only of "highly developed natures."

Chekhov had sufficient faith in the human race, though, to see modern culture as the starting point for a time "in the distant future [when] humankind will perceive the truth of the real God, that is, not make conjectures or search for the Almighty in the manner of Dostoevsky but perceive the Deity as clearly as they perceive that twice two makes four." See Chekhov, *Sochineniia*, 17:169. Also see Chekhov to Sergei Diaghilev, December 30, 1902, in *Pis'ma*, 11:106.

31. Chekhov to Suvorin, May 7, 1889, *Pis'ma*, 3:208.

32. Compare the remark of von Koren, the hero of the 1891 story "The Duel": "If you believe that there is a purpose for everything that happens in the world, it is obvious that nature is doing everything in its power to rid itself of all weaklings and organisms for which it has no use. Famines, cholera, influenza. . . . Only the healthy and strong will be left. And it is impossible not to believe in purposefulness." Chekhov, *Sochineniia*, 7:406–7. Also see Chekhov to Viktor Bilibin, March 11, 1886, *Pis'ma*, 1:212.

33. Chekhov to Suvorin, *Pis'ma*, March 28, 1894, 5:282.

an inner logic to the world that he once spent days devising a system to win at roulette in Monte Carlo.[34]

Even death Chekhov received with the stoic serenity of an agnostic. Unlike Bunin, he did not wish to live forever.[35] Rather, he faced his increasingly numbered days not only with a serene lack of faith but also with the time-honored knowledge that death is the ultimate—and inevitable—woe in life. "After summer, comes winter; after youth, old age; after happiness, unhappiness," Chekhov wrote to sister Maria in 1898. "Even if one were Alexander the Great, he cannot avoid death. One must be prepared for anything and, however sad it may be, to accept all as unavoidable and necessary. According to one's strength, one must fulfill one's duty—nothing more."[36]

Neither sickness nor death, though, could deter Chekhov for any length of time. With almost reckless indifference, he derided or dismissed his tuberculosis—a disease which ended his life at the age of forty-four—summoning forth disarming rationalizations even when coughing convulsed his body and blood streamed from his mouth. "There are times when I cough blood," he wrote to Elena Shavrova-Iust in 1897, "but it bears no relation to how I feel, and I go prancing about like an unmarried calf. . . . Oh, how fortunate I am not married yet. How convenient!"[37]

---

34. Potapenko recalled in his memoirs:

> Monte Carlo had a depressing effect on Chekhov, but it would be untrue to say that he was immune from the poison [of gambling]. Like every other writer, he dreamed of being able to write without having to earn a living. . . . For hours on end we pored over the paper with pencils in our hands, trying to find a system. . . . [When we thought we had found one] we went to Monte Carlo . . . and lost a few hundred francs. Once again we pored over the paper, writing down numbers. We tried another system. . . . We won for two days, but on the third we lost again. At this point, Chekhov refused to listen to my theories and sat down to work on his own system.
>
> Sometimes he refused to accompany me to Monte Carlo. I would go there alone, but an hour later, he appeared, looking a little embarrassed, stopping at one of the tables and watching the game for a long time as though checking up on some idea of his. Then he sat down, took out a few gold coins, and placed them in a special order on the roulette table. I believe he did win something. At this point, a gambler usually loses all self-control and becomes completely obsessed with the game. Not so Chekhov. One day he told me firmly that he was finished with the roulette, and he never returned there again. His common sense asserted itself, and, above all, he was ashamed to waste his time on trifles.
>
> (I. Potapenko, "Neskol'ko let s A.P. Chekhovym," in Kotov, *A. P. Chekhov*, 249–50)

35. "Death is terrible," Chekhov wrote in his notebooks. "But still more terrible is the feeling that one may live forever and never die." Chekhov, *Sochineniia*, 17:169.

36. Chekhov to Maria Chekhova, November 13, 1898, *Pis'ma*, 7:327. Compare Ivan Dmitrich's comment to Andrei Ragin in Chekhov's 1892 story "Ward No. 6" (Palata No. 6): "Hunger, cold, injury, loss, fear of death . . . why, these feelings are the very essence of being a man. They are the whole of life, these sensations are. Life may irk you, you may loathe it, but despite it, you must not." Chekhov, *Sochineniia*, 8:101–2.

37. Chekhov to Elena Shavrovna-Iust, October 29, 1897, *Pis'ma*, 7:88. Chekhov also refused all serious, sustained treatment for his affliction. "To treat my physical being fills me with

In one sense, Chekhov's tuberculosis was a blessing. Whether he looked past his steadily deteriorating condition with denial or fear, one thing is certain: he rebelled against his fate by living a "lie of health" to enjoy a semblance of happiness on earth. The life of an invalid was not for Chekhov. He never thought of entering a sanatorium; doctors and drugs were for his patients, not for him. Rather, his preference was to live life vigorously even at the risk of shortening it. Indeed, it was only by closing his eyes to his illness that Chekhov could maintain a desire for work, friends, and success. Pride and willpower drove him to overcome insurmountable obstacles. As if expecting a recovery, he planted gardens, entertained guests, and planned trips. Defying doctors, he traveled to savage Sakhalin and to cold and damp Moscow and St. Petersburg. Chekhov claimed improved health and even complete cures amid the sun, spas, and fermented mare's milk (*koumiss*) in such consumptive-friendly localities as the Crimea, the Caucasus, and Nice.[38] Even several days before he died in Badenweiler, Germany, he wrote his mother of physical resurrection and renewal, "My health is improving so rapidly that I will be entirely well within a week."[39]

It was also the writer's life-affirming imagination that caused Chekhov not only to write stories and plays but also to transform the terror of premature death into a mirage of purpose as well as of limitless time in which to make his mark on his world. "I am clever enough," Chekhov boasted to Suvorin in 1892, "not to lie or conceal my illness from myself or to cover it up with the rages of others, such as the ideas of the 'sixties' and the like. I will not throw myself down a flight of stairs like Garshin did, nor will I flatter myself with hopes for a better future. I am not to blame for my disease and it is not for me to cure myself [from this affliction]. So I must assume that this disease was not sent [to me] in vain, but that it is has good purposes that are hidden from us."[40]

During his last years, Chekhov brimmed with plans for new places to live and for fresh experiences to bring him new friends and literary material. Even when the bacillus had gotten the best of him, he wrote to Olga

---

repugnance," Chekhov wrote to Suvorin in 1891. "I will drink mineral water, but I refuse to let anyone examine me" (Chekhov to Suvorin, November 18, 1891, *Pis'ma,* 4:296–97). He similarly complained to Suvorin eight years later, "I am bored with the role of the man who, instead of living, 'vegetates for the sake of his health'" (Chekhov to Suvorin, April 2, 1899, *Pis'ma,* 8:43).

Such optimism did not mean, however, that Chekhov did not rebel against his fate. "Living with the idea that one must die is far from pleasant," he told Gorky, "but living and knowing that one will die before one's time is utterly ridiculous." Quoted in Gor'kii, "A. P. Chekhov," *Polnoe sobranie sochinenii,* 6:59.

38. See, for instance, Chekhov to O. Knipper, September 22, 1902, *Pis'ma,* 11:44.

39. Chekhov to E. Chekhova, June 13, 1904, *Pis'ma,* 12:123.

40. Chekhov to Suvorin, November 25, 1892, *Pis'ma,* 5:134.

Knipper on April 22, 1901, that he still wished "to swallow life at the rate of one tablespoon an hour."[41]

Death also confirmed Chekhov's agnosticism and doubt in an afterlife. Although he suffered greatly with the passing of family and friends—the premature (and tubercular) demise of his brother Nikolai was a key example—he became even more convinced that the absolute was unknowable, that human destiny opened onto a void, and that men and women must face the certitude of the coming night alone. Throughout his ordeal, Chekhov was an atheist in a foxhole. Even when he was in a clinic suffering from a hemorrhage and for the first time acknowledging his illness in an open and frank way, he refused to admit to Tolstoy the possibility of an afterlife. "Tolstoy and I had a most interesting conversation," Chekhov wrote to Mikhail Men'shikov in 1897, "interesting mainly for me, because I listened more than I spoke. . . . Tolstoy recognizes immortality in its Kantian form and assumes that humans and animals will continue to live in a principle (such as reason or love), the essence and goals of which are a mystery. I can imagine such a thing only as a shapeless, gelatinous mass absorbing my *I*, my individuality, my consciousness. I have no use for that kind of immortality. I do not understand it, and Lev Nikolaevich was astonished that I did not."[42]

Chekhov also departed from Bunin in that he did not shy away from those who had departed this world or who continued to suffer in it. He steeled himself to conduct autopsies; and, when he was in Sakhalin, he detailed the whipping of a prisoner in all its horror and gore. "The torturer stood to one side and struck the victim diagonally," Chekhov wrote in *The Island of Sakhalin (Ostrov Sakhalin)*.[43] "Every five lashes, he moved slowly to the man's other side, allowing him a thirty-second respite. The victim's hair soon stuck to his forehead. After only five or ten blows, his flesh, covered with welts from former beatings, first turned crimson and deep blue; then it began to peel. In screams and tears, the unhappy man cried out,

41. Chekhov to O. Knipper, April 22, 1901, *Pis'ma*, 10:15.

42. Chekhov to Men'shikov, April 16, 1897, *Pis'ma*, 6:332. It should be noted here that after Tolstoy's visit, Chekhov suffered a second serious hemorrhage.

Similarly, he told Suvorin, "I cannot console myself with the thought that [after death] I shall mingle with the sighs and torments of some universal life whose end is unknown to me."

At the same time, though, Chekhov could not fathom what he saw as the annihilation of death. "It is terrible to become nothing," he continued to Suvorin. "First you are carried off to the cemetery, then people go home and drink tea. . . . It is disgusting to think about it."

In fact, the "nothingness" of his physical end so terrified Chekhov that he had no choice but to see existence as negating the grave. "If after death the individual disappears," he continued to Suvorin, "there is no such thing as life." See Suvorin's diary entry, dated July 23, 1897, in A. Suvorin, *Dnevnik Alekseia Sergeevicha Suvorina* (Moscow: Nezavisimaia gazeta, 1999), 303.

43. Chekhov wrote *The Island of Sakhalin* between 1893 and 1895.

'Your Worship! Spare me, your Worship!' But then, after twenty or thirty blows, he started lamenting as if he were delirious or drunk, saying, 'I am an unfortunate man, a broken man. . . . Why are they doing this to me?' Suddenly his neck stretched out unnaturally, and I heard vomiting. . . . He did not say another word: he only moaned and wheezed."[44]

For the "humiliated and injured" of Russia, Chekhov took his vocation as a doctor to heroic lengths. Chekhov cared little for homegrown elites who saw folk suffering as sanctity and folk ignorance as bliss. Rather, the care and concern he had for his family he extended to the unfortunates of his land. Even as Chekhov was denouncing the folk in his stories, he took every measure to alleviate the suffering of workers and peasants. Chekhov never preached love for humankind; but he had an almost compulsive tendency for self-sacrifice, to give rather than to receive. He was, in fact, a real-life example of the character Mikhail Karlovich in his 1894 story *The Head Gardener's Story* (*Rasskaz starshego sadovnika*), who "was a consumptive and coughed, but when he was summoned to the sick, forgot his own illness and did not spare himself."[45]

Throughout his short life, Chekhov kept a watchful eye on the weak, lowly, and unprotected. He loved animals and the elderly. He never turned his back on petitioners and treated—often gratis—long lines of sick men, women, and children.[46] He built schools, libraries, and clinics; he organized relief during famines and epidemics; he conducted censuses and served in zemstvos and on local boards for education and health. His activities included even being the roving ambassador-patron for Taganrog, the (hated) city of his birth. More interesting, perhaps, Chekhov often regarded such efforts as more valuable and enduring than his stories and plays. "How good it would be," he noted in his diary, "if each of us left behind a school, a well, or something similar so that our lives would not slip into eternity without a trace."[47]

---

44. See Chekhov, *Sochineniia*, 15:337. Although Chekhov left the scene well before the ninetieth blow, he could hear the unfortunate man's cries throughout the town. Indeed, he seemed to have suffered an execution all his own. "For three or four nights thereafter," he wrote to Suvorin, "I dreamed of the torturer and of the repulsive flogging bench" (Chekhov to Suvorin, September 11, 1890, *Pis'ma*, 4:134).

45. Chekhov, *Sochineniia*, 8:344. Compare the remark of Chekhov's doctor, Isaak Al'tschuller: "Chekhov's kindness, his desire to be useful in anything, to help in trifles as well as in important matters, were most exceptional." I. Al'tschuller, "Vospominaniia I. N. Al'tschullera," *Literaturnoe nasledstvo*, 683.

46. He complained to Nikolai Leikin, "My patients are coming to me in droves and I am getting sick of the sight of them. During the summer, I had several hundreds of them and all I earned was one ruble." Chekhov to Leikin, September 14, 1885, *Pis'ma*, 1:159.

47. Chekhov, *Sochineniia*, 17:171.

Despite the marked disparity in their upbringing, personality, and worldviews, Bunin and Chekhov shared similarities that not only made for a solid friendship but also allowed Bunin to enter into Chekhov's world in a way that no one else could. Indeed, it was not for nothing that an autographed picture of Chekhov was displayed proudly on the marble fireplace in Bunin's apartment in Paris.[48] Both men adored intimate gatherings and groups. Indeed, for Bunin and Chekhov, homes full of family and friends were often crucial to their well-being. "I absolutely cannot live without visitors," Chekhov wrote to Suvorin in 1889. "When I am alone, I feel a kind of anxiety, as if I were sailing solo in a frail barge at sea."[49] With people they loved and admired, Bunin and Chekhov were often the life of the party. By their mere presence, they attracted and fascinated others. The two sparkled with wit, entered into lively discussions and disputes, and regaled colleagues with jokes and pranks. Chekhov actually convinced the nineteen-year-old (and naive) poet and short-story writer Tatiana Shchepkina-Kupernik that his marmalade-colored cat had sired his chocolate-tinged doves.[50] After all, who could doubt the authority of Chekhov?

Like Bunin, Chekhov was also adept at renditions of landowners, peasants, and other societal types. He and his younger colleague enthralled listeners with their readings and roles, their talent for drama and mime, and the depth and modulation of their voices. In fact, the two were such consummate actors that they considered joining dramatic troupes, including the company of the Moscow Art Theater.

For all their apparent gregariousness, though, Bunin and Chekhov were drawn from Leoncavallo's *Pagliacci;* they were clowns who, the more they laughed on the outside, the more they cried within. Innately sentimental and shy, they lived behind masks, even walls. Chekhov, for instance, often acted as an "observer, not an actor . . . distant and as it were senior . . . like an adult playing with children, pretending to be interested when he really was not."[51] Like his younger colleague, Chekhov was distressed by effusive demonstrations of emotion, sudden declarations which caught them unawares, and individuals who threw their arms about them without warning. The two were also uncomfortable with crowds. And, although they informed their works with people and incidents from their lives, they disliked writing

48. See V. Antonov, "I. A. Bunin vo Frantsii v gody voiny," *Inostrannaia literatura,* no. 9 (1956): 255.

49. Chekhov to Suvorin, June 9, 1889, *Pis'ma,* 3:233.

50. See T. Shchepkina-Kupernik, "O Chekhove," *Izbrannoe: Vospominaniia i portrety; Rasskazy i ocherki; Stikhotvoreniia; Dramaticheskie perevody* (Moscow: Sovetskii pisatel', 1954), 61.

51. Ibid., 199.

autobiographies for publishers. "I have a malady called autobiographopho-bia," Chekhov wrote to Grigory Rossolimo in 1899. "It is a genuine torture for me to read any details whatsoever about myself, to say nothing of writing them for the press."[52] Bunin and Chekhov cared little for standing out in gatherings, giving speeches or readings in public,[53] and receiving applause from groups.[54] With equal intensity, they hated the heat of the spotlight and the coldness of effusive praise. "Not even Shakespeare had to listen to the speeches that I heard [about my giftedness]," Chekhov complained to Leontiev-Shcheglov that same year, on the occasion of a banquet in the writer's honor.[55] Even those closest to Bunin and Chekhov did not know their minds, souls, and hearts. In fact, the two men remained enigmas to those who loved them most.

Not surprisingly, Bunin compares to Chekhov in that both were un-lucky in love and without families to call their own.[56] For them happiness was an illusion and life an entity bereft of lasting joy and light.[57] (Both men were enraptured by the book of Ecclesiastes and the *Meditations* of Marcus Aurelius.) It was the style of Bunin and Chekhov to search endlessly for something beyond their ken and to fear surrender to sorrow, passion, or joy. It was also their wont to complain of loneliness, of being "transplanted trees unsure as to take root or wither."[58] Indeed, it was more self-condemnation

52. Chekhov to Rossolimo, October 11, 1899, *Pis'ma,* 8:284. "Should we talk of personal life?" Chekhov also wrote to Nemirovich-Danchenko. "Yes, sometimes this can be interest-ing . . . but we become shy, evasive, insincere, the instinct of self-preservation restrains us and we get fearful. We are afraid that some Eskimo may overhear us, somebody who does not like us and whom we do not like." See Chekhov to Nemirovich-Danchenko, November 26, 1896, *Pis'ma,* 6:241–42.

53. Chekhov told Ertel', "I recite abominably. The main thing is that I am terrified. There's a complaint called 'fear of open spaces.' Well, I suffer from fear of the public and of publicity" (Chekhov to Ertel', March 4, 1893, *Pis'ma,* 5:181). He continued to Korolenko, "I do not recite in public. . . . If I do so, I find that after three or five minutes, my mouth dries up, my voice grows hoarse, and I cannot stop coughing" (Chekhov to Korolenko, February 19, 1896, *Pis'ma,* 6:123).

54. Such reticence, though, did not curb the happiness with which Bunin and Chekhov re-ceived honors for their writing. Both men received the Pushkin Prize in Literature and were elected as academicians to the Russian Academy of Sciences.

55. Chekhov to Leontiev-Shcheglov, February 18, 1899, *Pis'ma,* 3:157.

56. Bunin's son, Nikolai, died in 1905 at the age of five. Olga Knipper miscarried at least once in her short time with Chekhov.

57. It should be noted here that neither Bunin nor Chekhov was happy with this "realist" stance to life. For instance, Chekhov confessed to Leontiev-Shcheglov, "With me, a physician, there are . . . few illusions. Of course, I am sorry for such an approach to existence . . . since it somehow deprecates life." See I. Leontiev-Shcheglov, "Iz vospominanii ob Antone Chekhove," in Kotov, *A. P. Chekhov,* 405.

58. Chekhov to O. Knipper, February 10, 1900, *Pis'ma,* 9:45.

than comment when Chekhov wrote in his notebooks, "Just as I will be alone in my grave, so in essence will I be alone in life."[59]

Similar shortcomings—intellectual, physical, and mental—seized both men. Like Bunin, Chekhov was befuddled by foreign languages. "You probably know that I speak all languages except foreign ones," Chekhov wrote to Vasily Sobolevsky in 1897.[60] Physically, the two men suffered from hemorrhoids—in their view, the consequence of heavy drinking. "It is worse then syphilis," Chekhov had complained to Suvorin four years earlier, "the pain, itching, tension. I cannot sit or walk. My whole body is so sore that I feel like hanging myself."[61] Mentally, Bunin and Chekhov suffered from nervous strains, nightly terrors, and periods as manic-depressives: ecstatically high on good days and nearly suicidal on bad ones. Chekhov, for instance, paid a high price for his self-imposed restraint. The external prison to which his tuberculosis had confined him often paled to the psychic bars Chekhov erected about himself, breeding personal and professional torpor. "I have very little passion," Chekhov complained to Suvorin in 1889. "The fire in me burns with an even, lethargic flame. It never flares up or roars. That is why I never do anything notably intelligent or outstandingly stupid. That is also why I never end up writing fifty or so pages in one night, or get so involved in my work that I cannot fall asleep."[62] Chekhov's mental grid also moved him to ideas of premature age. What illness did to his body, darkness did to his mind. "In January I am turning thirty," he wrote to Suvorin in December 1889. "Hail, lonely old age; burn, useless life!"[63]

Bunin was like Chekhov in that he was also out of sync with life outside himself. Both were astonishingly "modern": new kinds of men, uncomfortable in their world, but refusing to compromise their views or to sentimentalize their unease. Humankind was for them deathly and dull, existence the stuff of "moral vomit":[64] a "melding succession of grayness . . . horrors, squabbles, and banalities . . . [in which] pharisaism, dull-wittedness, and tyranny reign not only in merchant homes and police stations . . . but also in science, literature, and with the younger generation."[65] As was the case to

59. Chekhov, *Sochineniia*, 17:86.

60. Chekhov to Sobolevsky, August 19, 1897, *Pis'ma*, 7:39.

61. Chekhov to Suvorin, April 26, 1893, *Pis'ma*, 5:204.

62. Chekhov to Suvorin, May 4, 1889, *Pis'ma*, 5:203.

63. Chekhov to Suvorin, December 7, 1889, *Pis'ma*, 5:300.

64. Chekhov to Alexander Chekhov, September 5–6 1887, in I. Ezhov, ed., *Pis'ma A. P. Chekhovu ego brata Aleksandra Chekhova* (Moscow: Gosudarstevennoe sotsial'no-ekonomicheskoe izdatel'stvo, 1939), 171.

65. See Chekhov to Maria Kiselyova, September 29, 1886, *Pis'ma*, 1:264; Chekhov to Alexei Pleshcheev, October 4, 1888, *Pis'ma*, 3:11.

Bunin, it seemed to Chekhov that his time on earth was, on the one hand, "suspended on the tooth of some monster," and on the other, "entangled in a great chain which [one] cannot sever but extend."[66] Even more darkly, perhaps, the two believed that the "damned questions" (*prokliatye voprosy*) of life resisted resolution. "We must declare point-blank," Chekhov wrote to Leontiev-Shcheglov in 1888, "that nobody can make heads or tails of anything in this world."[67]

Bunin and Chekhov could be ill at ease even with intimates. As much as they needed family and friends, they could be cold, petulant, and unyielding. They could also be heartily sick of the presence and demands loved ones made upon them. "My life bores me," Chekhov wrote to Suvorin that same year. "The long, stupid talks, the guests, the suppliants . . . not to mention people who borrow money indiscriminately, run off with my books, and waste my time. . . . In short my life is such a mess that I want to chuck it all and run. . . . All I need now is an unhappy affair."[68]

In fact, Bunin and Chekhov were so shocked by the treachery of the people whom they had seen as friends that they tended to receive humanity—and its vaunted ideals—with caution and restraint. "You are, I believe," Gorky wrote to Chekhov in 1899, "the first free man I have ever met who does not worship anything."[69] The literary world was a case in point. Although both men expected envy at their triumphs and schadenfreude at their tragedies, they were dumbfounded by the backbiting and ill will of

66. Chekhov, *Sochineniia*, 17:154. Also see Chekhov's 1896 story "House with a Balcony: The Story of an Artist" ("Dom s mezoninom: Rasskaz khudozhnika"), in Chekhov, *Sochineniia*, 9:184.

67. Chekhov to Leontiev-Shcheglov, June 9, 1888, *Pis'ma*, 2:283. Compare Olga's line at the end of *Three Sisters* (*Tri sestry*): "Oh, my dear sisters, our life is not yet at an end. Let us live! The music plays so gaily and joyfully, and it seems that in a little while we shall know why we live and why we suffer. If only we knew! If only we knew!" Chekhov, *Sochineniia*, 13:188.

68. Chekhov to Suvorin, December 23, 1888, *Pis'ma*, 3:100. "Oh, if only you knew how exhausted I am," Chekhov continued to Suvorin several years later. "Company, company, and more company. Every itinerant intellectual feels bound and beholden to look in on me, warm up, and sometimes even stay the night." Chekhov to Suvorin, December 8, 1892, *Pis'ma*, 5:139.

Chekhov, though, was not devoid of defense mechanisms. "When visitors come and begin to philosophize," he told Alexander Kuprin, "I take my field glasses and look, during the day at the sea, at night at the sky. Guests imagine that I am thinking about something deep and stop their discourse for fear of disturbing me."

[Kuprin continues,] " Soon a lady came in . . . and started at once to talk to Chekhov about his writing. For a long time Chekhov remained silent. Then he requested [to his sister], 'Masha, bring me my field glasses.'" A. Kuprin, "A. P. Chekhov," in Kotov, *A. P. Chekhov*, 146.

69. See M. Gor'kii, *Polnoe Sobranie Sochinenii: Pis'ma v dvadtsati chetyrekh tomakh*, 24 vols. (Moscow: Nauka, 1997–), 1:332, hereafter cited as *Polnoe Sobranie Sochinenii: Pis'ma*, with volume and page numbers.

literati and readers—"fungal growth," Chekhov called them[70]—over the peaks and valleys of their lives and careers. "I am surrounded by a dense atmosphere of extremely vague and incomprehensible hostility," Chekhov wrote to his sister, Maria, in 1891. "People give me meals and sing my praises, but they are ready to devour me. Why? Damned if I know. If I would put a bullet through my head, I would give nine-tenths of my friends and admirers a great deal of pleasure."[71]

Of course, Bunin mirrored Chekhov in his knowledge that they were not angels. Both men hated not only how money ruled their lives[72] but also how they became immersed in financial quagmires. Talk about funds made them uncomfortable; figures plunged them into childlike confusion; naïveté cast them as the pawns of unscrupulous friends, editors, and publishers.[73] Chekhov, for instance, bought properties sight unseen; he also gave large sums of money to people and institutions, worthy and otherwise. The more the wolf was at Bunin's and Chekhov's doors, though, the more profligate they were with cash on hand. Even in good times, they so relished earthly delights that they hovered close to fiscal ruin. "My money flies away from me like a wild fledgling," Chekhov complained to Avilova in 1899. "In two years' time, I will have to become a philosopher."[74] Two years later, he wrote to Suvorin, "To make a fortune, to escape the abyss of petty worries and fears, I have only one choice, an immoral one, to marry into wealth or to say that I wrote *Anna Karenina*."[75]

Angst over Russia further moved the two men to darkness, not light. As evidenced by such works as "The Peasants" ("Muzhiki"), "In the Ravine" ("V ovrage"), and *The Village (Derevnia)*,[76] Bunin and Chekhov were under no illusions as to *l'âme russe*, the state of imperial Russia, or the "messian-

---

70. Chekhov to Maria Chekhova, January 14, 1891, *Pis'ma,* 4:162.

71. Ibid., 4:161.

72. For instance, Chekhov wrote to Suvorin, "My soul has withered from the consciousness that I work for money and that money is the center of my activity. This gnawing feeling, together with my sense of justice, makes authorship a contemptible pursuit in my eyes. I do not respect what I write, and I am apathetic and bored [with life]." Chekhov to Suvorin, June 16, 1892, *Pis'ma,* 5:78.

73. For instance, Chekhov wrote to Olga Knipper, "I do not understand how my money disappears daily! I do not understand it at all! . . . Yesterday one person got a hundred rubles, today another came to say good-bye and took ten from me. I gave a hundred to still a third, promised a hundred to another, and fifty to someone else. All this must be handed over when the bank opens tomorrow." Chekhov to O. Knipper, September 9, 1901, *Pis'ma,* 10:76.

74. Chekhov to Avilova, March 23, 1899, *Pis'ma,* 8:133–34.

75. Chekhov to Suvorin, July 24, 1891, *Pis'ma,* 4:251.

76. Chekhov's "The Peasants" appeared in 1897 and "In the Ravine" in 1900. Bunin's *The Village* was published in 1909 and 1910.

ism" of their homeland. "Russia is nobody's country," Chekhov wrote in his notebooks, "an enormous plain peopled by mischievous men."[77]

Although apolitical by nature, Bunin and Chekhov rallied against all forms of national injustice. The excesses of autocracy disgusted them; the lethargy of bureaucrats and petty officials raised their ire.[78] The *poshlost'* or "vulgarity" of the bourgeoisie turned their stomachs; the worsening state of the peasantry anguished their souls. The two were particularly horrified by the new industrialists and capitalists. In their view, factories and railways posed the same threat to the homeland in the cities as did peasant-Pechenegs in the steppes.[79]

United in their hope for a homeland ruled by law,[80] they knew that the "purely Russian traits of lethargy, excitability, and guilt,"[81] together with the national penchant for extremes of all kinds,[82] would leave their country as

---

77. Chekhov, *Sochineniia*, 17:93.

78. Consider this anecdote from Chekhov's notebooks: "The new governor made a speech to his clerks. He called the merchants together—another speech. At the annual prize-giving of the secondary school for girls—a speech on true enlightenment. To the representatives of the press—a speech. He called the Jews together: 'Jews, I have summoned you. . . .' A month or two passes—he does nothing. Again he called the merchants together—a speech. Again the Jews: 'Jews, I have summoned you. . . .' He has wearied them all. At last he said to his Chancellor, 'No, this work is too much for me. I shall have to resign.'" Chekhov, *Sochineniia*, 17:159.

79. See Masha's remarks to the Doctor in Chekhov's 1896 work "My Life" ("Moia zhizn'") in Chekhov, *Sochineniia*, 9:253.

80. See Chekhov to Suvorin, March 4, 1899, *Pis'ma*, 8:113: "A state should be founded on definite legal relationships. If it is not, it is a bogeyman, an empty sound producing an imaginary fright." Also see Chekhov to Suvorin, April 2, 1899, *Pis'ma*, 8:143: "When people lack the right to express their ideas freely, they vent their opinions irately, in anger, and often—from the point of view of the government—in a form that is ugly and appalling. Grant the freedoms of press and conscience and you will have the peace and quiet you desire."

Ever the optimist, though, Chekhov did not expect a revolt in Russia, hoping against hope that his homeland would move toward enlightened liberalism. "There will never be a revolution in Russia," Chekhov wrote to Pleshcheev (Chekhov to Pleshcheev, February 9, 1888, *Pis'ma*, 2:195). "Do you want me to tell you something?" he asked Kuprin. "In ten years Russia will have a constitution" (Kuprin, "A. P. Chekhov," 242).

81. "Russians are strange creatures," Chekhov told Gorky. "They are like a sieve—everything passes through them. In their youth, they fill themselves greedily with anything they come across so that after thirty years, nothing remains but a kind of gray rubbish. . . . In order to live well and humanly, one must work with love and faith. But we Russians, we can't do it. . . .

"Russians eat and drink enormously of nice things, like to sleep in the daytime, and snore in their sleep. They marry to have houses looked after and keep mistresses to have prestige in society. Their psychology is that of a dog: when beaten, they whine shrilly and run into their kennels. When petted, they live on their backs with their paws in the air and wag their tails." See Gor'kii, *Polnoe sobranie sochinenii*, 6:52. Also see Chekhov to Suvorin, December 30, 1888, *Pis'ma*, 3:115.

82. For instance, regarding the Russian quest for faith, Chekhov wrote in his notebook in early February 1897: "Between 'there is a God' and 'there is no God' lies a great expanse

depressing and dark as medieval Rus' had been. The hero in Chekhov's 1894 story "The Student," wincing in the cold gusts on a bleak Good Friday, reflects that "just such a wind had blown in the days of Ryurik, Ivan the Terrible, and Peter the Great. . . . Then there had been the same ruined thatched roofs, the same ignorance and misery, the same desolation on all sides."[83] Even worse, perhaps, Bunin and Chekhov intuited the cruelties of the Soviet era. "Under the banner of learning," Chekhov warned Alexei Pleshcheev in 1888, "there will be a time in Russia when art and freedom of thought will one day be ruled by such toads and crocodiles as were unknown even in Spain under the Inquisition. Yes, you just wait! Narrow-mindedness, enormous pretensions, excessive self-importance, a total absence of any literal or social conscience: these things will do their work. . . . [There] will spawn an atmosphere so stifling that every healthy person will be bloody well nauseated by literature, while every charlatan and wolf in sheep's clothing will have a stage on which to parade his lies and hypocrisy."[84]

Particularly irksome to Bunin and Chekhov were the homespun remedies by which citizens sought to rescue their country from the abyss—the herdlike cliques and crowds, causes and cults that opposed everything under the Russian sun and that, at every turn, threatened violence and even more severe strictures. "People who are united by opinions or common causes," Chekhov wrote to Pleshcheev in 1888, "condemn free and broad thought, especially if such individuals are unimaginative and unintelligent."[85]

Bunin concurred with Chekhov in his respect for intelligence but dislike of the intelligentsia. Indeed, the two had nothing but contempt for the idle minds, empty hearts, and loose tongues that, they believed, marked the purportedly elite and erudite in their land. Self-styled angst—*morbus fraudulentus*, Chekhov once diagnosed[86]—was the order of the day. "Our intellectuals," Chekhov complained to Suvorin in 1889, "are wood lice . . . and snails. . . . [They are] apathetic, cold-blooded . . . unpatriotic, gloomy, and colorless. Idle philosophers and freeloaders, they grouse all the time, visit fifty-kopeck brothels, and get drunk on one glass of vodka. They also renounce *everything*, since it is easier for their lazy brains to reject than affirm."[87]

---

through which the sincere sage traverses with great difficulty. The Russian, though, knows only one of these two extremes, if only because the middle ground does not interest him. Hence he usually knows nothing or very little." Chekhov, *Sochineniia,* 17:33–34.

83. Chekhov, *Sochineniia,* 10:306.

84. Chekhov to Pleshcheev, August 27, 1888, *Pis'ma,* 2:316–17.

85. See Chekhov, to Pleshcheev, January 23, 1888, *Pis'ma,* 2:83.

86. See Gor'kii, *Polnoe sobranie sochinenii,* 6:51.

87. Chekhov to Suvorin, December 27, 1889, *Pis'ma,* 3:308–9. "To hell with the philosophy of the great men of this world!" Chekhov continued to Suvorin two years later. "All great wise

Even worse, perhaps, was the outrage of Bunin and Chekhov over dinners and other formal occasions at which writers and intellectuals fiddled while Russia burned, that is, they denounced the suffering of the folk but ate and drank to excess, attended hand and foot by the very unfortunates with whom they claimed kinship. Chekhov, having returned from a sumptuous banquet celebrating the anniversary of the emancipation, jotted in his diary in 1897, "[The whole thing] was boring and ridiculous. [Everyone] eating, drinking champagne, making noise, and giving speeches on the 'people's' self-awareness, freedom, and the like, while slaves in frock coats, serfs even now, bustle about the table and coachmen wait outside in the cold. Why, it is like lying to the Holy Spirit."[88]

Among Russian writers and intellectuals, several groups particularly galled Bunin and Chekhov. Instructors of higher learning earned their contempt. "I have my knife out for professors," Chekhov wrote to Suvorin in 1899. "Like authors, they have no caring and much self-importance."[89] Students fared even worse if only because, while in school, they rebelled "to look like heroes and to have an easier time with young ladies,"[90] but, out of it, they abandoned their radicalism for families and careers as "doctors, owners of dachas, greedy officials, and thieving engineers."[91] The nadir for Bunin

---

men are as despotic as generals . . . because they are confident of their impunity. Diogenes spat in people's beards knowing the he would not be called into account. Tolstoy calls doctors scoundrels and flaunts his ignorance of important issues because he knows that . . . no one will report him to the police or denounce him in the papers." Chekhov to Suvorin, September 8, 1891, *Pis'ma,* 4:270.

Further, Chekhov sought to solve in his typically swift and pragmatic way the agony and angst of Russian intellectuals. As the so-called Grouch advises a bored intellectual in Chekhov's 1891 story "In Moscow" ("V Moskve"), "Take a length of telephone wire and hang yourself on the nearest pole." Chekhov, *Sochineniia,* 7:500.

88. Chekhov, *Sochineniia,* 17:25. Chekhov also had little use for the rapid transit of Russian intellectuals from excitement to disillusionment and pity. He wrote to Suvorin on December 30, 1888:

> In a fit of enthusiasm, a man who has only just left the classroom undertakes a burden beyond his strength. He takes up a school, the peasant question, rational farming, and *The Herald of Europe.* All in one breath, he speechifies, writes to the ministry, fights evil, and applauds good. If he falls in love, it must absolutely be with some bluestocking or neurotic . . . or a prostitute, whom he saves. . . .
>
> But hardly does he reach the age of thirty or thirty-five when he begins to feel exhaustion and boredom. His mustache has hardly reached its full development when he declares authoritatively, "Don't get married, old man . . . profit by my experience," or, "What is liberalism after all?" (Chekhov to Suvorin, December 30, 1888, *Pis'ma,* 3:109–10)

89. Chekhov to Suvorin, November 27, 1899, *Pis'ma,* 3:294.
90. See A. Serebrov-Tikhonov, "O Chekhove," in Kotov, *A. P. Chekhov,* 300.
91. See Chekhov to Ivan Orlov, February 22, 1899, *Pis'ma,* 8:101.

and Chekhov, though, was socialists, particularly Marxists with their "arrogant physiognomies."[92] The cholera epidemic of 1892, for instance, caused Chekhov to condemn not only how socialists moved disaster to discontent but also how they wreaked an Edenic future from an earthbound present. "If our socialists exploit the epidemic for their own ends," Chekhov wrote to Suvorin in 1892, "I will have nothing but contempt for them. Repulsive means for good ends make the ends themselves repulsive. . . . Why assure the folk that they are right to be ignorant and that their crass prejudices are the holy truth? Can a beautiful future really expiate a base lie? Even if I were promised a hundredweight of bliss for a pennyweight of lies, I would never disgrace the present for the sake of the future."[93]

If Bunin and Chekhov often regarded both modernity and their lives as "imprisonment," "exile," and "execution," they also had three escapes from their everyday distress.

The first was travel. Bunin shared with Chekhov a love for the nomadic life. Neither could remain still for any length of time. The two were comfortable more with boats and trains than with estates and homes; they believed that happiness and health lay just beyond whatever they were doing or wherever they were. Some inner urge or wanderlust kept pushing the two forward, their wish being to live vicariously; they sought to flee the routines, responsibilities, and muddling bedlam of life, to appear as Buddhalike or Christlike seeker-wanderers, to lose themselves in existence, and to embrace every experience and pleasure in their race against time and other enemies who, they believed, would truncate their lives in a quick and merciless way. "Life is short," Chekhov wrote to Suvorin in 1892, "I long terribly for a steamer and for freedom. The pious, ordered life disgusts me."[94]

Bunin and Chekhov also revered the same places as repositories for their images and ideals. Despite their disparate attitudes toward God and death, both men were fascinated with cemeteries. Wherever they were, they sought out final resting places, deciphering the inscriptions on the tottering headstones and wondering about the strangers beneath them. In cemeteries, Chekhov wrote in his 1898 work "Ionych," "every poplar tree exudes mystery; and the gravestones, faded flowers, and the autumnal fragrance of leaves breathe pardon, sadness, and peace."[95]

Further, Bunin shared with Chekhov a love for the same cities and re-

92. See Chekhov to Leonid Sredin, December 26, 1900, *Pis'ma,* 9:164.

93. Chekhov to Suvorin, August 1, 1892, *Pis'ma,* 5:101.

94. Chekhov to Suvorin, May 28, 1892, *Pis'ma,* 5:70.

95. Chekhov, *Sochineniia,* 10:31. "Chekhov told me that he loved cemeteries," Grigory Rossolimo also recalled in his memoirs, "especially in the winter when the graves could hardly

gions in both Russia and the world. Ukraine captured their minds and hearts. Nice delighted their senses with its sea, flowers, and civility.[96] "In Nice," Chekhov wrote to his brother Ivan, "every dog has the whiff of civilization . . . the chambermaid smiles like a duchess . . . and even beggars are addressed as 'Monsieur' or 'Madame.' "[97] Venice, if not all of Italy, restored their faith in civilization and humankind. "Never in my life have I seen a city more remarkable than Venice," Chekhov wrote to Ivan. "The fascination, the glitter, the exuberance. . . . A Russian, poor and humble, can very easily go out of his mind in this world of beauty, freedom, and wealth. One feels like staying here forever."[98]

It was Ceylon, however, which most impressed Bunin and Chekhov as paradise[99] on earth—but in ways which spoke to the heart of the difference between the two men. If in Ceylon Bunin saw himself as a second Adam seeking Buddhist-style enlightenment in a world gone awry, Chekhov looked to the isle to pursue more earthly delights. "When I have children," he confided to Suvorin in 1890, "I will tell them, not without pride, 'Listen, you sons of bitches! When I was a young man, I had sex with a black-eyed Hindu girl, and guess where? In a coconut grove on a moonlit night.' "[100]

Despite their taste for the excesses of Europe and Asia, they always returned to their Russian roots.[101] The lavish nature and buildings, the culture and food of both East and West—"artichokes, truffles, and all sorts of nightingale tongues," Chekhov wrote to his family in 1891[102]—not only left the two with physical (and metaphysical) stomachaches but also gifted them with a longing for the simpler if more elemental things of the land of their birth. Both Bunin and Chekhov suffered from contradictory impulses: the more they headed off to distant places, the more they returned to the safety of familiar ground, to the realization of how unalterably Russian they were. "Men who tie boa-constructors around their waists," Chekhov complained to his family that same year, "ladies who kick their legs to the ceiling, flying

---

be seen under the deep drifts of snow." G. Rossolimo, "Vospominaniia o Chekhove," in Kotov, *A. P. Chekhov,* 466.

96. It is a quirk of fate that Bunin got to see more of Nice than he had planned. He spent the years of World War II in Grasse, twelve miles west of the city.

97. Chekhov to Ivan Chekhov, October 2, 1897, *Pis'ma,* 7:64.

98. Chekhov to Ivan Chekhov, March 24, 1891, *Pis'ma,* 4:202.

99. See Chekhov to Leontiev-Shcheglov, December 10, 1890, *Pis'ma,* 4:143.

100. Interestingly, this section of Chekhov's letter to Suvorin appears as an ellipsis (Chekhov to Suvorin, December 9, 1890, *Pis'ma,* 4:140). It does appear, however, in Chekhova, *Pis'ma,* 3:146.

101. Chekhov made five excursions to Europe.

102. Chekhov to his family, April 15, 1891, *Pis'ma,* 4:217.

people, lions, cafés, elephants, dinners, luncheons—all begin to sicken me. It is time I went home. I want to work."[103]

L'âme russe seized Bunin and Chekhov in yearnings for cabbage soup, church bells,[104] journeys through native steppes, and preferences for native writers and artists. "Russian painters are more solid than French ones," Chekhov pronounced summarily to his family in 1891. "Compared with the French landscape painters I saw yesterday, Levitan is a king."[105] In fact, several days before Chekhov died in Badenweiler, he complained to sister Maria, "I cannot get used to all this German peace and quiet. There is not a sound inside or out except when a band with no talent strikes up at seven in the morning and noon. Nowhere is there a drop of giftedness or good taste, only great quantities of honesty and order. There is a good deal more talent in Russia."[106] Most of all, Bunin was drawn homeward with Chekhov by the ultimate hallmark of patriarchal Russia: the images and ideals of the estate. "I terribly love anything that is called an estate in Russia," Chekhov wrote to Nikolai Leikin in 1885. "The word still has not lost its poetic sound."[107]

Bunin and Chekhov also traveled spiritually. Indeed, they were as comfortable in psychic worlds as they were in real ones. Even when the two seemed absorbed by people and events, they often assumed fixed-state stares and turned inward, seized by singular emotions and thoughts, on the one hand, and by unfinished manuscripts or new contexts for works, on the other. Without the slightest warning, they often broke off conversations or left festivities to enter into their souls or to exit to a secluded place to jot down the phrases and ideas that had come to them.[108]

A second avenue of escape for Bunin and Chekhov from their troubles was the beauty of the natural and human worlds. The two believed that

---

103. Chekhov to his family, April 24, 1891, *Pis'ma*, 4:222.

104. "Love for church bells is all that remains to me of my faith," Chekhov once told Alexander Vishnevsky. See A. Vishnevskii, "Nezabvennoe," *Solntse Rossii*, no. 228 (June 1914): 34.

105. Chekhov to his family, April 21, 1891, *Pis'ma*, vol. 4:220.

106. Chekhov to Maria Chekhova, June 16, 1904, *Pis'ma*, 12:123–24.

107. Chekhov to Leikin, October 12, 1885, *Pis'ma*, 1:167.

108. Maxim Kovalevsky, in his memoirs, writes, "During our walks together, Chekhov often fell silent, as though preoccupied with his own thoughts. At such times, he was probably dwelling upon a story he had just written." M. Kovalevsky, "Ob A. P. Chekhove," in N. Gitovich, ed., *A. P. Chekhov v vospominaniiakh sovremennikov* (Moscow: Khudozhestvennaia literatura, 1986), 362.

Potapenko concurs. "Creativity never left Chekhov for a minute," he wrote in his memoirs. "It often turned out that during a noisy conversation, he disappeared suddenly but returned right away. He had been in his study to write down the two or three lines that happened to appear in his head. Such a thing he did often in the course of the day." Potapenko, "Neskol'ko let s A. P. Chekhovym," 244.

flowers, trees, and the sea whispered truths that were eternal and sublime and that pointed to the triumph of beauty over bestiality and of the present over the future and the past.[109] Nature also offered a healing, if at times heady, sense of freedom, peace, and renewal to the stagnation, chaos, and death of life. As Bunin and Chekhov saw it, the universe showed a profound disregard for the fleeting affairs of humankind. "For many thousands of years," Chekhov wrote in his 1888 story "The Steppe" ("Step'"), "stars and the deep mysterious sky have been indifferent to the short lives of men."[110]

Although Chekhov was a man of science, he was no Bazarov, content to view the world only from a microscope. In fact, to Leontiev-Shcheglov, he regretted how science so "desiccated" life that he could no longer look at the moon as something "terribly mysterious and unattainable."[111] Throughout his life, Chekhov took great pleasure in his surroundings. "God's world is good. Only one thing is bad: we ourselves," he wrote to Suvorin in 1890.[112] In fact, Chekhov was often so moved by what he saw in forests and fields that he was prepared to cast aside his religious skepticism and to agree with Bunin on the existence of eternal life. "Looking at spring," Chekhov asserted in the same letter to Suvorin, "I have a dreadful longing that there should be a paradise in the other world."[113]

Bunin echoed Chekhov, though, in wanting bliss in this life, not the next. Both men loved to cast themselves as singular Adams in self-styled Edens. At times, their joy was spiritual: elusive and mystical. Chekhov, for instance, could be like the poor seminarian in "The Student," who, having told the story of Peter's denial of Christ to simple folk, finds that he is seized by an "inexpressible, sweet expectation of happiness, an unknown and mysterious joy . . . and [the idea] that life is rapturous, marvelous, and full of meaning."[114]

Other times, though, the happiness of Bunin and Chekhov was physical. The more the two tasted of the good things of life, the more they wanted

---

109. See Chekhov to Suvorin, March 17, 1892, *Pis'ma*, 5:25.

110. Chekhov, *Sochineniia*, 7:65.

111. See I. Leontiev-Shcheglov, "Iz vospominanii ob Antone Chekhove," *Ezhemesiachnye literaturnye i populiarno-nauchnye prilozheniia k zhurnalu 'Niva,'"* no. 6 (June 1905): 238–39.

112. Chekhov to Suvorin, December 9, 1890, *Pis'ma*, 4:140.

113. Ibid. Compare the rhapsody of the hero in Chekhov's 1898 story "Ionych," over a moonlit cemetery "where there is no life, but where in every dark poplar and in every grave one feels the presence of a mystery which holds out the promise of a quiet, beautiful, everlasting life." Chekhov, *Sochineniia*, 10:31.

Similarly, when Chekhov visited the crater of Mount Vesuvius and heard the "roar of Satan . . . the terrifying sounds of breakers and beating, of thunder clapping, trains pounding, and boards falling," he was also ready to "believe in Hell." Chekhov to his family, April 7, 1891, *Pis'ma*, 4:212.

114. Chekhov, *Sochineniia*, 8:309.

them. Throughout their lives, Bunin celebrated existence with Chekhov as pagan-hedonists who loved wine, women, and song and who grabbed at whatever good things life afforded them. Their appetites could be gargantuan. "I do nothing but wander about the orchard and eat cherries," Chekhov wrote to Leikin in 1897. "I pick about twenty cherries and put them in my mouth all at once. It is tastier that way."[115] The writer of *The Cherry Orchard* was a particularly colorful meld of cultured and crass. "I should now like carpets, an open fireplace, bronzes, and learned conversation," he wrote to Suvorin in 1891. "Alas! I shall never be a Tolstoyan! In women I love beauty above all things, and in the history of mankind, culture [as it is] expressed in carriages with springs, and keenness of wit!"[116]

When Bunin and Chekhov were happy in life, they vaunted what they saw as the best qualities of their race. To play with a popular saying, they believed that when humankind was bad, it was very bad, but when it was good, it was better. As they saw it, men and women harbored the fundamental goodness of the human heart: "health, intelligence, talent, inspiration, love, and the most absolute freedom imaginable, freedom from violence and lies."[117] Also, in their thoughts on social change, Bunin joined with Chekhov to champion the triumph of the individual, not the masses. Life in their homeland, they believed, would improve only when select beings took an active part in national betterment. "I see salvation in individuals," Chekhov wrote to Ivan Orlov in 1899, "people who are scattered here and there, all over Russia. Be they intellectuals or peasants, no matter how few they are, they are the ones who really matter. Their role in society may be inconspicuous . . . but despite all obstacles . . . their work is clearly to be seen."[118]

The third avenue of release for Bunin and Chekhov from their woes was their fictional works. Both men were strong-willed, self-disciplined, and extraordinarily resilient individuals who despised laziness in themselves and others[119] and who believed in the value of productive, meaningful effort as a remedy not only for their own ills but also for the failings of society. As they saw it, the only cure for despair was work without ambition or hope of recompense. "One must work," Chekhov told Suvorin in 1890, "and to hell with everything else."[120]

---

115. Chekhov to Leikin, July 4, 1897, *Pis'ma,* 7:22.

116. Chekhov to Suvorin, August 30, 1891, *Pis'ma,* 4:267.

117. Ibid.

118. Chekhov to Orlov, February 22, 1899, *Pis'ma,* 8:101.

119. For instance, Chekhov wrote to Lika Mizinova, "I hold that true happiness is impossible without idleness. My ideal is to be idle and love a fat girl. My greatest pleasure is to sit and do nothing. . . . But I am a writer, so write I must." Chekhov to Mizinova, March 27, 1894, *Pis'ma,* 5:281.

120. Chekhov to Suvorin, December 9, 1890, *Pis'ma,* 4:140.

Of course, the ultimate bond between Bunin and Chekhov was their love for literature. The two relished their avocation as writers, and so the thrills and spills of their bohemian-like calling were for them exhilarating alternatives to what they saw as the staid dreariness of philistine and family life. "My soul longs for breath and height," Chekhov declared to Suvorin in 1892. "There is nothing more banal than bourgeois life with its two-kopeck pieces, absurd conversations, and useless, conventional virtues."[121] Even the struggles in their early years—the groping for a "voice,"[122] the abuse of critics,[123] and the need to write *na zakaz* or "on order"[124] and in haste, "as if eating pancakes," Chekhov recalled[125]—came to be seen by them as formative trials by fire through which they forged their craft.[126]

Further, Bunin concurred with Chekhov in approaching their calling as writers with an almost religious fervor. As much as the two loved fun and good times, they embraced a monastic ideal in their writing. "If I were a landscape painter, I would lead an ascetic life," Chekhov told Suvorin in 1895. "I would have intercourse once a year and food once a day."[127] More seriously, he wrote to his colleague a year later, "If monasteries accepted the irreligious and permitted abstention from prayer, I would become a monk."[128]

121. Chekhov to Suvorin, June 16, 1892, *Pis'ma,* 5:78.

122. Not surprisingly, both men were often mortified by their early works. "The new edition of my works," Bunin told Andrei Sedykh on November 1, 1935, "does not include a great many of my first stories. . . . The reason for this is because . . . I remember that Chekhov once told me, 'I was in Yalta when a new collection of my works appeared. Of course, I was very happy. . . . But after some time, I happened to be in Moscow . . . and wanted a bowl of soup. So I went out and the first thing I saw was my work in a lowly bookstall. . . . I almost got sick to my stomach right then and there. . . . 'To hell with the soup, to hell with the book, too!' I thought. . . . 'I have to get out of here.' . . . It is the same way with me and my early works." See A. Sedykh, "Ivan Bunin rasskazyvaet o Tolstom," *Poslednie novosti,* November 1, 1935, 3.

123. "To Mr. A. Ch——v," a critic wrote to the writer on December 21, 1880, "You are withering without having flowered. A great pity." N. Gitovich, *Letopis' zhizni i tvorchestva A. P. Chekhova* (Moscow: Gosudarstvennoe izdatel'stvo khudozhestvennoi literatury, 1955), 44–45.

124. While proud of surviving their literary boot camp, both authors were later embarrassed by the quality of their early works. For instance, Chekhov flushed red at confessions that he had never worked "on a single story for more than a day." He also often denounced the "hodge-podge," "tripe," and "literary excrement" he had written as a student. See Chekhov to Leikin, October 7, 1884, *Pis'ma,* 1:127; Chekhov to Alexander Chekhov, January 4, 1886, *Pis'ma,* 1:177; Chekhov to Dmitri Grigorovich, March 28, 1886, *Pis'ma,* 1:218–19.

125. See Chekhov to Viktor Bilibin, January 4, 1886, in Chekhova, *Pis'ma,* 134.

126. In this aspect, Chekhov far outstripped Bunin. In his early years, Chekhov seemed to write effortlessly. For instance, by the age of twenty-seven, he had written more than six hundred stories. Such fluidity with the pen, though, had an undesired if not unexpected result: Chekhov was far more unsure of himself as a writer than Bunin and had to work long and hard to develop the simple fluidity that marked his later writings.

127. Chekhov to Suvorin, January 19, 1895, *Pis'ma,* 6:15.

128. See Chekhov to Suvorin, December 1, 1895, *Pis'ma,* 6:104–5.

Bunin and Chekhov also realized that they had entered literature at a time of vast changes in the national written expression. The giants of Russian letters had exited the literary stage. Fyodor Dostoevsky had died in 1881, Ivan Turgenev in 1883. Leo Tolstoy had moved from writer to prophet. In the ensuing void, Bunin stood alongside Chekhov; they regarded themselves as transitional figures whom God and fate had chosen to continue "classical" Russian literature.[129] More important, perhaps, the two considered it their self-appointed duty to steer the literary tradition through what they regarded as the swirling chaos of modernism and to bequeath it, safe and sound, to the next generation of writers. Indeed, the advice Bunin and Chekhov gave to would-be authors and artists drew from their own hard-earned lessons in writing. The experiences of life, captured succinctly, were the ultimate goal. "Do not invent sufferings you have not experienced and landscapes you have not seen," Chekhov cautioned his brother Alexander in 1886, "for a lie in a story is a hundred times more boring than one in a conversation."[130] To Maria Kiselyova that same year, he wrote, "Do not forget that brevity is the mother of all virtues. The moment you come to page eight [in your story] . . . stop!"[131]

Both men also agreed that writers should be calm and collected in their writing. The more tragic the fictional character or situation, they believed, the more detached the writer should be. "If you want your readers to pity the unfortunate and down-and-out in your stories," Chekhov advised Avilova in March 1892, "try to be colder so as to underscore their grief. All your heroes weep, and you sigh with them. Be colder."[132] He continued to Avilova in April of that same year, "One may weep and groan over one's stories, one may share the heroes' sufferings; but one should do so without letting the reader know. The more objective you are, the more powerful the impression."[133]

Regarding their national literature, Bunin agreed with Chekhov on many writers and works. The two cared little for Ivan Goncharov, especially *Oblomov*.[134] Beyond *Fathers and Sons*, they also rejected Turgenev,[135] espe-

---

129. As if aware of his transitional status, Chekhov wrote to Leontiev-Shcheglov, "In our talents there is much phosphorous but no iron. Perhaps we are beautiful birds and sing well, but eagles we are not." Chekhov to Leontiev-Shcheglov, January 22, 1888, *Pis'ma*, 2:180.

130. See Chekhov to Alexander Chekhov, April 6, 1886, *Pis'ma*, 1:230.

131. Chekhov to Kiselyova, September 29, 1886, *Pis'ma*, 1:264.

132. Chekhov to Avilova, March 19, 1892, *Pis'ma*, 5:26.

133. Chekhov to Avilova, April 29, 1892, *Pis'ma*, 5:58.

134. In what had to be the ultimate self-effacement, though, Chekhov believed that "Goncharov is ten times more talented than I." See Chekhov to Suvorin, May 4, 1889, *Pis'ma*, 3:203.

135. "Dear me, what a magnificent novel *Fathers and Sons* is," Chekhov wrote to Suvorin. "Bazarov's illness is so powerfully done that I felt weak when I read it. I even had a feeling I had

cially his heroines. "Pythian priestesses . . . impossibly affected and false," Chekhov noted to Suvorin in 1893. "When you think of Tolstoy's Anna Karenina, all of Turgenev's gentlewomen with their seductive shoulders are not worth a damn."[136] Bunin and Chekhov were also irritated by Fyodor Dostoevsky. "Prolix and pretentious," Chekhov once said of the writer.[137] Most interesting, perhaps, they shared a grudging admiration for Gorky, delighting in his proletarian flamboyance but dismayed by his politically tinged, if heated art.

Bunin and Chekhov, though, loved Mikhail Lermontov, Nikolai Gogol, and Mikhail Saltykov-Shchedrin. They revered Tolstoy as an artist[138]—even *Resurrection* (*Voskresen'e*) enthralled them[139]—but although the two had been Tolstoyans in their youth,[140] they were now bored by his philosophy of art[141] and aghast at many of his thoughts on literature and life. Bunin con-

---

caught the infection from him. And Bazarov's end? And his old parents? And Kukshina? It's all devilishly well done. A work of genius." Chekhov to Suvorin, February 24, 1893, *Pis'ma*, 5:174.

136. Ibid. Chekhov was so annoyed with critics who drew parallels between his work and Turgenev's that he consigned to the writer the same fate he feared for himself. "Only an eighth to a tenth of what Turgenev wrote will survive," Chekhov wrote to Olga Knipper on February 13, 1902. "All the rest will be buried in archives twenty-five to thirty-five years hence." Chekhov to O. Knipper, February 13, 1902, *Pis'ma*, 10:194.

137. Chekhov, though, did credit Dostoevsky for understanding the Russian psyche. "We are such a bone-lazy people," he once told Serebrov-Tikhonov. "We have even infected nature with our laziness. Look at this stream—it is too lazy to move. And see how it twists and turns, and all because of laziness. All our famous 'psychology,' all that Dostoevsky stuff [*dostoevshchina*] is part of it, too." Chekhov to Serebrov-Tikhonov, March 5, 1889, *Pis'ma*, 3:169; Serebrov-Tikhonov, "O Chekhove," 301.

138. "Tolstoy, that Tolstoy!" Chekhov wrote to Suvorin. "He is no mere man . . . but a Jupiter!" (Chekhov to Suvorin, December 11, 1891, *Pis'ma*, 4:322). It should be noted that beyond Tolstoy's fiction, what impressed Chekhov most was the devotion of Tolstoy's daughters toward the great writer. "A man can deceive his fiancée or mistress as he likes," Chekhov observed, "and, in the eyes of a woman in love, even a donkey appears as a philosopher, but daughters are quite a different proposition." Chekhov to Suvorin, October 26, 1895, *Pis'ma*, 6:87.

139. "I have just read *Resurrection*," Chekhov wrote to Gorky. "Everything in it, with the exception of the rather obscure and artificial relations between Nekhlyudov and Katya, struck me by its richness, strength, and breadth . . . as well as by the insincerity of a man who is afraid of death but, not wanting to admit such a thing, clutches desperately to the texts from the holy writ." Chekhov to Gorky, February 14, 1900, *Pis'ma*, 9:53.

140. "Tolstoy's philosophy had a powerful effect on me . . . for six or seven years," Chekhov wrote to Suvorin, "but it was not Tolstoy's premises . . . that affected me, but rather his manner of expression, good sense . . . and hypnotic qualities. . . . But now Tolstoy has already passed out of my life. He is no longer in my soul. Rather, he has left me saying, 'I leave your house empty.' So I am free of this tenant." Chekhov to Suvorin, March 27, 1894, *Pis'ma*, 5:283.

141. For instance, Chekhov wrote to Ertel', "Tolstoy's idea [about the demise of contemporary art] is not new. It has been reiterated in various forms by clever old men in every

curred with Chekhov, of course, on such Tolstoyan sociopolitical tenets as hatred of violence, love for the poor, and desires for justice and moral perfection, on the one hand, and such artistic concepts as Tolstoy's dislike for the young decadents and symbolists, particularly for what he saw as their posturing in art, on the other. Dmitri Merezhkovsky and Zinaida Gippius, for instance, were for Chekhov (and Bunin) frauds. Leonid Andreev was an "artificial nightingale."[142] Read one page of the writer, Chekhov told Bunin, and "you need to take a two-hour walk in the fresh air."[143] Similarly, Chekhov told Gorky, "I have been thinking of Balmont's poem, 'The Fragrance of the Sun' ('Aromat solntsa'). It is a silly thing. In Russia the sun smells of Kazan soap, but here it stinks of Tatar sweat."[144]

Bunin joined with Chekhov, however, in distaste for Tolstoy's idea of nonresistance to evil. They also disliked the writer's cult of the folk as an answer to the problems of the world. "I have peasant blood flowing in my veins," Chekhov wrote to Suvorin in 1894. "So I am not the one to be impressed by peasant virtues. . . . War and the legal systems are evil, true, but does this mean that I should wear bast shoes and sleep on a stove alongside the hired hand and his wife?"[145] He continued to Serebrov-Tikhonov, "The Russian peasant was never religious. Long ago he shoved the devil under the sweating bench into the steam bath."[146] Further, whereas Tolstoy believed that society should live the life of peasants, Bunin and Chekhov believed that peasants should live the life of society. As the character Masha asserts in Chekhov's 1896 story "My Life" ("Moia zhizn'"), the two men agreed that when people work, dress, and eat like peasants "they somehow lend support to those heavy clumsy coats, ghastly huts, and stupid beards."[147]

Bunin and Chekhov also disliked how Tolstoy preached abstinence from earthly joys in this life to enjoy spiritual ones in the next. "Something in me protests [against Tolstoy]," Chekhov continued to Suvorin in 1894. "My sense of fair play tells me that there is more love of humanity in steam and electric-

---

century. Old men have always been inclined to think that the end of the world is at hand, that morals have sunk to the ne plus ultra, that art has grown shallow and threadbare, that people have grown weak, and the like. Lev Nikolaevich is out to convince everybody . . . that art in our time has entered its final phase and that it is stuck in a blind alley from which it has no way out." Chekhov to Ertel', April 17, 1897, *Pis'ma*, 6:333.

142. See Chekhov to Gorky, July 29, 1902, *Pis'ma*, 11:13.

143. Quoted in I. Bunin, *Okaiannye dni* (Moscow: Sovetskii pisatel', 1990), 118.

144. In his 1904 and 1915 versions of his memoirs of Chekhov, Bunin included this comment from the writer: "Tell me, do you like the poetry of Alexei Tolstoy? In my opinion, he is an actor. As a youth, he put on operatic costume and wore it for the rest of his life." See Bunin, "Pamiati Chekhova," 249 (see preface, n. 2).

145. Chekhov to Suvorin, March 27, 1894, *Pis'ma*, 5:283.

146. Quoted in Kotov, *A. P. Chekhov*, 299.

147. Chekhov, *Sochineniia*, 9:259.

ity than in chastity and abstention from meat."[148] Tolstoy's willful obscurantism over matters of the flesh was a particular thorn in Chekhov's professional side. "The one thing I am unwilling to pardon in Tolstoy," he wrote to Pleshcheev in 1890, "is his audacious handling of topics about which he knows nothing and which, out of obstinacy, he does not wish to understand. His opinions of syphilis . . . and of women's aversion to sexual intercourse . . . are not only debatable but also expose him as an ignorant man who has never taken the trouble to read what the specialists have written about such things."[149]

Despite their self-appointed safeguarding of the national canon, Bunin and Chekhov saw themselves as outsiders in the Russian literary world. They had little use for their colleagues or their lifestyles or beliefs. "Russian writers," Chekhov wrote to Suvorin in 1889, "live in drainpipes, eat slugs, and make love to sluts and laundresses. They know nothing of history, geography, or the natural sciences."[150] They are also horrified at what they considered to be the moral and aesthetic stagnation of their confreres. "In our time," Chekhov wrote to Suvorin in 1892, "there is a lack of spirits that intoxicate and subjugate. Tell me sincerely who among my contemporaries . . . has given to the world so much as one drop of alcohol? Are not Korolenko, Nadson, and all the playwrights nowadays producing a sort of lemonade? . . . It is a sour, flaccid, boring time."[151]

It was thus both personal temperament and public circumstances that led Bunin and Chekhov to opt for absolute freedom and independence in art. With their shared dislike for organizations and groups, they cared little

---

148. Chekhov to Suvorin, March 27, 1894, *Pis'ma*, 5:283–84.

149. Chekhov to Pleshcheev, February 15, 1890, *Pis'ma*, 4:18. Tolstoy returned the charge. "Chekhov's medicine is a hindrance to him," he told Gorky. "If he had not been a doctor, he would have written much better" (Gor'kii, "Lev Tolstoi," *Polnoe sobranie sochinenii*, 16:305).

"I am afraid that I will never be a Tolstoyan!" Chekhov confided to Suvorin. "What I love best about women is their beauty, and about the history of humankind and culture—carpets, carriages with springs, and keen minds" (Chekhov to Suvorin, August 30, 1891, *Pis'ma*, 4:267).

Chekhov had additional bones to pick with Tolstoy. More specifically, Chekhov believed that Tolstoy's discounting of science, medicine, doctors, and the like promoted obscurantism and hindered the well-being of society. He also had little empathy for Tolstoy's severe guilt over being a landowner, since he took a "capitalist" pride in his possessions.

Chekhov also disliked Tolstoy's authoritarianism, particularly the often high-handed way in which the great writer blessed, condemned, and forgave humankind. Indeed, the very fact that Tolstoy was turning his back on literature to venture into more worldly spheres, Chekhov regarded both as a sign of creeping senility and as a betrayal not only of the great writer's talents but also of Russian literature as a whole.

It should be noted that Chekhov, in his conversations with Tolstoy, rarely got a word in edgewise with the great writer but received his proclamations with passive resistance. Simply put, throughout their relationship, the wide-eyed prophet and the courteous skeptic maintained a respectful distance from one another.

150. Chekhov to Suvorin, May 15, 1889, *Pis'ma*, 3:217.

151. Chekhov to Suvorin, November 25, 1892, *Pis'ma*, 5:133–34.

for literary theories, schools,[152] and the biases of "thick" journals.[153] "When people talk to me about what is artistic and inartistic, or stageworthy and unstageworthy," Chekhov wrote to Leontiev-Shcheglov in 1890, "or about tendencies, realism, and the like, I am at a loss as to what to say. So halfheartedly I nod a reply with half-truths which are not worth a farthing. I divide all works into two kinds: those I like and those I do not. I have no other yardstick. If you ask me why I like Shakespeare and do not like Zlatovratsky, I will have no answer. Perhaps I shall grow wise in time and acquire a criterion, but meanwhile all aesthetic discussions just exhaust me and seem like continuations of the scholastic disputes with which people wearied themselves in the Middle Ages."[154]

The literary success Bunin shared with Chekhov in life did not mean, though, that they were content with themselves as artists, or that they did not suffer abuse from both without and within. They took pride in their achievements, true; but it also seemed that for every step forward the two took in the delight and growth of their talent, they took one back in doubt and despair over their gifts.

From within, both men experienced dark nights of the soul regarding themselves and their work. Chekhov, for instance, saw himself as a "complete ignoramus . . . [who] longed to hole up somewhere . . . and learn

---

152. Chekhov told Leontiev-Shcheglov:

We cannot all feel and think alike, for our aims are different; or else we have no aims, we know each other very little or not at all, and there is nothing that could unite us in a single group. But do we want such a group? I do not think so.

To be of assistance to a fellow writer, to respect his personality and his work, not to spread all sorts of tales about him, to envy him his success, to lie to him and play the hypocrite, it is necessary . . . to be merely a human being. Let us be ordinary men, let us cultivate the same attitude to everybody, and then we shall not want any artificially contrived solidarity. As for the desire to establish professional solidarity among a small circle of writers, it would only result in unintentional spying, suspiciousness, and control, so that, without wishing it ourselves, we should have founded something that resembled the Society of Jesus. (Chekhov to Leontiev-Shcheglov, May 3, 1888, *Pis'ma*, 2:203)

153. Chekhov wrote to Yakov Polonsky:

A stifling, clannish spirit reigns in all our "thick" journals. Perhaps there was some sense to it when monthly periodicals were edited by . . . Belinsky, Herzen, and the like, people who not only paid decently but also attracted, taught, and educated you. But now when ["thick" journals] are edited by . . . literary dachshunds (I cannot help feeling that dachshunds with their long bodies, short legs, and pointed muzzles are a cross between professors, who are civil servants, and dull-witted men of letters) . . . they will create an entire order which will succeed in perverting literary tastes and views to such a degree . . . that we will not be able to recognize them. (Chekhov to Polonsky, January 18, 1888, *Pis'ma*, 2:177–78)

154. Chekhov to Leontiev-Shcheglov, March 22, 1890, *Pis'ma*, 4:44.

everything from scratch."[155] Most serious, perhaps, were the moments when both Bunin and Chekhov were utterly repulsed by their craft. "I have lost all taste for writing and do not know what to do," Chekhov wrote to Avilova in 1898. "When I write or think about what I ought to write, I feel as nauseated as if a cockroach has just been removed from my soup."[156]

Bunin and Chekhov were also alike in their fear that after their deaths, their works would be confined to oblivion. "I have cleared the way for writers . . . to [reach] the hearts of decent people," Chekhov confided to Suvorin in 1888. "For the present, this is only my own merit . . . this is my own worth. . . . Everything I have written, everything I have received the [Pushkin] prize for . . . will live no more than ten years in people's memories."[157]

From without, both Bunin and Chekhov suffered at the hands of readers and reviewers who, confounded by the artistic originality and independence of the two men, sought numerous and often cruel ways to force them into conventional modes of art, thinking, and acceptance. They both were exasperated and chagrined by audiences who, accustomed to the grandeur of the Russian novel, sought "tendencies" in their writing and wrongly regarded their maverick status as vaunting a worldview which— despite the protests of the two men to the contrary[158]—smacked of self-indulgence, conservatism, and indifference to the problems of the day.[159] "But in this story do I indeed not—from beginning to end—protest

155. See Chekhov to Suvorin, circa December 20, 1889, *Pis'ma*, 3:304.

156. Chekhov to Avilova, July 1898, *Pis'ma*, 5:49. Similarly, Chekhov had written to Suvorin, "I am well over thirty and feel as if I were nearly forty. I have grown crassly indifferent to everything in the world. . . . I get out of bed and go to bed feeling as if I had lost all interest in life. It is either . . . excessive fatigue or some kind of unconscious . . . process which novelists call a spiritual upheaval." Chekhov to Suvorin, April 8, 1892, *Pis'ma*, 7:244.

157. Chekhov to Suvorin, October 10, 1888, *Pis'ma*, 3:23. Chekhov was awarded the Pushkin Prize in 1888, Bunin in 1903, 1907, and 1915. It should also be noted that Chekhov was so convinced of Korolenko's superiority to him as a writer that when he was informed of having won the Pushkin Prize, he insisted that he would accept the honor only if he could share the money from the award with his admired colleague. See Chekhov to Alexander Chekhov, October 21, 1887, *Pis'ma*, 2:134.

158. In an early version of his memoirs on Chekhov, Bunin recalled, "I never saw Chekhov in an evil frame of mind. And if he ever became irritated, he got hold himself in an amazing type of way. I remember how he once became . . . [when a critic] talked about his pessimism, as well as about his 'indifference' to social and moral questions [in art]. His response to the reviewer he uttered in two severe and thoughtful words. 'Complete idiot!' Chekhov said." Bunin, "Pamiati Chekhova," 262.

159. In his memoirs, Lazarev-Gruzinsky recalls, "Among Chekhov's precepts for writers . . . the admonition against tendencies was the most frequent. Chekhov was such a fervent enemy of tendentiousness . . . that he reverted to the subject with a kind of passionate insistence. . . . What was it that caused Chekhov to do such a thing? In my opinion, it was his reaction as a writer to the reproaches of 'indifference,' 'apathy,' and 'lack of principle' showered upon him by

against lying?" Chekhov wrote to Pleshcheev in 1889. "And, in truth, is this not a 'direction'?"[160] A year earlier, he told the same addressee, "When I draw my 'types,' I do not think of liberal or conservative tendencies but of stupidity and pretensions."[161]

The public at large was thus seen by Bunin and Chekhov as "less than house spirits (*domovye*) . . . uneducated, ill-mannered . . . unscrupulous and insincere."[162] Russian readers, the two insisted, were the willing captives of "vulgar writers . . . who fanned the hypocrisy of the bourgeois with their narrow virtues"[163] and with their willingness to stay within the confines of conventional (read: nonthreatening) art. "New forms of literature produce new forms of life," Chekhov wrote in his notebooks. "That is why they are so revolting to the conservative mind."[164] For Bunin and Chekhov, aesthetics should reflect and raise the hopes of society. When Chekhov heard the news that Gorky intended to replicate the Moscow Art Theater with a "people's theater" in Nizhnyi Novgorod, he declared to Nemirovich-Danchenko, "People's theaters and people's literature are just foolishness. They are something to sweeten up the people. Gogol should not be lowered to the level of the people; rather, they should be raised to his."[165] In fact, it was one of Chekhov's most cherished beliefs that "culture and the commune were incompatible."[166] Even worse for Bunin and Chekhov, perhaps, were the editors and reviewers who, for political or aesthetic reasons, classified both the personalities and works of the two men with labels that were simplistic, contradictory, and demeaning. "The people I fear the most," Chekhov confessed to Pleshcheev in 1888, "are those who see me as either liberal or conservative. I am neither a liberal nor a conservative, nor a gradualist nor a monk. . . . I should like to say that I am a free artist and nothing else."[167]

If Bunin and Chekhov took solace both from work and from one another, it was also because they practiced their craft in similar ways. Declaring that "subjects [*siuzhety*] were rubbish,"[168] both chose stories over sagas and shunned grandiose theories and ideas. "I finished a boring story in which

---

Mikhailovsky, Skabichevsky, and other critics." A. Lazarev-Gruzinskii, "A. P. Chekhov," in Kotov, *A. P. Chekhov*, 444.

160. Chekhov to Pleshcheev, September 1889, *Pis'ma*, 2:404.

161. Chekhov to Pleshcheev, September 1888, *Pis'ma*, 3:19.

162. See Chekhov to Suvorin, December 23, 1888, *Pis'ma*, 3:98.

163. See Chekhov to Suvorin, August 15, 1894, *Pis'ma*, 5:311.

164. Chekhov, *Sochineniia*, 17:158.

165. Chekhov to Nemirovich-Danchenko, November 2, 1894, *Pis'ma*, 11:294.

166. Chekhov to Suvorin, January 17, 1899, *Pis'ma*, 8:24.

167. Chekhov to Pleshcheev, October 4, 1888, *Pis'ma*, 3:11.

168. "I. A. Bunin o Chekhove," *Iuzhnyi krai*, July 4, 1914, 2; as quoted in V. Geideko, *A. Chekhov i Iv. Bunin* (Moscow: Sovetskii pisatel', 1976), 274.

I attempted to philosophize a little," Chekhov complained to Leontiev-Shcheglov in 1888, "but it turned out to be resin with vinegar."[169] Similarly, Chekhov wrote to Olga Knipper on April 20, 1904, "You ask what life is. That is like asking what a carrot is. A carrot is a carrot, and there is nothing more to know."[170]

The reason for such "objectivity" in art, Bunin and Chekhov agreed, was simple. Both men, together with the people and times they portrayed in their works, were "modern," that is, they were devoid of worthy goals, ideas, or myths with which to live life. "We [writers] paint life as it is, but beyond that, we do nothing at all," Chekhov told Suvorin in 1892. "Flog us, but we can do nothing more."[171]

In the absence of things great and grand, Bunin shared with Chekhov a focus on "prosaics," that is, on what they regarded as the more revealing and relevant minutiae of existence. With each passing year, they saw more clearly the relationship between literature and life. Existence, they believed, lacked spectacular events, high-flown phrases, and great sorrows and joys. People, fictional and otherwise, who knew the purpose of life, were to be pitied, not praised. Rather, Bunin and Chekhov believed that life featured only small canvases on which gray areas and rhetorical questions moved to ideological paradoxes and benign absurdities.

Gifted with extraordinary insight and intuition, Bunin and Chekhov could grasp a person's "prosaics" in a flash. A veined leg or a pockmarked nose was all they needed to spin entire stories and to comment insightfully on existence. Their senses moved at will between warmth and cold, lightness and dark, virtue and vice. Their eyes scoured mansions and huts, their noses sniffed flowers and dung, their tongues savored shrimp and snow. Like Bunin's, Chekhov's hands stroked fur and flesh, and his ears picked up on gossip, tuned in on intonations, and delighted in accents from all over Russia and the world. "No one can write so simply about simple things as you can," Gorky told Chekhov in 1900. "Your tales are exquisite vials filled with the smells of life."[172]

The creative goal that Bunin shared with Chekhov was simple: they wished that when "their readers closed their eyes, they would see pictures."[173] Any item—the smaller and more insignificant the better—was for

---

169. Chekhov to Leontiev-Shcheglov, April 18, 1888, *Pis'ma*, 2:249.

170. Chekhov to O. Knipper, April 20, 1904, *Pis'ma*, 12:93.

171. Chekhov to Suvorin, November 25, 1892, *Pis'ma*, 5:133.

172. Gor'kii, early January 1900, *Polnoe Sobranie Sochinenii: Pis'ma*, 2:8.

173. Chekhov to Alexander Chekhov, May 10, 1886, *Pis'ma*, 1:242. Similarly, Chekhov wrote to Alexander Zhirkevich, "Above all, a description of nature must be so vivid that the reader can conjure up your landscape immediately after he has read it and closed his eyes. But the piling

them impetus to original and independent art. In a meeting with Nikolai Teleshov, for instance, Chekhov pointed to a greasy spot on the wall: the resting place of cabbies for their tired heads. "Now here you complain there are few themes [for art]," Chekhov scolded his colleague. "But is this [spot] not a suitable subject? . . . At first, there seems to be nothing interesting about it. But if you look closely, you will find something in it, something *all its own,* something which no one else has found or described."[174]

In their "prosaic" focus, also, Bunin and Chekhov rejected both the larger-than-life characters of Dostoevsky or Tolstoy, as well as the activist-rebels of Gorky and other proletarian writers. From their stories they struck "virtuous peasants, devoted slaves, moralizing old ladies, kind old nurses, rustic wits, red-nosed captains, and the 'new' people."[175] Rather, Bunin was drawn, as was Chekhov, to the "loose change" of society, to the pitiful characters who laughed only when they hurt and who groped their way through life, equipped only with enough intelligence, knowledge, and emotion to regret the past, abuse the present, and disavow the future. The works of Bunin and Chekhov featured gentry ruined by the emancipation, peasants crushed by poverty and ignorance, and professionals trapped in staid careers. They relished the torments of individuals burning in their private hells: husbands and wives caught between stifling marriages and painful affairs; bachelors and old maids torn between clinging to old ways and striking out for a new life; parents, clergy, and officials abusing the weak but idolizing the strong; and students vacillating between ethereal illusions, on the one hand, and the earthly allures of sex and sin, on the other. With heroines, however, both writers were of two minds. Their stories featured a roving, if patriarchal, eye for the ladies. "Describe your women in such a way," Chekhov told Lazarev-Gruzinsky in 1888, "that the reader feels your tie is off and your waistcoat is open. With women and nature . . . let yourself go."[176] Yet their works also exposed the dark side of sexuality: the ruthless exploitation of one being over another, often ending in violence and death. The lot of the heroines in Bunin and Chekhov, though, mirrored the fate of their heroes. Metaphorically speaking, both sexes were doomed to trudge an endless dirty road, to face a prison wall, or to endure a pointless life. "Your talent has brought to light the lives and the very souls of the simple and most ordinary human be-

---

up of such features as twilight, leaden hues, ponds, dampness, the silveriness of poplars, horizons with storm clouds, sparrows, distant meadows—that is not a picture because no matter how hard I try, I cannot visualize it as a harmonious whole." Chekhov to Zhirkevich, August 2, 1895, *Pis'ma,* 6:47.

174. Quoted in N. Teleshov, "A. P. Chekhov," in Kotov, *A. P. Chekhov,* 165.

175. Chekhov to Suvorin, March 11, 1889, *Pis'ma,* 3:178.

176. See A. Chekhov, *Perepiska Chekhova v trekh tomakh,* vol. 1 (Moscow: Nasledie, 1966), 446.

ings," Pyotr Kurkin wrote to Chekhov. "The streets are full of such people, and every one of them bears with him a particle of the existence you describe."[177]

For Bunin and Chekhov, less was always more. Although both men called themselves realists, they shunned "Turgenev-like descriptiveness."[178] Rather, Bunin and Chekhov saw themselves as closet impressionists who relished light touches, pastel dabs, and evanescent hints and who chose the veiled gossamer of memory, not the harsh glare of life.[179] "You are killing realism," Gorky wrote to Chekhov in early January 1900. "And you will succeed, too—for good, forever. . . . After the most inconsequential of your stories, everything else seems coarse, written with a log instead of a pen."[180]

Finally, in their mature writing, both Bunin and Chekhov were perfectionists, obsessive-compulsives of the first order. They labored painfully to create simple and sober styles—"ascetically austere and direct," Chekhov told Bunin[181]—as well as to minimalize their presence in their tales. To the exasperation of editors and publishers, the two missed deadlines and fretted over commas and semicolons. "In a work of art," Chekhov told a beginning writer in 1897, "punctuation often plays the part of musical notation. It demands instinct and experience, not knowledge from a textbook."[182] Many times also, Bunin joined with Chekhov in squeezing their works so dry of what they thought was excess that they wound up with paragraphs, not pages.

In *About Chekhov,* Bunin sought to articulate three facets of his relationship with the writer. In the first, Bunin looked to Chekhov as an older brother-mentor who offered wisdom and companionship in both literature and life.

177. Quoted in V. Ermilov, *A. P. Chekhov* (Moscow: Sovetskii pisatel', 1959), 436.

178. Chekhov to Suvorin, February 24, 1893, *Pis'ma,* 5:175.

179. For instance, Chekhov wrote to Fyodor Batiushkov, "I can write only from recollections. I have never written straight from nature. I need to let a subject strain through my memory until only what is important or typical remains as on a filter." Chekhov to Batiushkov, December 15, 1897, *Pis'ma,* 7:123.

180. Gor'kii, *Polnoe Sobranie Sochinenii: Pis'ma,* 2:8. Compare Tolstoy's remark to Alexander Goldenweiser: "In Chekhov everything is real to the verge of illusion. His stories give the impression of a stereoscope. He throws words about in an apparent disorder, and, like an impressionist painter, he achieves wonderful results by his touches." A. Gol'denveizer, *Vblizi Tolstogo* (Moscow: Gosudarstevennoe izdatel'stvo khudozhestvennoi literatury, 1959), 68–69.

Also compare Vladimir L'vov-Rogachevsky's remark that in the work of Bunin and Chekhov, one feels the "beginnings of the new realism which makes use of the great work by the poet-symbolists." V. L'vov-Rogachevskii, "Simvoliki i nasledniki ikh," *Sovremennik,* no. 7 (1913): 307.

181. Bunin, "Pamiati Chekhova," 249.

182. Chekhov to Rimma Vashuk-Neishtadt, March 28, 1897, *Pis'ma,* 6:318.

In the second, Bunin regarded Chekhov as a doppelgänger or alter ego in which everything Bunin said and believed about the writer, he also said and believed about himself. And in the third, Bunin looked to Chekhov as a national treasure who needed to be preserved not from the ravages of time but, as noted previously, from the views of Westerners, Soviets, and émigrés who, in Bunin's opinion, were distorting or misinterpreting key aspects of his life and work.

Bunin realized, of course, that with *About Chekhov*, he had set about a difficult task. Even before he could establish credibility with the stances he had assumed for himself as to the object of his affection, he had to deal with several aspects of Chekhov's life and work which he found unpalatable or difficult to accept.

A first challenge for Bunin in *About Chekhov* was the objectivity he needed to maintain toward the subject of his study. As much as Bunin wanted to identify with Chekhov personally, he sought to keep his distance socially and aesthetically. First and foremost was the fact that Chekhov was from the very folk whom Bunin, as an aristocrat, had disliked before the revolution and whom he despised after. In fact, so convinced was Bunin of the answer to the question—"What good could come from [Chekhov's birthplace] Taganrog?"—that he cast aside both the Russian and Ukrainian origins of the writer's family. Rather, calling attention to the pronounced cheekbones, large mouths, and somewhat slanted eyes of the clan, Bunin pronounced the Chekhovs "people from the East": Mongols. (In truth, the often grim portraits of Chekhov and his family gave Bunin some evidence for such an assertion.) Bunin, though, was enough of a gentry writer to realize that select individuals of the folk could teach him much about literature and life. And, when he was with Chekhov and his family, he was gracious to admit both to himself and to the readers of *About Chekhov* that Mongols could be nice people, too.

Bunin sought to keep an even further distance between himself and Chekhov aesthetically. As noted earlier, he agreed with Chekhov on what both men saw as key bases in art. What Bunin abhorred, though, was the widespread consensus that he was a clone of the writer: a "Chekhov light" who duplicated the writer's content and form but lacked independence and originality. Bunin realized that in the all-too-close association of himself with his "elder brother," he had an uphill battle to fight. Throughout the lives of both writers—and after—critics commented on Bunin's relish for Chekhov's alleged "melancholic late-autumn days": scenes in which an eerie stillness and silvery shadows embraced fallen leaves, moonlit lakes, and empty homes, rendering everything as "strange, lonely . . . and helpless."[183] Alexander Izmailov wrote in the *Exchange News* (*Birzhevnye vedomosti*) in

183. Gor'kii, "A. P. Chekhov," *Polnoe sobranie sochinenii*, 6:54.

1

1912, "One cannot talk about Bunin without disturbing the splendid shadow of Chekhov. . . . Body and soul, Bunin is part of Chekhov's generation, his mood, his likes and dislikes."[184]

Such closeness, though, Bunin accepted only to an extent. "Did Chekhov influence me as a writer?" Bunin responded to a question posed by an interviewer from the *Odessa News* (*Odesskie novosti*) in 1914. "No, I was engrossed by him; I was enraptured by him; but I never wanted to write like he did. . . . Chekhov influenced me, but the influence was not direct."[185] On a stronger note, he added later, "I state without hesitation that there has never been anything of Chekhov in my works."[186] It also should be noted that Bunin did not always approve of his colleague's writings. "Chekhov has several stories that I simply adore," he told Alexander Bakhrakh, "but he also has much that I find unacceptable. I have just now finished rereading a collection of his stories, and it was remarkable how many of them were weak and contrived. For instance, Chekhov writes, 'There was a storm in his soul.' Such phrases I would have struck out with a pencil."[187]

A second—and more problematic—issue in Bunin's study of Chekhov was the elder writer's love life, particularly his tie to Lydia Avilova. The facts are these: When the twenty-nine-year-old Chekhov met Avilova on January 24, 1889, he was first capturing public notice as a potentially great writer. He had already published three volumes of short stories, including some of his most famous ones, such as "The Steppe." The object of his future fascination was four years younger, the wife of a man working in the Ministry of Education (whom she did not love). Avilova was tall and statuesque, with rosy cheeks, big blue eyes, and luxurious hair worn in long thick braids. She was also the mother of a small child. (Two more were to follow.) Like a heroine in one of Chekhov's stories, though, Avilova was bored with domestic life. She nourished ambitions not only of becoming a writer primarily of children's stories but also of having Chekhov at her side in whatever physical or spiritual capacity life would allow them.

---

184. A. Izmailov, "Iubilei I. A. Bunina," *Birzhevnye vedomosti*, October 27, 1912, 3. Comparisons between the two men became even more pronounced with the publication of Bunin's *The Village*. For instance, on March 2, 1910, a critic for the newspaper *Morning Russia* (*Utro Rossii*) posited similarities between Bunin's Tikhon Krasov and Chekhov's Lopakhin. "Utro," *Utro Rossii*, March 2, 1910, 3.

Also compare Bunin's (undated) complaint to his nephew, Nikolai Pusheshnikov: "All my life people have pecked at me for the Chekhovlike things in my works!" Quoted in A. Baboreko, "Chekhov v perepiske i zapisiakh Bunina. Novye materialy," *A. P. Chekhov: Sbornik statei i materialov* (Simferopol': Krymizdat, 1962), 27.

185. Quoted in A. Ninov, "K avtobiografii I. Bunina," *Novyi mir,* no. 10 (1965): 230.

186. Quoted in I. Gazer, "A. P. Chekhov i Bunin,"*Sbornik statei i materialov,* no. 3 (Rostov-na-Donu: Rostovskie knizhnoe, 1963), 198.

187. A. Bakhrakh, "Chetyre goda s Buninym," *Russkie novosti*, November 9, 1945, 5.

When in 1947 Bunin first read Avilova's memoirs in Kotov's *Chekhov*, he was surprised, even shocked, by revelations that Chekhov and Avilova had had a discreet—and five-year-long —"love story." To hear Avilova tell it, the two had been attracted to each other so strongly that, in the period from 1889 to 1894, they had regularly fought urges to throw caution to the winds and to seek a new life together. Even more revealing, perhaps, was Avilova's assertion that the hopeless love between the two had forced Chekhov to Sakhalin.

Bunin was not alone in his amazement about a tie between Chekhov and Avilova—and with good reason. Almost without exception, scholars of Chekhov doubt many of Avilova's assertions about her "affair" with the writer. They point out that her recollections, written in 1943—thirty-nine years after Chekhov's death and a year before Avilova's own passing—suffer lapses in time, space, and truth. Further, the facts of the alleged relationship between Chekhov and Avilova cause investigators into the writer's life and work to assert no tangible evidence of love between the two. They claim that despite the supposed fireworks that marked Chekhov and Avilova's first en-counter—"a rocket exploded in my soul . . . brightly, joyfully, triumphantly, rapturously," she wrote in her memoirs—Chekhov did not respond to her subsequent letter, nor did he make any attempt to see her a second time. In fact, it was a full three years later that Chekhov contacted Avilova with a rather brash apology, saying that "he had forgotten her name . . . since he had thrown the letter away and pocketed the stamp. . . . [That was his usual response to] requests, especially when they come from ladies."[188]

Aficionados of Chekhov's life and work also record not only other year-long silences in correspondence and meetings but also discrepancies and omissions, implausibilities and illogicalities surrounding the chronotopes in-forming the relationship. They call into question Avilova's assertion that the two engaged in a secret correspondence. They wonder why Chekhov never mentioned an attraction to Avilova in conversations or letters with family and friends (Bunin included). More seriously, perhaps, scholars who have stud-ied the alleged attraction between Chekhov and Avilova note the striking variance between the prolonged and passionate outbursts Chekhov pur-portedly made at various intervals in Avilova's memoirs and the actual casual and bantering letters he wrote to his supposed "love." In fact, in his corre-spondence with Avilova, Chekhov was often not only brusque with the love-struck woman but also critical of her writing. "Your laziness and lack of ex-perience and confidence stand out on every line you write," he wrote to

188. Chekhov to Avilova, March 19, 1892, *Pis'ma,* 5:27.

Avilova in 1897. "You do not work on your sentences. You must. That is what makes art."[189] Further, investigators of Chekhov and Avilova find fault with the conversations between the two. They note that Chekhov's purported parleys with Avilova are often out of character with both the content and the form of his discourse, that is, his discussions with his "love" about their encounters in other lives and their slow but steady progress to each other over time.

Scholars of Chekhov's life and work, though, overlook a number of facts in their investigation of the writer and Avilova. First and foremost, there is considerable evidence that the two had a brief but intense attraction. True, Chekhov was not the aggressor in the relationship, but at its inception he was sufficiently intrigued—and discreet—to find out more about Avilova. "If you should happen to be at the office of the *Petersburg Gazette*," Chekhov wrote to his brother Alexander in 1894, "try and find out the address of Lydia Avilova, the sister of Mrs. Khudyakova. And please, find out quietly, without any talk."[190]

Further, hearsay of a liaison between Chekhov and Avilova was legion. Sergei Rachmaninoff witnessed a scene in which Tolstoy, as a guest in Chekhov's house, chided the writer openly for his behavior. "Why are you courting another man's wife?" Tolstoy asked Chekhov, adding, "That is not proper!"[191] The most colorful rumor, though, was the one that had reached Avilova's husband and that she, in abject terror, reported to Chekhov—that Chekhov, in a drunken moment, had announced publicly to friends that he intended to seduce Avilova, have her divorce her husband, and marry her himself. (Chekhov denied the allegation.)[192]

---

189. Chekhov to Avilova, November 3, 1897, *Pis'ma*, 7:93–94. Compare earlier remarks by Chekhov on Avilova's writing: "To sum up, you are talented, but too heavy, to put it vulgarly, flabby. You belong to the ranks of flabby writers. Your style is as precious as an old man's" (Chekhov to Avilova, February 15, 1895, *Pis'ma*, 6:25).

Chekhov, though, did sometimes apologize to Avilova for the harshness of his criticism: "I often hear so many good things about you that I become sad . . . when I think of the uncalled-for severity with which I chastised you. We are old friends, after all; and, at the very least, I would like to have it remain that way. . . . I always read your stories with great pleasure" (Chekhov to Avilova, July 10, 1898, *Pis'ma*, 7:237).

190. Chekhov to Alexander Chekhov, December 30, 1894, *Pis'ma*, 5:350.

191. It should be noted that investigators into the tie between Chekhov and Avilova have been unaware of Tolstoy's interest in the liaison. See Muromtseva-Bunina's diary excerpt, dated August 6, 1930, in M. Grin, *Ustami Buninykh: Dnevniki Ivana Alexeevicha i Very Nikolaevny i drugie arkhivnye materialy v trekh tomakh*, 3 vols. (Frankfurt am Main: Posev, 1977–81), 2:228.

192. "What is this fantasy of yours?" Chekhov wrote to Avilova. "My dignity forbids me to justify myself. . . . As far as I can judge, it is all gossip. Am I correct? If you trust me as earnestly

Second, for all the ups and downs in their relationship, Chekhov and Avilova kept passing each other like ships in the night or, more darkly, like moths about a flame. Avilova was one of the precious few who not only defended Chekhov's *The Seagull* in print after its disastrous 1896 debut in St. Petersburg but also proclaimed the writer as a new kind of dramatist for the Russian theater.[193] The two also kept up a voluminous correspondence. As much as Chekhov refused to acknowledge, much less accept, Avilova's love, he was unwilling to cast her off forever. In response to her complaints about his indifference, his harshness about her writing, and his unwillingness to accept her many invitations, Chekhov wrote to Avilova in 1898, "If my letters are sometimes harsh and cold, it is my frivolous nature that is to blame."[194]

Even when the relationship had ended, Chekhov could not leave Avilova in peace. In 1899, he asked Avilova to assist him in finding stories of his that had been published in the *Petersburg Gazette* (*Peterburgskaya Gazeta*) and which he wished to include in a complete edition of his works. Avilova agreed gladly. She also began a new correspondence with Chekhov that patched up the differences between the two and that was more relaxed and confiding than it had been previously. "You are very kind to me," Chekhov wrote to Avilova. "I have said it a thousand times and I will say it once again." Two months later, he continued, "When shall we see each other? I must see you to put into words how infinitely grateful I am to you [for your assistance] and how much, indeed, I would like to see you."[195] In fact, Chekhov felt sufficiently comfortable with Avilova to invite her and her three children for coffee and buns at the train station whence the four of them had planned to leave for the country. Even Chekhov's final letter to Avilova—a response to her congratulations on his marriage to Olga Knipper[196]—is sufficiently ambiguous to suggest both sorrow and regret

---

as you do the gossips, I ask you not to believe all the bad things said about people in Petersburg. Or if you must believe them, believe them all, wholesale, e.g., my marriage into five million rubles, my affairs with the wives of my best friends, and the like. But for heaven's sake, do calm down. . . . Think of me what you will." Chekhov to Avilova, March 19, 1892, *Pis'ma*, 5:27.

193. See L. Avilova, "Pis'mo v redaktsiiu," *Peterburskaia gazeta*, October 20, 1896. Curiously, the text of Avilova's letter has been published only recently. See "Avilova i Chekhov na fone 'Chaiki'," *Nauka*, no. 1 (2001): 31–33.

194. Chekhov to Avilova, July 10, 1898, *Pis'ma*, 7:237.

195. Chekhov to Avilova, February 18, 1899, *Pis'ma*, 8:94; Chekhov to Avilova, April 27, 1899, *Pis'ma*, 8:159.

196. It should be noted that Olga Knipper was taking no chances with Avilova's reentry into Chekhov's life. Even before Olga had married Chekhov, she wrote to the writer on March 2, 1901: "I have just received a letter from Avilova, you seem to know her. She wishes . . . a ticket to the *Sisters*. I replied politely that I could not get her one." See A. Derman, ed., *Perepiska A. P. Chekhova i O. L. Knipper v trekh tomakh*, 3 vols. (Moscow: Mir, 1934–36), 1:340.

that he had been unwilling or unable to realize a life together. "I repeat that I am very grateful for your letter," Chekhov wrote to Avilova in summer 1901. "I have always wanted to make you happy, and I would gladly have done so [if I could]."[197]

Chekhov did not pursue his attraction to Avilova for several reasons. As evidenced by his brother Alexander's liaison with a married woman, he would have faced insuperable difficulties in obtaining a divorce for Avilova from the ecclesiastical courts. He already had numerous responsibilities and worries, his often dysfunctional family being a key burden. Chekhov was also marriage shy, the lamentable union of his parents and the squalid ties of his brothers to common-law wives and mistresses presenting him with more than ample evidence against the institution of wedlock.

Further, it was not for nothing that in both serious and humorous moments, Chekhov called Avilova "little mother" (*matushka*).[198] He was too upright, cautious, and discreet to enter into an affair with a woman who had children.[199] He also did not wish to risk being the object of scrutiny and scandal in the Russian literary world or to suffer the potential misery that so many of his philandering characters in love with married women endure in his fiction.

Finally, it must be noted that in his relationships with members of the opposite sex, Chekhov was alternately honorable and shabby, prudish and prurient. With his increasingly debilitating illness, he fretted not only over his willingness to commit to a long-term relationship but also over his ability to function as a husband and a father in any capacity for any length of

---

197. Chekhov to Avilova, summer 1901, *Pis'ma*, 10:33. As Avilova tells it, her story with Chekhov did not end with the writer's death. For instance, as evidenced by papers in her personal archive, Avilova claimed that several years after Chekhov's passing, Chekhov's sister, Maria, presented her with an innocent-looking bundle: Chekhov's letters to Avilova over the course of their relationship.

"Maria Pavlovna told me," Avilova wrote, " that they had been tied with a ribbon and kept in her brother's desk." Avilova, though, chose not to keep the missives. "Without reading them," she continued, "I threw them into the oven. Now I very much regret what I did. But I could not bear asking myself over and over again as to why Chekhov had collected and kept the letters." See L. Avilova, "A. P. Chekhov i L. Avilova," in *Perepiska A. P. Chekhova v trekh tomakh*, 3 vols., ed. V. Vatsuro et al. (Moscow: Nasledie, 1996), 1:555.

198. See, for instance, Chekhov to Avilova, March 9, 1899, *Pis'ma*, 8:121.

199. Consider Muromtseva-Bunina's remark as to Chekhov's concern for Bunin's own marital difficulties. "Not long before his passing," she wrote in her memoirs, "Ivan Alexeevich told me that Anton Pavlovich had once delicately broached this aspect of his [Bunin's] life, noting that his son would suffer very much from a divorce [from his wife, Anna Tsakni]. Having told me this, he smiled and said, 'This is the influence of Avilova as I now understand it.' It was she who told Chekhov, 'After all, there would have to be some sacrifice. First of all, there are the children. One need not feel sorry for oneself, but think about the victims. After all there would invariably be sacrifices.'" V. Muromtseva-Bunina, *Zhizn' Bunina* (Paris: n.p., 1958), 129.

time. "My health is like that of an old man," Chekhov wrote to his future bride, Olga Knipper, in 1901, "so with me [as a husband], you will be acquiring more of a grandfather than a spouse."[200] He continued to his wife in 1902, "By the time our baby is a year and a half old, I will be a bald graybeard with not a tooth in my head."[201] Even when Olga praised him as her "superman," Chekhov replied with typical irony, "Yes, your superman who runs so often to the bathroom."[202]

Chekhov also believed that women should be accorded dignity and respect. To his brother Alexander, who had recently paraded drunk and half naked in front of his new mistress and his children, Chekhov wrote in 1889, "You will pardon my saying so, but treating women, no matter who they are, in such a way, is unworthy of any decent, loving human being. What heavenly or earthly power has given you the right to make slaves of your family? Reproaches, a raised voice, constant profanity of the most vile kind, eternal complaints about a life of forced and loathsome labor—are these not the expressions of blatant despotism? . . . No, it is better not to love at all than to love with a despotic love."[203]

Despite such noble sentiments, Chekhov often received members of the opposite sex with patriarchal attitudes. Here he was no shrinking violet. Indeed, he believed that women were literally his for the taking. "There is no need to put girls on a pedestal," he wrote to Alexander in 1877, "but there is no need to run after them either."[204] Even as a youth, Chekhov filled his letters and diaries with boasting that he had "mastered the secrets of love at

200. Chekhov to O. Knipper, March 16, 1901, *Pis'ma,* 9:229. Throughout his life, Chekhov often doubted his sexual prowess. For instance, he told Suvorin that regarding his manly capabilities, he was as much like the insatiable Catherine the Great as a "nut was to a warship" (Chekhov to Suvorin, January 21, 1895, *Pis'ma,* 6:18).

Compare also Chekhov's comments on Clotilde, the heroine of Zola's 1893 novel, *Doctor Pascal:* "Clotilde is like Abishag, the 'cat' that kept old King David warm. I feel sorry for Abishag because her earthly destiny was nothing more than that. Abishag may not have composed the psalms, but, in the eyes of God, she is probably purer and more beautiful than the abductor of Uriah's wife. Abishag is a human being, an individual, she is young and naturally desires youth, and forgive me, but you would have to be a Frenchman who, in the name of some damned principle or other, turns her into a hot-water bottle for a gray-haired Cupid with stringy rooster legs. . . . Old King David straining himself in the embrace of a young girl is a melon that has already known the frost of an autumn morning and is still hoping to ripen. But every fruit has its season" (Chekhov to Suvorin, November 11, 1893, *Pis'ma,* 5:244).

201. Chekhov to O. Knipper, September 10, 1902, *Pis'ma,* 11:35.

202. Chekhov to O. Knipper, November 8, 1903, *Pis'ma,* 11:302. Bunin was more blunt. He told Vladimir Zenzinov, "I do not understand how Knipper could get into the same bed with Chekhov. Well, maybe the first time was all right. . . . But after, he was in such a state. . . ." Quoted in V. Zenzinov, "Zapisi: Besedy s I. A. Buninym," *Novyi zhurnal,* no. 81 (1965): 274.

203. Chekhov to Alexander Chekhov, January 2, 1889, *Pis'ma,* 3:121.

204. Quoted in Ezhov, *Pis'ma Chekhovu ego brata,* 43.

thirteen"[205] and that he had triumphed over ballerinas, actresses, and "tarts."[206]

His views of marriage were equally circumspect. Legal unions between men and women, Chekhov believed, tied the knot in a stultifying way. As he saw it, wedlock meant "face-powder . . . curl-papers . . . copper saucepans, and untidy hair."[207] His fear was also for a loss of independence, specifically, the incursions on his creativity, privacy, and peace of mind which, he claimed, marriage would bring to him. "Very well, I will marry if you so desire," Chekhov half joked to Suvorin in 1895. "But under the following conditions: Everything must continue as before. In other words, she must live in Moscow and I in the country, and I will go and visit her there. I will never be able to stand the sort of happiness that lasts from one day to the next, from one morning to the next. . . . I promise to be a splendid husband, but give me a wife who, like the moon, does not appear in the sky every day. I will not write any better for being married."[208] (As the adage goes, Chekhov should have been more careful what he wished for, if only because with his marriage to Olga Knipper, his dream came true.)

If women were for Chekhov objects of persiflage, marital bonds were for him items of fear and scorn. Like many characters in his stories, Chekhov loved to be in love,[209] especially if the object of his affection had a wild and impulsive nature, so different from his own. He relished a flirtation there, a summer romance there. One only had to sit in a haystack for several hours, he told Leontiev-Shcheglov in 1894, "to imagine oneself in the embraces of a naked woman."[210] Chekhov also delighted when several women lusted after him at the same time. He was the "admiral"; they were his "squadron." Indeed, it spoke volumes about Chekhov's stance toward women and love when he titled a picture of himself with a wry face and several actress-friends "The Temptation of Saint Anthony."[211]

Without the slightest hesitation or regret, though, Chekhov held the

---

205. Chekhov to Serebrov-Tikhonov, February 22, 1892, *Pis'ma*, 4:362.

206. Chekhov to Pleshcheev, November 13, 1888, *Pis'ma*, 3:68.

207. See Chekhov's 1891 story "The Duel" ("Duel'") in Chekhov, *Sochineniia*, 7:356; and his 1893 work "An Anonymous Story" ("Rasskaz neizvestnogo cheloveka") in *Sochineniia*, 8:157.

208. Chekhov to Suvorin, March 23, 1895, *Pis'ma*, 6:40.

209. "I have no desire to marry," Chekhov told Suvorin. "Who needs it? [Such a thing] would just get in the way [of my life]. Falling in love [with someone], though, would not" (Chekhov to Suvorin, October 18, 1892, *Pis'ma*, 5:117). He continued to Kovalevsky, "The very role of a husband terrified me, for there is something grim about it, like the role of a captain. Lazy as I am, I prefer a much easier role" (Chekhov to Kovalevsky, January 29, 1898, *Pis'ma*, 7:162).

210. Chekhov to Leontiev-Shcheglov, July 5, 1894, *Pis'ma*, 5:304.

211. It was not for nothing, therefore, that an exasperated Olga Knipper wrote to Chekhov on March 1, 1901, "Don't dare to sign yourself 'the monk'—I do not like monks." Quoted in Derman, *Perepiska Chekhova i Knipper*, 1:347.

line against enduring ties and commitment. As much as he loved being with women, he also loved being without them. "I do not intend to get married," he wrote to Suvorin in 1891. "I should like to be a little, bald man sitting at a big table in a fine study."[212]

It comes as little surprise, therefore, that Chekhov deflected the amorous claims of Lydia Avilova, Lika Mizinova, Olga Knipper, and countless others with mock imprecations, gallant ruses and quips, and expressions that bordered on the salacious and obscene. The outpourings of emotion and love his heroes conveyed to his heroines Chekhov withheld in the encounters with the ladies in his life. The more interest members of the opposite sex showed in Chekhov, the more evasive and mocking he became. To their brash, winsome, melancholic, and tragic ways, he responded with mock laments that he was ugly, old, and useless. "I love you," Chekhov wrote to an exasperated Olga Knipper in 1901, "but you need a husband or, rather, a spouse with muttonchops and the cockade of an official. But what am I? Nothing special."[213] (As will be seen, Chekhov made a similar remark about cockades to Avilova.)

If Chekhov's admirers wished to see him as passionate and adventurous, he desired just the opposite: he wanted his ladies to be beautiful and charming, intelligent and gay, but to keep their distance and accept his circumspect affection and posturing. "I love you passionately, like a tiger," he wrote in jest to Mizinova in 1891, "and I offer you my hand."[214] To their detriment and misery, Mizinova, Avilova, and others saw such avowals as heartfelt, not humorous. For them, Chekhov seemed to possess some precious, vital secret which he might, perhaps, one day divulge to the right person. In fact, nothing spurred them to greater effort and frenzy than their sense that Chekhov could manage quite well without them.

To the consternation of the women in his life, Chekhov acted as an affectionate if flippant elder brother who engaged them in metaphorical bouts, on the one hand, of hide-and-seek and of catch-me-if-you-can, and on the other, of advance-and-retreat games of chess in which he and his partner swore both devotion and indifference to one another before they moved, inevitably, to checkmate. Although flattered by the love of Avilova and company, Chekhov neither encouraged nor discouraged women in their quest.[215]

212. Chekhov to Suvorin, May 10, 1891, *Pis'ma,* 4:227.
213. Chekhov to O. Knipper, January 2, 1901, *Pis'ma,* 9:172.
214. Chekhov to Mizinova, summer 1891, *Pis'ma,* 4:256.
215. In this Chekhov recalls Gurev, the hero in his 1899 story "A Lady with a Dog" ("Dama s sobakoi"): "He always seemed to women other than what he was, and they loved in him a man who instead of being himself was someone created by their own imagination, someone they had eagerly sought all their lives; even later, when they saw their mistake, they went on loving him. And not one of them had been happy with him. Time passed, and he went on meeting women,

Indeed, he seemed to delight in the ambiguity, the dithering, the badinage, the strained explanations, the bumbled encounters, the moments of illusory bliss, anticipation, and reminiscence, and finally, the drama-laden misunderstandings that he had with women who, like soldiers in a battlefield, threw themselves at him. Like the hero in his 1891 story "My Wife" ("Moia zhena"), Chekhov took great if perverse pleasure when a woman told him how wicked he was.

True, Chekhov apologized profusely whenever his devotees, lachrymose and worse, accused him of condescension, insensitivity, and indifference, and of casting them as spectators rather than actors in the relationship. He begged their forgiveness at charges that he was fitful and phlegmatic, egotistic and egregious, callous and cruel. Chekhov, though, did not change his behavior toward women. Indeed, the more Avilova and others refused to accept defeat and insisted on commitment—or at the very least, some affirmation that they existed as more than amusements and ornaments in his life—the more playful Chekhov became[216] but the more he dug in his heels, beat a hasty retreat, or fled from the scene entirely.[217]

Chekhov's sudden exit from St. Petersburg immediately after meeting Avilova may be seen as a typical response to the stimulus of potential passion and love. Overwhelmed by the success of his play *Ivanov*, one week after his first encounter with Avilova, Chekhov may well have been hinting at even stronger distress when he wrote to Elena Lintaryova in 1889, "I simply had to leave [St. Petersburg] at all costs. I ran away from strong sensations like a coward from a battlefield."[218] Even more intriguing, perhaps, are Chekhov's remarks about wives. Someone may have very much been on Chekhov's mind when, in a letter to Kiselyova in 1890, speaking specifically about Kiselyova's five-year-old daughter, he asked in a quasi-Freudian slip, "Was my future wife from whom I was running away to Sakhalin satisfied with the present I gave her?"[219] Four months later, Chekhov came even closer pub-

having affairs, and parting, but he had never loved; call it what you please, but it was not love." Chekhov, *Sochineniia*, 10:142–43.

216. For instance, to an anguished Avilova, Chekhov wrote, "I have nothing more to write about, but as you want to see my signature with the long tail upside down, like the tail of a suspended rat, and as there is no room for the tail on the other page, I have to go over this page. Keep well. I press your hand and thank you from the bottom of my heart for your letter" (Chekhov to Avilova, July 10, 1898, *Pis'ma*, 7:238).

217. Chekhov sometimes expressed regret over his unattached state: "I am afraid of a wife and domestic routine which would cramp me, but [marriage] might be better than to drift about on the sea of life, tossing in the frail skiff of profligacy. I have already gotten over loving mistresses" (Chekhov to Suvorin, November 10, 1895, *Pis'ma*, 6:94).

218. Chekhov to Lintaryova, February 11, 1889, *Pis'ma*, 3:149.

219. Chekhov to Kiselyova, January 28, 1890, *Pis'ma*, 4:12.

licly to acknowledging the object of his affection when he wrote to Leikin, "When I start living like a human being, that is, when I have a place of my own and my own wife, not someone else's, when, to put it, I am not bothered by trivia and petty worries, I shall take up comic writing again."[220]

The same untrammeled simplicity Chekhov sought in his fiction, he also wanted in his life. His final letter to Avilova, written five months before he died, crystallized what he sought for both himself and the women in his life: "I wish you all the best, and I hope that you will be happy and have a less complicated view of existence because life is probably a good deal simpler than you make it out to be. Does it really deserve all the anguished meditations we Russians waste on it? Nobody knows."[221] Avilova, though, was unmoved by such a send-off. "I read that letter a hundred times," she recalls in her memoirs of the writer. " 'Life is simple, and our painful musings count for nothing,' he wrote. It seemed to me that [when he wrote this] his face had a bitter smile, and that he was looking into the past, at himself."

Bunin, of course, was well aware of the difficulties Avilova posed in her memoirs. He felt compelled, though, to include Avilova's recollections about Chekhov for a key reason: because, unlike investigators into the relationship between the two, Bunin knew Avilova personally, particularly the strengths and weaknesses of her character. Also, like Chekhov, Bunin was under no illusions about Avilova as a writer. He told his nephew, Nikolai Pusheshnikov, in 1917, "Avilova is akin to Turgenev and Chekhov. I am not talking about talent, of course. She did not give her life over to writing. She could not tie that tight knot which all writers must do, nor could she endure all the torments connected with the literary craft."[222] Bunin, though, saw that with Avilova, still rivers ran deep. Avilova, he continued to Pusheshnikov, "lived a complex and mysterious life. She was like a cup that was filled to overflowing."[223] A month later, Bunin continued to his nephew, "I remember Avilova as a young girl. She was pale all over, but with rosy cheeks, blond hair, and shining eyes.

220. Chekhov to Leikin, May 22, 1889, *Pis'ma*, 3:219.

221. Chekhov to Avilova, February 14, 1904, *Pis'ma*, 12:35. Perhaps Chekhov's most graphic summary of his conflicted attitude toward Avilova, women, and marriage is the idea for a play which he proposed to Stanislavsky immediately before the writer's death. In this work, a scientist, disappointed by a phlegmatic or unfaithful wife, travels to the far north where, in the final act of the piece, he stands alone on the bridge of his icebound ship and sees his wife's ghostly shadow hovering over him in the unearthly Arctic twilight.

222. Quoted in Baboreko, "Chekhov i Bunin," *Literaturnoe nasledstvo*, 402.

223. Quoted in ibid. It should be noted that Muromtseva-Bunina also knew and esteemed Avilova. "I was struck by how different Avilova was from other women writers," she wrote in the introduction to *About Chekhov*. "She was modest and poised; she could argue and listen to others. Also, her literary tastes, along with her views of writers and people, coincided with those of Ivan Alexeevich." Muromtseva-Bunina, introduction to *O Chekhove*, 23 (see preface, n. 4).

Unlike any of my colleague-writers at the time, she possessed such tact, such an elusive flair [for life]."[224] Bunin had good reason for such a view. Whereas other critics were seriously misreading the content and form of his work, Avilova was one of the precious few who discerned the innovations of his art. "I have read your book," she wrote to Bunin in 1915. "Do you want me to explain to you what you are doing to literature? . . . At first I thought that you were 'distilling' your stories only as a matter of taste . . . and that you were ridding them . . . of tenderness, music, and warmth. . . . But then it suddenly occurred to me that you were extracting from your works . . . all that was relative and false. . . . Ungird your belt, Ivan Alexeevich, your path is clear."[225]

Bunin's prolonged focus on the relationship between Chekhov and Avilova in *About Chekhov* also requires explanation. For one thing, Bunin's claim that he did not know of a tie between Chekhov and Avilova was, at best, a half-truth. In a work entitled *About Chekhov: Recollections and Articles*, published in Moscow in 1910 (and edited by Avilova herself!),[226] Bunin's and Avilova's recollections on the writer appeared as the first two pieces in the collection. Doubtless, Bunin had to have read Avilova's account of her flirtation with Chekhov at the masquerade ball, an event upon which she expanded in her recollections for Kotov and which Bunin reproduced in *About Chekhov*. For instance, Avilova, masking herself as an individual by the name of "X.," asked the writer, "Do you still love me?" Initially, Chekhov fended off the question, claiming uncertainty as to whether Avilova really was the "X." she had claimed to be. Almost immediately, though, Chekhov told Avilova that he knew her true identity.[227] In Avilova's 1910 memoirs also, Bunin had to have read still further evidence of Avilova's closeness to Chekhov, particularly in a scene in which she visits the ailing writer in Moscow and which, like that of the masquerade, reappears (with minor variations) in both Avilova's and Bunin's later recollections of the writer.

For another thing, Bunin did not, as some critics have asserted, accept without reservation Avilova's contention that she was the great love of Chekhov's life.[228] His decision, though, to structure a good part of *About*

---

224. Quoted in Baboreko, "Chekhov i Bunin," 402. Bunin also commented to Muromtseva-Bunina after a meeting with Avilova in 1915, "Imagine what she must be suffering. She has not seen anything, she does not know anything, but her hair is gray. She talked a great deal about my works. She thinks that I am founding a school of writing. . . . She shows a rare understanding, a precise sense for things" (Bunin, *O Chekhove*, 25).

225. Quoted in Gazer, "A. P. Chekhov I Bunin," 216.

226. See L. Avilova et al., *O Chekhove: Vospominaniia i stat'i* (Moscow: Sovremennoe tvorchestvo, 1910).

227. Avilova, "Moi vospominaniia," 10.

228. See E. Simmons, *Chekhov: A Biography* (Chicago: University of Chicago Press, 1962), 260.

Chekhov not only about the relationship between Chekhov and Avilova but also about Avilova herself helped him realize several key goals. By publishing the letters Avilova had written to him both in her years as a Soviet citizen and as an émigré, Bunin wished to cast the woman as an individual who, in the face of adversity, had shown admirable courage, resilience, and strength, and who, more important, had put family first and foremost in her struggle to survive political and social change. Also, by focusing on the relationship between Chekhov and Avilova, Bunin wished to present the two as a star-crossed pair who, not unlike the characters in the fiction of both Chekhov and himself, were fated to know happiness only for the moment, not for life. To that end, therefore, Bunin focused on interludes when the two set aside their other lives so that they could dine at a party or a banquet; or ride in a carriage late at night; or talk behind masks at a ball; or appear as a family at a train station. The dynamics of such meetings were also typical of Bunin and Chekhov. When Chekhov and Avilova were not keeping up a brave front when he was sick in a hospital, or a semblance of propriety when guests appeared unexpectedly at Avilova's home, the two were misreading each other's codes, cues, and declarations of love. As Avilova suggests in an edition of her memoirs that was published after Bunin's death, Chekhov and Avilova bore an affinity to Alekhin and Anna Luganovich in Chekhov's 1898 piece "About Love" ("O liubvi"). In that work, neither character can pursue whatever attraction exists between them; so the two go their separate ways, knowing that their future will be as pallid as their present and past. Indeed, it is perhaps the bitterest irony in Chekhov's life that when Avilova, in her well-wishing to the writer on his upcoming marriage to Olga Knipper, signed her letter as "Luganovich," Chekhov responded by signing his return missive to her as "Alekhin."[229]

Whether Chekhov loved Avilova is not the key issue for Bunin; rather, it is Chekhov's moments first of frivolity and joy and then of sorrow and resignation with Avilova that claimed his attention and that showed both to the readers of *About Chekhov* as well as to himself how the curse of love ate away at Chekhov's heart in much the same way as the scourge of disease eroded his body.

In the three stances that Bunin adopted toward the writer in *About Chekhov*, the first one is by far the most poignant and poetic. That is, as the

---

229. Chekhov to Avilova, late May–September 1901, *Pis'ma*, 10:33. The final chapter of Avilova's memoirs was published in N. Gitovich, ed., *A. P. Chekhov v vospominaniiakh sovremennikov* (Moscow: Gosurdarstvennoe izdatel'stvo khudozhestvennoi literatury, 1960), 287–93.

230. Critics unanimously concur on Bunin's singular closeness to Chekhov. Donald Rayfield, for instance, calls Bunin the "Peter of the Chekhovian Church." D. Rayfield, *Chekhov. A Life* (New York: Henry Holt and Co., 997), 487. Also see Simmons, *Chekhov*, 524.

self-styled younger brother of the object of his study, Bunin claimed an access to Chekhov that no one, except perhaps his mother, sister, and wife, possessed.[230] He had good reason for such a view. Be it in Moscow or the Crimea, Bunin was often Chekhov's singular and constant companion. The two enjoyed one another's company's immensely. "I have been at your brother's . . . for days on end, of course, at his invitation," Bunin wrote to Maria Chekhova in 1901. "He has been very affectionate with me, and I have found it very pleasant to be with him. He will not let me go; that is why I am still here. . . . May God grant him a thousand healthy years."[231] Several days later, he continued to Teleshov, "Chekhov has kept me here in Yalta. I have spent a marvelous week with him. If only you knew what kind of person he was."[232]

During visits, Bunin and Chekhov discussed literature, came up with plots for stories, traded jokes and pranks, and acted out roles. They laughed at each other's expense and lamented their lot in the world. More revealingly, perhaps, there were also times when the two understood each other before they spoke, or completed each other's sentences, or merely communed in silence. Only Bunin, it seemed, could bring a twinkle to Chekhov's otherwise sad eyes, if only because he could read aloud one of the writer's stories in a masterful way[233] or because he appeared to the writer as "Monsieur Bouquichon," the tag being taken either from a foppish manager on a nearby estate or from a French marquis Chekhov had once seen in a newspaper (sources vary). When Bunin and Chekhov were together, "one often heard bursts of loud laughter," Chekhov's sister, Maria, recalled.[234] Indeed, with his younger colleague, Chekhov assumed a playfulness he rarely showed to other people in his life. "Happy New Year!" he wrote to Bunin in 1902. "I wish that you become famous throughout the entire world, that you meet the very best women around, and that you win two hundred thousand rubles [in a lottery]."[235]

Not surprisingly, Bunin prevailed upon Chekhov in a way that no one else could. It was at his urging that Chekhov agreed to sit for a portrait by the artist Pyotr Nilus, an idea he had rejected previously.[236] Given the closeness between the two men, it is no surprise that whenever Bunin took leave of the writer, Chekhov always pressed him to stay longer and demanded further vis-

231. Bunin to Maria Chekhova, February 18, 1901, in Baboreko, "Chekhov i Bunin," 396.

232. See A. Baboreko, "Pis'ma I. A. Bunina," *Na rodnoi zemle* (Orel: Orlovskaia pravda, 1956), 305.

233. Quoted in Teleshov, "A. P. Chekhov," 170.

234. See Maria Chekhova, "Iz dalekogo proshlogo," 356 (see preface, n. 1).

235. Chekhov to Bunin, January 15, 1902, *Pis'ma*, 10:169.

236. Sadly, the sittings were suspended with Olga's repeated bouts with illness. Nilus, though, later finished the portrait from his sketches and photographs of the writer.

its from his younger colleague. In fact, there were times in the last years of Chekhov's life years when Bunin was the only visitor he wanted to see.

The respect and support was mutual. For all their differences, Chekhov was one of the first to sense Bunin's talent as a writer. He not only cleared the path for Bunin's entry into the Russian literary world, but he was also instrumental in securing the 1903 Pushkin Prize for his younger colleague.[237] Chekhov's belief in Bunin as an artist continued until the last days of the writer's life. In fact, immediately before departing for Badenweiler, where he died, Chekhov had his younger "brother" very much in mind. "Tell Bunin," Chekhov beseeched Teleshov, "that he must write and write. A great author will emerge from him. Yes, tell him that for me. Do not forget."[238]

Chekhov's support of Bunin was returned tenfold. Whenever Bunin spoke of his personal time with the writer, it was invariably amid "all in the family"—"I am one of the family at the Chekhovs'," he boasted to his brother Yuly in 1901[239]—an arrangement that remained in force even when Chekhov was in Europe or no longer among the living. Bunin was a surrogate son to Chekhov's mother, Evgenia, often residing alone with the woman when Maria and her siblings were elsewhere.

Bunin was also a devoted brother—and perhaps more—to Chekhov's sister, Maria. "I am paying court to Maria Pavlovna Chekhova," Bunin wrote to Yuly in 1900.[240] Ten months later, he continued to a friend, "Maria Pavlovna is a rare girl."[241] If Maria also called Bunin "Bouquichon" (and later "Don Zinzaga"), Bunin responded by naming her "Amaranta."[242] He often flirted openly with Maria, escorted her to parties and gatherings, and wrote her affectionate notes. He also dedicated at least one story to Maria[243] and, in her name, penned such ditties as:

> Snow falls, blizzards blow
> I have fled down to the south.

---

237. Also see Bunin's letter to Chekhov, dated April 30, 1901, in which he informed Chekhov that he had sent to the writer both a collection of his verse entitled *Falling Leaves* (*Listopad*) as well as his translation of Longfellow's *Hiawatha* (*Pesn' o Gaiavate*) as materials for consideration for the prize. (Both works earned Bunin the award, the first of three times to be accorded this distinction.) See Bunin to Chekhov, April 30, 1901, in Vatsuro et al., *Perepiska*, 3:519. See also Chekhov to Anatoly Koni, May 6, 1901, *Pis'ma*, 10:22.

238. See Teleshov, "A. P. Chekhov," 180.

239. Baboreko, "Pis'ma Y. A. Bunina," 305.

240. Quoted in Baboreko, "Chekhov v perepiske i zapiskakh Bunina," 29.

241. See Bunin's letter to a friend, written in early February 1901, in Baboreko, "Chekhov i Bunin," 388.

242. Don Al'fonso Zinzaga and Amaranta are characters in Chekhov's 1880 story "Wives of Artists" ("Zheny artistov").

243. See, for instance, Bunin's 1902 story "The Meeting" ("Svidanie").

> But the cold is still my foe.
> Bunin and I look at the views.
> All day long we stoke the stoves
> And go for walks like little ewes.[244]

As would any protective spouse or sibling, Bunin routinely lied to Maria about the state of her brother's health. "You worry about Anton Pavlovich in vain," he wrote to his "Amaranta" when she was away from Yalta in 1901. "I am hiding nothing from you . . . [when I say that] never has your brother given such an impression of the most robust health."[245]

Bunin also used Maria as a sounding board for his sorrows and joys. Just as Chekhov turned to his sister in his sojourns away from home, Bunin also wrote to her to record both agony and astonishment in his travels throughout Russia and the world. "Again I am on my way, my endless way," he wrote to Maria in 1902, "and today I do not have a single person nearby whom I could call a close relative. I feel like crying from loneliness. Indeed, the people who are close to me number no more than ten in the entire world. You are one of them."[246] Nine years later, he told Maria, "God knows where I am—in Africa, among the Somalians who go about completely naked and who are chocolate-colored from head to toe (with terrible manes and covered with lime, to boot). If they do not eat me up, I will write to you from Ceylon."[247]

Maria, it should be noted, was flattered by Bunin's attention and appeals. "I am leaving for Yalta in two weeks," she wrote to Bunin in 1901, "and I cannot imagine life without you! With whom will I walk on the embankment; with whom will I read in the evening?"[248] In Chekhov's absence from his home, Bunin lived downstairs next to Maria and worked in her brother's

---

244. Another of Bunin's improvisations was perhaps more to the point:

> Guliai, guliai, Masha
> Poka volia nasha—
> Kodga zamuzh otdadut,
> Takoi voli ne dadut!

> Go about, Masha
> Go about while you can
> Before someone forces you
> Upon some man!
> (Maria Chekhova, "Iz dalekogo proshlogo," 357)

245. Ibid., 359.
246. Ibid., 362.
247. Bunin to Maria Chekhova, February 20, 1911, in A. Baboreko, "Iz neopublikovannoi perepiski Bunina," *Vremia* (Smolensk: Smolenskoe otdelenie Soiuza pisatelei, 1962), 102.
248. The relationship, though, was not destined to last. In fact, letters from Maria to Bunin

sunny study. He was more than happy with the arrangement. Bunin wrote to Chekhov (who was in Nice at the time) that same year:

> I am writing . . . to thank you for your hospitality [of your family]. The village where I had been living . . . was a veritable north pole . . . blizzards, snow, and a yellowish metallic sun that shone dimly in a wide frosty circle. I got bored quickly . . . and so, when I received the invitation from Maria Pavlovna, I left for Yalta with the greatest of pleasure.
> Yalta is very quiet. The weather is mild, and I have rested thoroughly in your home. . . . Mornings, my room is full of sunlight; your study . . . is even better: cheerful and spacious. The big, beautiful window casts green, blue, and red reflections on the wall and floor. I love colored windows, but at dusk, they seem so sad. Your study is so simple and lonely when you are far away. . . .
> I hear from Maria Pavlovna that you are working. I wish you good spirits and peace. I am also scribbling away and reading, and I am living peacefully and well.[249]

---

and Olga Knipper hint at an unhappy love affair. (Rayfield also suggests an intervention by Chekhov; see archival materials as quoted in Rayfield, *Chekhov: A Life*, 523, 563.)

"Dear Bouquichon," Maria wrote to Bunin in summer 1902, "I was very sad when you left. . . . Of course, it would be nice to be one woman in ten, but nicer still to be the only one, to combine the Yakut girl, the Temir girl, the Sinhalese girl, etc." In November of the same year, Maria wrote to him, "Darling Bouquichon, What has happened? Are you ill? You have vanished and God knows what I am to think! I have been very ill. . . . Is it a new love affair? Your Amaranta" (Baboreko, "Iz neopublikovennoi perepiski Bunina," 93–94).

It should also be noted that in exile, Bunin turned against Maria. In an interview with Zenzinov on March 31, 1934, he charged that Maria "had lost her mind"; she was accommodating the Bolsheviks in order to keep alive the memory of her brother and his work (see Zenzinov, "Zapisi," 272–73). Specifically, Maria had ceded the bulk of Chekhov's archive to Soviet authorities and was serving as the director of the A. P. Chekhov Home-Museum in Yalta, a position that she held from 1921 until her death in 1957.

What Bunin did not know, though, is that Maria, especially in the early years of Soviet power, often feared for her life. In 1920, the Bolsheviks had searched her home at least ten times and had even issued an order for her arrest. See G. Shaliugina and A. Golovacheva, "M. P. Chekhova," *Chekhovskie chteniia v Yalte: Chekhov i XX vek; Sbornik nauchnykh trudov* (Moscow: Nasledie, 1997), 241, 242, 245.

249. Baboreko, "Iz perepiski," 200. Similarly, Bunin wrote to Alexander Fyodorov in an undated missive, "My days here [with the Chekhovs] flow by in a kind of poetic intoxication. Here, in the mountains, everything is in a constant state of flux—the snows, the storms, the fogs—but now, for the most part, we have a sun, the joyous, turquoise sea, and the gulf of the sea down below. If only you knew what a view I have [from] my windows. . . . Anton Pavlovich is well and working. His family is enchanting. Today his sister, Maria Pavlovna, came to stay. She is a close friend and a rare type of girl! . . . I am writing a lot of verse, beginning a number of stories. I also read . . . and dream." See Baboreko, "Bunin i Chekhov," 396.

Also, more than once, Bunin was drawn into family dramas—Chekhov's sudden marriage to Olga Knipper being a prime example. On the one hand, Bunin was the first to receive written declamations from Chekhov not only about his marriage to Olga but also his wavering over his decision. "I have changed my mind about marrying," Chekhov wrote to Bunin in 1901 (two months before his actual union with Knipper), "I do not want to . . . but just the same, if I must, I will."[250] (Ironically, Bunin was undergoing his own divorce from his first wife, Anna Tsakni.) On the other hand, Bunin had to confront both his dislike of Olga Knipper[251] and his uneasiness over her union with Chekhov. Bunin also had to face the anger, hurt, and resignation of Maria, who had sacrificed her own happiness (and chances at marriage) for the well-being of her brother.[252] Only half-jokingly did Maria tell Olga that her new sister-in-law was not unlike the vile Natasha in *The Three Sisters*.[253]

250. Chekhov to Bunin, March 25, 1901, *Pis'ma,* 9:235. Bunin also told Zenzinov:
   Chekhov did not want to marry for anything in the world. But then he told only me, "You know, I have decided to marry."
   I replied, "Well, marriage is a good thing. God grant you happiness."
   He said, "I am marrying a German. . . . A Russian washes her face, but my intended washes her neck, behind her ears, her entire body. She is squeaky-clean. And the house will be clean, too. But there won't be any children crawling around the floor in my study and upsetting things."
   As he spoke, though, Chekhov had a somewhat confused look on his face. He wanted to hear my opinion. But what was I supposed to say to him? Of course, I understood everything that he was telling me. (Zenzinov, "Zapisi," 274)

251. For instance, Bunin told Zenzinov that Knipper was "very good-looking . . . but somehow wooden . . . and not particularly bright" and that she has married Chekhov "from ambition" (Zenzinov, "Zapisi," 273–75).
   Muromtseva-Bunina also did not care for Olga Knipper. "Yesterday Olga Leonardovna Knipper visited us," Muromtseva-Bunina wrote in her diary on October 28, 1919. "She was very sweet and friendly; she spoke intelligently, but I got the impression that she had nothing in her soul, that she was like a house without a foundation . . . with a cellar stocked with provisions and good wine. The Bolsheviks have been very courteous to her, so she does not see them as we do." Quoted in Grin, *Ustami Buninykh,* 319.

252. Bunin, feigning surprise at Chekhov's marriage to Olga Knipper, wrote to Maria in early June 1901, "Having arrived in Moscow, I just received the unexpected news about Anton Pavlovich. I happened to be at the home of [Knipper's mother] Anna Ivanovna Knipper, and she told me that your brother left [for his wedding] in a very happy frame of mind. . . . From the bottom of my heart and in all respects, I wish that it all will turn out well for *every one of you*" (Chekhov, *Pis'ma,* 10:318).

253. It should be noted, though, that eventually Maria and Olga settled into a friendship that survived two world wars and three Russian revolutions and that continued into the late 1950s, when both women were in their nineties. See Maria Chekhova to O. Knipper, May 30, 1901, in O. Knipper-Chekhova, *Vospominaniia i stat'i: Perepiska s A. P. Chekhovym,* vol. 2 (Moscow: Iskusstvo, 1972), 24.

To Maria, Bunin had always shown intuition, affection, and tact. Now, with Anton married to Olga, Bunin was the recipient of Maria's shock and despair. "I am in a murderous mood," Maria lamented to Bunin on June 6, 1901. "I keep thinking that my life is a disaster. The reason, in part, is my brother's marriage. It all happened so abruptly! . . . For a long time I was distraught and wondered how Olga could have let someone so ill experience the shock of such a thing; but, in the end, everything seems to have turned out well." And, in an obvious cry for help, Maria continued, "And so I ask you, Bouquichonchik, to find me a husband, one who is generous and rich. I do not wish to continue writing now, though I enjoy talking to you very much. I am terribly depressed because of Antosha and Olechka."[254]

On the other hand, Chekhov wrote to Bunin in playful joy over his hasty union. "Tomorrow I am leaving for Yalta," he wrote to Bunin several weeks later, "where you may send your congratulations on my legal marriage. You have heard, have you not, that I have been married off? Well, I am now engaging lawyers and suing for divorce."[255]

It should be noted that Bunin also served as an unofficial spokesman for the Chekhovs, informing friends and colleagues of developments in the household or taking on detractors of the writer's life and work, especially those who wished to see Chekhov as declining, physically as well as aesthetically. "Chekhov is much better now," Bunin told an interviewer from *Odessa News* in 1902. "Recently I read a letter he had sent to his sister, Maria Pavlovna, and which is filled with happiness and cheer."[256] Bunin continued as Chekhov's spokesman even after the writer's death. For instance, he told an interviewer

254. See archival materials in Rayfield, *Chekhov: A Life,* 541. Several days later, Maria continued to Bunin, "Anton keeps writing everything will remain the same. Like hell it will. I want the reality, not the picture. Maria Chekhova, "Iz dalekogo proshlogo," 362.

To Maria's request for a husband, Bunin replied on June 7, 1901, "Find you a husband now? I can do nothing of the sort! Let's wait until winter when I will be spending almost all my time in Moscow" (ibid).

It should be noted that Chekhov's mother was less than thrilled with the news. As Bunin noted to Zenzinov, " 'An actress for a wife!' Evgenia lamented, 'What kind of life will they have! She will live in Moscow, but Antosha will be in Yalta. An actress in Moscow always has lovers!' " (quoted in Zenzinov, "Zapisi," 274).

255. Chekhov to Bunin, June 30, 1901, *Pis'ma,* 10:50.

256. Quoted in Baboreko, "Chekhov v perepiske," 21. Similarly, Bunin told a reporter from *Odessa News* on July 2, 1914, "What is the most valuable thing about Chekhov? Why, everything about him! His unique talent for artistic portraits . . . his noble simplicity, his lack of anything bookishness or false, and his wonderfully precise and harmonic forms—all are worthy of admiration. Especially dear is Chekhov's clear, sober, and unusually bright mind—especially when now everything just the opposite is the case. . . . Chekhov still has not been understood as he should be. He is an extremely unique and complex individual." Quoted in Baboreko, "Chekhov v perepiske," 26.

from *Odessa News* in 1914, "How Chekhov would have suffered if he had lived to see the third and fourth Dumas . . . the Sanins . . . the vile cries about the Sun . . . and the days of glory for Purishkevich, Rasputin, Max Linder, Iambo the elephant, and Igor Severianin!"[257]

What Bunin said about Chekhov in the early twentieth century, he continued to say at its midpoint. Particularly delightful in Bunin's fraternal, bird's-eye view of Chekhov are the many vignettes of the writer which render parts of *About Chekhov* as an intimate family album of Chekhov's life and work. It should be noted that in his close-ups of the writer, Bunin called only minimal attention to the writer's illness. The key tragedy of Chekhov's life, though, must have been hard for him to ignore. Doubtless, in his time with Chekhov, Bunin had to have seen in his colleague and friend what others did. He had to have been pained by Chekhov's sunken chest, hollow cheeks, and bloodless lips. He had to have been anguished by the way his "elder brother" spoke with a slow and husky voice, or how he pulled his cap down low over his eyes, or how, like an old man, Chekhov took tiny steps up stairs or inclines, with frequent stops to catch his breath. Bunin also had to have looked the other way when Chekhov, after a fit of coughing, first disposed of blood and spittle in a paper cone or a leather-covered flask and then, having regained his breath, readjusted his pince-nez and smiled a weary or embarrassed smile. Further, it also must have been Bunin's response to his ailing colleague to have spent hours distracting Chekhov with cheerful conversation and activity whenever he encountered the writer in bouts of lethargy and indifference, his cane between his legs and his eyes looking off into the distance.

Much as Bunin liked horror and gore, he chose a different tack with his subject in *About Chekhov*. Chekhov believed that people should not parade their misfortunes, and Bunin followed suit. His approach was to highlight Chekhov's stoicism, docility, and courage in the face of death. Any other route, perhaps, would have been too painful for Bunin not only in portraying his "elder brother" but also in extending the ravages of sickness and old age to his own declining state in life.

During his frequent visits to Chekhov's household, therefore, Bunin chose to note Chekhov's unassuming manner, his exquisite courtesy, and his

---

257. Quoted in I. Gazer, "A. P. Chekhov I. A. Bunin," *Literaturnyi muzei A. P. Chekhova Taganrog: Sbornik statei i materialov*, vol. 3 (Rostov-na-Donu: Rostovskoe knizhnoe izdatel'stvo, 1963), 197. As to Bunin's references in the citation, Balmont wrote "Let Us Be Like the Sun" ("Budem kak sontse") in 1902. Also, Iambo the elephant was, between the years 1908 and 1912, the focus of intense interest with the Russian public if only because the animal was reputed to have been losing its sanity during that time.

mania for order and decorum. Moments between the two moved at will between good and bad, simple and complex. Bunin laughed both at Chekhov's mischievousness and at his almost morbid fear of appearing before anyone without a waistcoat and tie. He grimaced at his colleague's struggle for success as an artist, on the one hand, and for inner peace and happiness, on the other. Bunin also recorded how, with his "brother," light often flashed through the darkness. Melancholy over personal and professional fate gave way to laughter over an anecdote, tale, or verse. Annoyance at all forms of posturing ceded to pleasure over well-crafted sentences and plots or gatherings that were simple, genuine, and relaxed. Particularly important to Bunin were the "prosaics" of Chekhov's life: Chekhov tending his garden; Chekhov freeing a mouse; Chekhov fretting about clothes for a visit to Tolstoy; Chekhov demanding a moonlit ride; Chekhov offering contradictory opinions on life after death; Chekhov fearing what people would say after his passing. These were images in which Bunin's jottings captured Chekhov as painfully human, a writer who indeed was "like everyone else" in his passage through life.

In the second stance, Bunin looked to Chekhov as mirror of himself. Specifically, he sought to correct the popular image of the two as "brothers" of another sort, which maintained that they were the voice of "dying Russia": passive and melancholy individuals who sang wistful melodies in minor keys. Rather, Bunin presented Chekhov as an individual who, above all, believed that human dignity—his own and others'—was both the ultimate seedbed and the sanctuary for all endeavors in literature and life. The object of Bunin's affection is seen as holding forth to family and friends about belief in self, about courage in the face of adversity, and about good breeding and respect for others, for their lifestyles and their beliefs. Bunin shows Chekhov to be equally forceful in his views about art: the need to tell the truth, no matter how painful or unpleasant, so as to evoke his own version of *épater le bourgeois*—he wished to shock readers out of their deathlike stupor and self-denial and to force them to look, without dissembling, at both the beauty and the ugliness of life.

In the third and final stance, Bunin strove to rectify what he considered misunderstandings of Chekhov and his work. Above all, Bunin wished to present Chekhov as a secure master of prose but an insecure practitioner of the theater. He had much evidence for such a view. Throughout his life, Chekhov maintained a tortured relationship with the stage. He hated with a passion the institutional aspects of Russian drama. National theater was for him a "nasty disease of the cities," the province of "grocers, not writers."[258]

258. Chekhov to Leontiev-Shcheglov, November 7, 1888, *Pis'ma*, 3:56; Chekhov to Suvorin, November 7, 1888, *Pis'ma*, 3:60.

The egos and intrigues of actors and directors, the vulgarity and fickleness of the audience, the limitations of the Russian repertoire were for him items of withering contempt. No idol of the stage—Russian or otherwise—was spared Chekhov's wrath. Actresses were "cows" and "Machiavellis in skirts."[259] Even the legendary Sarah Bernhardt was for Chekhov a fraud. "All of Bernhardt's tears, her dying convulsions, and her acting are nothing but an irreproachably and cleverly learned lesson," a brash twenty-year-old Chekhov wrote in a review. "There is not a trifle in her parts, big or little, which has not gone a hundred times through the purgatory of labor."[260] There were even times in Chekhov's life when he so equated the evils of the theater with the failings of society that he put a pox on both houses. "I am in absolutely no mood for theaters or humanity," Chekhov wrote to Kiselyova in 1887, "they can both go the devil!"[261]

To his further woes with Russian drama, Chekhov suffered the abuse of actors, spectators, and critics who disliked what they saw as his disregard, even contempt, for the conventions of theatrical content and form, as well as his entry into what they saw as a strange anticlimactic, antiromantic, and antidramatic world. These three groups were distressed that in his plays, Chekhov preferred humdrum to histrionics, whimpers and sighs to bangs and blows. "Against all the rules of dramatic art," Chekhov told Suvorin in 1895, " I begin my plays in *forte* but end them in *pianissimo.*"[262] In Chekhov's dramas, also, action was replaced by atmosphere; events by feelings; and dialogue and declamation by pauses, allusions, and conversations that were detached, skewed, and incoherent, that moved along parallel lines, and that only hinted at things of earthshaking importance.

It was the discourse of Chekhov's plays that proved particularly vexing for his audiences. The moralizing and didactic mania which raged in Russia at the time had not spared the theater. Spectators wished to see characters who were virtuous and self-sacrificing, energetic and honest. They yearned to hear soliloquies on human dignity, freedom, and happiness in order to appease their conscience—and then to continue living as they liked. Chekhov, though, would not pander to the public. "Be faithful to your wife, say your prayers. . . . Make money, love sports, and all is for the best in this world and the next," Chekhov told Suvorin, again in 1895. "The bourgeoisie loves so-called 'positive' types and novels with happy endings because, in a soothing

259. Chekhov to Suvorin, December 17, 1888, *Pis'ma*, 3:87.

260. Chekhov, *Sochineniia*, 16:15. "Widows' tears, orphans' tears, everyone's tears," Chekhov wrote to his brother Alexander, "all this has been portrayed long ago" (Chekhov to Alexander Chekhov, April 11, 1889, *Pis'ma*, 3:188).

261. Chekhov to Kiselyova, September 13, 1887, *Pis'ma*, 2:119.

262. Chekhov to Suvorin, November 21, 1895, *Pis'ma*, 6:100.

way, they suggest that one can make money while preserving one's innocence and remain happy while behaving like a swine."[263]

The abuse of individuals on both sides of the theater often eroded Chekhov's faith in himself as a dramatist. It became almost axiomatic that, beginning with *The Wood Demon* and ending with *The Cherry Orchard*, Chekhov proclaimed that he was a "mediocre dramatist"[264] and that, even if he "lived to age seven hundred,"[265] he was through with the theater and would return to prose. "It seems that I am not meant to be a playwright," he told Suvorin in 1895. "But I do not despair, because I keep writing stories. In that domain, I feel at home. But when I write a play, I feel discomfort, as if somebody is poking me in the back."[266] Rehearsals of Chekhov's dramas often ended in anger; premieres drove him into despair. Small wonder, therefore, that every time Chekhov sat in a theater, he had a "feeling that someone in the balcony was about to yell 'Fire!'"[267] It also comes as little surprise that in a letter written in 1898, Chekhov told Shavrova-Iust, "I have had such bad luck in the theater that if I were to marry an actress, she would probably give birth to an orangutan or a porcupine."[268]

Bunin chose to ignore why Chekhov, in his stance toward the theater, often moved from hate to love. The reason is simple. For Bunin, the focus was intellectual: he wanted to show Chekhov as an exemplar of prose, not drama. For Chekhov, the focus was emotional: even though he believed that the theater was a "snake that sucked one's blood,"[269] he simply could not exorcise the smell of greasepaint from his nose—or heart. As a youth, he had captivated family and friends with various scenes and roles. He had staged mock weddings and trials. He had incurred "Homeric laughter"[270] with guises and roles, including those of a provincial mayor, padded with pillows and adorned with medals; an aging sacristan, seeking promotion to deacon from his bishop; and a street urchin, dressed in rags and begging for alms. In

263. Chekhov to Suvorin, April 18, 1895, *Pis'ma*, 6:54.

264. Chekhov to Elena Shavrova, November 18, 1895, *Pis'ma*, 6:90.

265. See Suvorin's diary excerpt, written on October 17, 1896, in Suvorin, *Dnevik Alekseia Sergeevicha Suvorina*, 256.

266. Chekhov to Suvorin, December 13, 1895, *Pis'ma*, 6:108.

267. Chekhov to Suvorin, March 13, 1898, *Pis'ma*, 7:185.

268. Chekhov to Shavrova-Iust, December 26, 1898, *Pis'ma*, 7:380.

269. Quoted in Leontiev-Shcheglov, "Iz vospominanii," in Kotov, *A. P. Chekhov*, 409 (see preface, n. 3).

270. A. Drossi, "Iunye gody A. P. Chekhova," *Solntse Rossii*, no. 228 (1914); as quoted in V. Feider, ed., *A. P. Chekhov: Po vospominaniiam, dnevnikam i pis'mam* (Leningrad: Akademia, 1928), 325.

fact, so convincing was Chekhov in this last guise that he once fooled his uncle Mitrofan into giving him money for the poor.[271]

As an adult, Chekhov was fascinated with both the challenge and the difficulty of writing drama. He cherished the direct, almost blood relationship between himself and his audience, a quasi-gladiatorial combat in which he challenged his viewers to forget their troubles and to take on those of his characters. For Chekhov, frequent if legendary successes before large auditoriums of people provided much more rousing and intoxicating thrills than the subtle satisfactions afforded by a piece of delicate prose penned in the solitude of his study. Indeed, it was not lighthearted boasting when Chekhov told Olga Knipper in 1903, "If I had the strength, I would write not one but twenty-five dramas."[272]

In another telling omission in *About Chekhov*, Bunin declined to discuss the ludicrous way in which the object of his study exited from this life. When Gorky and several friends gathered to meet the train that had transported Chekhov's body from Badenweiler to Moscow, they were aghast to learn that the coffin had traveled in a dirty green car with a sign FOR OYSTERS in large letters on the door. Even worse, perhaps, the mourners were shocked to hear a military band strike up a funeral procession, a memorial for a General Keller who had been killed in Manchuria and whose body had arrived in Moscow at the same moment as that of the beloved writer.

To the further chagrin of Gorky and company, the onlookers who attended Chekhov's remains were like characters of his fiction come to life. There was a fat constable on an imposing white horse. There were several lawyers who, "dressed like newlyweds" in shiny shoes and bright ties, chatted about the intelligence of their dogs and the relative merits of their dachas. There was a woman wearing a purple dress and carrying a lace parasol who noted to an old man in horn-rimmed glasses, "What a nice, witty man he was!"[273]

Gorky was particularly outraged by the incident. "I felt like screaming, weeping, and bawling with indignation and wrath," he wrote to his wife, Ekaterina Peshkova.[274] In truth, neither Gorky nor Bunin nor any other

---

271. Among Chekhov's best tableaux was the "oriental" scene he staged with Isaac Levitan, in which Chekhov, dressed as a Bedouin tribesman, "shoots" Levitan, a Muslim pilgrim rapt in prayer.

272. Chekhov to O. Knipper, March 4, 1903, *Pis'ma*, 11:179.

273. Gor'kii, "A. P. Chekhov," 56.

274. See Gorky to Peshkova, July 11, 1904, in Gor'kii, *Polnoe Sobranie Sochinenii: Pis'ma*, 4:103.

writer or reader of Russian literature should have been surprised that the homeland marked the passing of a great artist in such a shocking and vulgar way. After all, could they not see that the absurdities surrounding Chekhov's journey home mirrored the idiocies of Russian life highlighted so frequently in their works?

Perhaps it is an epigraph written by Chekhov that best summarizes both his and Bunin's approach to life. When in early 1898 an individual by no less notable name than Onegin asked Chekhov to sign his album, a calendar-like affair replete with literary excerpts and citations, he became an unexpected witness to the writer's philosophy of life. On the page in which Chekhov was asked to put his signature was this epigraph from Lermontov: "Believe me—happiness is there only / Where we are loved, where we are believed."[275] To this, Chekhov responded, "Where we are loved, where we are believed, such things we find dull; but we are happy there where we ourselves love and where we ourselves believe. Anton Chekhov."[276] In one fell swoop, Chekhov set aside assessments that he was inert, passive, and unloving; rather, he charted a life plan for himself, and hopefully, his fellow readers, to follow. As always, he found a willing student in Bunin. Indeed, it was Bunin's enduring love and belief in Chekhov that afforded to him a prominent if posthumous role in the collective memory of the writer. As an early sign of the post-Stalinist thaw that would ultimately bring down the Soviet state, Bunin's recollections of Chekhov were included in the third (1954) edition of *Chekhov as Recalled by His Contemporaries.*

275. The citation is from Lermontov's 1833 work *Khadzhi Abrek.*
276. See A. Suvorin, *Dnevnik A. S. Suvorina* (Moscow: L. D. Frenkel', 1923), 180; and Gitovich, *Letopis' zhizni,* 504–5.

About Chekhov

Chapter One

    I OFTEN ASKED Evgenia Yakovlevna [Chekhov's mother]
and [his sister] Maria Pavlovna:
    "Tell me, did Anton Pavlovich ever cry?"
    "Never," they responded firmly.
    I find such a thing remarkable.[1]

Chekhov was born on the shallow shores of the Sea of Azov,[2] in a provincial
and, at that time, remote city.[3] His squalid environs had to have influenced his
innate melancholy in a significant way.[4] It also always seemed to me that, judging by the faces of his commoner-relatives—their pronounced cheekbones
and somewhat narrow and slanted eyes—the sad, despondent temper of his

---

    1. Chekhov himself was aware of his inability to cry. "Old writers love to weep," he told
Ignaty Potapenko, "but I cannot do such a thing." See I. Potapenko, "Neskol'ko let s A. P.
Chekhovym," in Kotov, *A. P. Chekhov*, 240 (see introduction, n. 34).

    2. The Sea of Azov is north of the Black Sea, approximately six hundred miles south of Moscow.

    3. Chekhov was born in Taganrog, a town on the northeast shore of the Sea of Azov. Once a
bustling port, it had by the 1850s turned into a ghost town, having ceded its position and
prowess to nearby Rostov-on-Don to the east and Odessa to the west. The unpaved streets were
riddled with potholes, mud, and grass. Water was scarce and polluted.

    A large part of the population in Taganrog was foreign: Italians, Germans, English, and
a substantial number of Greeks who, as shipowners, grain merchants, and owners of import-
export firms, controlled the economic life of the city.

    The thirty or so thousand Russians in Taganrog—unskilled workers, shopkeepers, steve-
dores, and petty clerks—barely eked out a living. Trapped and resigned to their fate, they were
joined by the convicts who, chained to wagons like horses, dragged flour in carts from ware-
house to prison. Locals in Taganrog lived in small, dilapidated houses with moth-eaten awnings,
tiny gardens, and common latrines. They rendered nothing sacred or private via gossip and
news filled with envy and spite. They were also host to cruel spectacles; for example, prisoners
were flogged or executed in public squares; stray dogs were beaten to death with clubs and
sticks; young girls occasionally were kidnapped for Turkish harems.

    Chekhov never got over his dislike of Taganrog. In fact, the only saving grace about the place
was the surrounding sea, its sights, smells, and sounds becoming a hallmark of his writing.

    4. Bunin is correct here. For Taganrog, Chekhov felt disgust and affection, revolt and resig-
nation. He wrote to Nikolai Leikin, "Sixty thousand inhabitants and all they do is eat, drink, and

personality was rooted in an ample Eastern legacy. With the years, Chekhov resembled his family more and more; and, as is the case with people from the East, he aged very early in life, physically and spiritually. True, consumption is consumption, but it was not the only reason why, at only forty years old, Chekhov's lined, yellowish face began to resemble that of an elderly Mongol.

As regards Chekhov's childhood, there was the provincial, philistine poverty of his family. His mother was quiet, with a compressed mouth and straight tense lips.[5] His father was "frenzied and severe," a beast who forced his older sons to sing in evening church choirs. He tormented his offspring with late-night rehearsals[6] and demanded that they, from a tender age on, take their turns as the "master's eyes and ears" in his shop.

Antonsha suffered most of all. His observant father noticed immediately that he could rely upon his son. So, whenever the old man had to go off somewhere, the boy had to mind the store more often than his brothers. But his father's actions had this beneficial result: if there had been no church choirs or rehearsals, there would not have been such stories as "The Sacred Night," "The Student," "The Sacred Mountains," "The Archbishop," and perhaps, "The Murder."[7] [Without such exercises] Chekhov would not have acquired his keen knowledge of religious services and of simple-souled people.

Taking care of his father's shop also gave Chekhov an early awareness of people. It forced him to become an adult, since the store was a meeting place for the citizens of Taganrog, monks from Greece, and the peasants of the surrounding regions.[8]

---

reproduce. They have no other interests. . . . There are no newspapers or books. . . . There are also no patriots or businessmen or poets. There are even no decent bakers" (Chekhov to Leikin, April 7, 1887, *Pis'ma*, 2:54; see introduction, n. 2). Indeed, it comes as little surprise that Taganrog would be the prototype for what Chekhov later called a "deaf town" (*glukhoi gorod*) in his sketches and stories of Russian life.

It should be noted, though, that in his later years, Chekhov became a tireless benefactor for Taganrog. For example, he not only patronized its regional museum but also presented hundreds of books to the library there.

5. Bunin's statement is surprising since Chekhov's mother, Evgenia Yakovlevna, was a gentle and simple soul, beloved by everyone, including Bunin himself.

6. Actually, the spiritual situation in the Chekhov home was far worse—and more bizarre than Bunin describes. A religious fanatic, Pavel Chekhov forced his children not only to attend church in both morning and evening but also to reenact the liturgies at home during the day. In these encounters, Pavel dressed as a priest and even swung a censer. He also ordered his wife and offspring to sing hymns, lie before icons, and beat their heads against the floor in solemn praise to God.

7. Chekhov wrote "The Sacred Night" ("Sviataia noch'") in 1886; "The Sacred Mountains" ("Sviatye gory"), later retitled "Baby's Breath" ("Perekati-polia"), in 1887; "The Student" ("Student") in 1894; "The Murder" ("Ubiistvo") in 1895; and "The Archbishop" ("Arkhierei") in 1902.

8. Bunin has forgotten to mention that the foreign community—the often wealthy Italian, German, and Greek merchants—gave a veneer of culture to Taganrog, endowing the city with fine homes, a library, a symphony orchestra, and a cathedral.

Of course, besides minding the store, Chekhov had other ways of learning about people. From the time he was sixteen years old, he lived among strangers and earned his own keep.[9] As a student in Moscow, he knocked about working for the "tabloid press" which exposed wide human inadequacies and even vices. . . .

I have always been struck by how Chekhov, before he was even thirty years old, could write such pieces as "A Boring Story," "The Princess," "On the Road," "Cold Blood," "The Slough," "Member of the Choir," and "Typhus."[10] Even in his youth, he astounded readers not only with his artistic talent but also with his knowledge of life and his profound understanding of the human soul.

Of course, Chekhov's career as a doctor gave him much in this regard. . . . "My knowledge of medicine," he often said, "saved me from many mistakes, mistakes that even Tolstoy himself could not avoid, for instance, in his story, *The Kreutzer Sonata.*"[11]

If it had not been for his tuberculosis, Chekhov would never have abandoned medicine. He loved to treat people; he valued his calling as a doctor highly. Indeed, it was not for nothing that on [his wife] Olga Leonardovna's passport, he had written "physician's wife."[12]

---

9. Bunin's allegation is true. In 1876, Evgenia took Maria and Mikhail (Ivan was farmed off to a relative) to Moscow to join both her unemployed husband—who, seeking to hide from creditors in Taganrog, had left for the capital earlier—as well as her two feckless sons who ostensibly were attending school there. For the next three years, Chekhov supported both himself and his family by tutoring and selling what remained of their possessions. Although desperately poor, lonely, and bored, Chekhov not only completed his formal schooling but also learned valuable lessons in independence and self-reliance.

10. Chekhov's "On the Road" ("Na puti"), "The Slough" ("Tina"), and "Member of the Choir" ("Khoristka") appeared in 1886; "Cold Blood" ("Kholodnaia krov'") and "Typhus" ("Tif") in 1887; "The Princess" ("Kniaginia") in 1888 and 1889; and "A Boring Story" ("Skuchnaia istoriia") in 1889.

11. Chekhov continued:

> Medical study has exercised a serious influence on my literary activity. It has considerably widened the area of my observations. It has enriched me with knowledge whose true value to me, as a writer, can be appreciated only by another doctor. It has also helped to guide me in the right direction, and it is probably thanks to my medical knowledge that I have avoided many mistakes.
>
> Familiarity with the natural sciences and with the scientific method has always kept me alert, and I have tried wherever possible to take scientific data into account. And when and where that has not been possible, I have preferred not to write at all. (Chekhov to Grigory Rossolimo, October 18, 1899, *Pis'ma,* 8:284)

12. For instance, Chekhov wrote to her, "At first I wanted to list on your passport as the 'wife of an honored academician,' but then I thought it would be more pleasant to have you as the 'spouse of a physician.'" Chekhov to O. Knipper, September 4, 1901, *Pis'ma,* 10:72.

Writing in such journals as *Alarm Clock*, the *Spectator*, and *Fragments*[13] taught Chekhov the art of the sketch: he was not allowed to exceed a hundred lines![14]

The brevity of the poetic line taught me the same thing.

Chekhov's personality was entirely like his mother's (an Asian).[15] His edifying tone was the one thing he inherited from his father.[16] One has to read only several of the writer's letters to his brothers.

Still as a high school student, Chekhov wrote to his younger brother, Misha—Anton was seventeen, Misha was twelve—about the fact that Misha had called himself an "inferior and inconspicuous little tyke": "So you think you are not worth much? Not all Mishas are alike, brother. Do you know where you should acknowledge your insignificance? Before God, and, perhaps, before the mind, beauty, and nature. But you do not want to do such a thing before people; in their midst you must acknowledge your worth. . . . Know that an honest person is not an insignificant entity. Do not confuse the need 'to submit or to be resigned' with the 'consciousness of one's inferiority.'"[17]

Chekhov often told my friends, the Elpatievskys, "I have not sinned against the fourth commandment."

While still a high school student, Chekhov wrote to his cousin in a letter dated July 29, 1877, "For me, my father and mother are the only people in the entire world whom I will never pity. If I ever stand tall in this world, it is because of them. They are wonderful people. Their love for their children

13. *Alarm Clock* (*Budil'nik*) was a satirical journal published in St. Petersburg from 1865 to 1871 and in Moscow from 1873 to 1917. *Spectator* (*Zritel'*) was an illustrated humorous publication that came out in Moscow between 1881 and 1885. *Fragments* (*Oskolki*) was a magazine that appeared in St. Petersburg from 1881 to 1916 and which is said to have published more than two hundred of Chekhov's stories between 1881 and 1887.

Such magazines were popular with readers and reviewers because public taste had become both frivolous and vulgar in the wake of the 1881 assassination of Alexander II and the ensuing reaction of Alexander III. *Alarm Clock*, *Spectator*, and *Fragments* often featured stock characters from vaudeville—bumbling officials, idiotic law-court clerks, clumsy dentists, and befuddled cuckolds—all bearing ridiculous names and enduring absurd situations but also serving as seedbeds for the heroes and heroines of Chekhov's mature stories and plays.

14. Bunin's statement is true. In his early years as a writer, Chekhov could be appallingly verbose and repetitive in his work.

15. There is no evidence for such an assertion.

16. About the influence of his parents on his life, Chekhov once said, "Our talent came from our father, our soul from our mother" (quoted in Sakhorova, *Vokrug Chekhova*, 53; see preface, n. 1). Further, from his father Chekhov received his fervent belief in education, from his mother the resolve both to endure and to hold the family together at all costs.

17. Chekhov to Mikhail Pavlovich Chekhov, early April 1879, *Pis'ma*, 1:29.

alone exceeds all praise, transcends all the shortcomings that arose from their impoverished life, and prepares the gentle and short journey which they, like few others, believe and hope for."[18]

Chekhov was that rare type of writer who began his career without ever thinking that he would be a writer, or even a great one.

Chekhov had to write under the following conditions: "In the room next to me, father is reading aloud *The Engraved Angel* [19] to my mother. . . . Someone is winding up the Victrola and I hear *La Belle Hélène.*[20] . . . I want to run off to our dacha, but it is already one in the morning. In such wretched circumstances, I find it difficult to write something."[21]

It was only from 1885 on, when . . . Anton Pavlovich became a doctor, that he had his own room: a study with a fireplace.

His vivacity and ability to work were remarkable. After all, notwithstanding all his writing, he graduated from the most difficult department at the university.[22]

Below is a remarkable letter from Chekhov to his older brother, Alexander, dated February 20, 1883, and concerning Alexander's illicit marriage to his wife.[23] (The church consistory at Tula [24] had forbidden the woman to marry after her divorce.) Chekhov's father had reacted negatively to the couple's living together outside of wedlock, and Alexander Pavlovich was suffering greatly. "I do not know what you want from father," Chekhov wrote. "He opposes smoking and living together outside of marriage. Do you want him to be something other than he is? You can get away with this escapade with mother and auntie, but not with him. He is as stubborn as an Old Believer.[25] He believes

18. It should be noted here that Chekhov's noble sentiments for his father are colored somewhat by the fact that at the time, he was appealing to a cousin for assistance in finding a job for the man. See Chekhov to Mikhail Mikhailovich Chekhov, July 29, 1877, *Pis'ma,* 1:25.

19. Nikolai Leskov wrote *The Engraved Angel* (*Zapechatlennyi angel*) in 1873.

20. Jacques Offenbach penned his successful operetta *La Belle Hélène* in 1865.

21. In this letter, written in mid-August 1883, Bunin omits other distressing details. Chekhov continues, "The fledgling of an itinerant kinsman is screaming in the room next door. . . . Even worse, the man keeps coming up to me and starts discussing medicine: 'My daughter must have the colic. That is what is making her scream.' . . . I promise myself never to have children." Chekhov to Leikin, August 1883, *Pis'ma,* 1:81, 82.

22. At the time, the medical faculty of the university was in its prime, presenting its students with a difficult five-year course of study, which was quite at variance with the school's other programs in literature and law.

23. Alexander had fallen in love with a married woman whose husband had refused to give her a divorce and with whom, along with her child, he now lived in a common-law arrangement.

24. Tula is located approximately 120 miles south of Moscow.

25. Old Believers (*Starovery*) were seventeenth-century schismatics who, for political, social, and religious reasons, revolted against both the Russian church and state.

that one can do nothing worse than to live together in an unmarried state; he cannot be persuaded otherwise. He is a truly forceful personality. No matter how sweetly you may write to him, he will exude eternal sighs, will write one and the same thing, and worst of all, will suffer at what you are doing."

At the end of the letter, Chekhov adds, "I confess that I am extremely ill at ease with the family. Generally speaking, I am a nervous type. I am coarse and sometimes unjust in my actions with others."[26]

Chekhov always took himself in hand before he moved on to others. . . . But he was innately hot-tempered.

It is remarkable how Anton Pavlovich, as a twenty-six-year-old doctor, could explain the nature of good breeding in a letter to his brother Nikolai in March 1886:

> People of good breeding must satisfy the following conditions: (1) They must respect the human personality, and always be tolerant, mild, courteous, and flexible; (2) They must respect another's property, and pay their own debts; (3) They do not lie even in trifles; (4) They do not talk openly about their personal matters, when they are not asked about them; (5) They do not debase themselves to seek someone's pity; (6) They are not vain. The handshake of some drunken Plevako[27] does not impress them; (7) If they have talent, they respect . . . and sacrifice everything for it. They are fastidious; (8) They acquire an ethical sense. They do not need to bed women. Precisely because they are artists, they need freshness, humanity, and the ability to be a mother, not a whore. They need to work constantly day and night, to read and study endlessly, and to possess a firm will . . . for every hour is valuable to them.[28]

Before 1885 Chekhov . . . knew only one contemporary writer—Leskov, whom he loved dearly. On a trip to Moscow in 1883, the two had drunk a great deal, with Leskov anointing Chekhov just as "Samuel did to David."[29]

[As a young man] Chekhov once moved to an apartment . . . which was located right below the premises of an eating house which its owner rented

---

26. At the same time, though, Chekhov also supported Alexander against Pavel. In the same missive, he continued, "What do you care what some bigot thinks about your private life? Let him think what he likes. . . . Every man has a right to live with anyone he likes and how he likes" (Chekhov to Alexander Chekhov, February 20, 1883, *Pis'ma*, 1:56).

27. Fyodor Plevako, a famous lawyer in Russia in the 1890s, was also an inspiration for Bunin's 1925 *The Elagin Affair* (*Delo korneta Elagina*); the story is rooted in Plevako's stirring but unsuccessful defense of an army officer who had murdered his mistress (allegedly at her own request).

28. Chekhov to Nikolai Chekhov, March 1886, *Pis'ma*, 1:223–24.

29. Bunin forgets to mention that in their meeting, the self-proclaimed "mystical" Leskov made the prophecy that Anton would die before brother Alexander. (Leskov was correct.

out for weddings and funeral dinners. Anton Pavlovich wrote, "At dinner time, wakes; at night . . . death and conception."[30]

At the end of March, Chekhov received a letter from Grigorovich, who forced him to think about himself as a writer.[31]

On March 28, 1886, Anton Pavlovich replied:

> If I have a talent that I should respect, I confess that, in all honesty, I have yet to do so. I sense that I had talent, but I have grown used to seeing it as paltry. . . . All my close friends regard my writing with condescension. In a friendly type of way, they tell me not to give up my real job for scribbling. . . .
>
> I do not remember any story that took me more than a day to write. My story "The Huntsman,"[32] which you liked, I wrote when I was in a dressing room at the beach. I write in much the same way as a reporter talks about fires . . . mechanically, half-consciously, without caring in the least about the reader or myself.[33]

By the way, I should mention that I do not like "The Huntsman." I find it to be a weak story.

[In 1886 also] Chekhov received a letter from his close acquaintance M. V. Kiselyova regarding his story "The Slough":[34]

> Although I am convinced that very few others will agree with me, I did not at all like the feuilleton which you sent me. It is well written, and male readers will regret that fate did not push them into the arms of a similar Susanna who would enjoy their wild behavior. Women will secretly envy her, but the

---

Alexander died in 1913, nine years after Anton.) See Chekhov to Alexander Chekhov, October 1883, *Pis'ma*, 1:88.

30. Chekhov to Leikin, January 19, 1886, *Pis'ma*, 1:186. Bunin, though, does not know or cares not to mention that the hospitable Chekhovs were soon holding parties and evenings to rival the proceedings in others parts of the building in which they lived.

31. Bunin's comment is true. Up to this point, Chekhov had written solely for supplemental income and lacked the advice and encouragement of established writers to adopt a more serious attitude toward his art.

"You have genuine talent," Grigorovich wrote to Chekhov on March 25, 1886, "a giftedness which places you in the front ranks among writers in the new generation. . . . Cease to write hurriedly. . . . Save your impressions for a mature, finished work, written not in one setting but during the happy hours of inspiration. . . . [In the end] one such work will be valued a hundred times higher than a hundred fine stories scattered among the newspapers at various times." Quoted in Vatsuro et al., *Perepiska*, 1:290 (see introduction, n. 197).

32. Chekhov's "The Huntsman" ("Eger'") appeared in 1885.

33. Chekhov to Grigorovich, March 28, 1886, *Pis'ma*, 1:217–18.

34. Chekhov wrote "The Slough" ("Tina"; also known in English as "The Mire") in 1887.

majority of the public will read the story with interest and say, "This Chekhov is something else. He writes in a such a bold and daring way!"

Perhaps such responses and the 115 rubles that you got for your story will satisfy you; but personally speaking, I was annoyed by your piece, that a writer of your talent, that is, someone whom God has so blessed, would show me only a "pile of manure."

The world swarms with dirt and scoundrels, both male and female, and the impressions which they evoke are not new. That is why readers are so grateful to have a writer who leads them to a stinking manure pile but who suddenly pulls pearls from it, thereby making them wonder if it really had been a manure pile in the first place. Give me those pearls so that all the dirt of my surroundings will recede into my memory. I am fully in my rights to ask such a thing from you. I will not even begin to read writers who cannot find or stand up for individuals amid four-legged animals. . . .

Perhaps it would be better for me to hold my tongue; but I have had this wild wish to swear at you and at your vile editors, who ruin your talent with their indifference. If I were an editor, I would, for your own benefit, tear up this feuilleton . . . for it is really repulsive. Let others write these type of things—those hacks and other untalented *tutti quanti* who are poor in spirit and abused by fate.[35]

Only three weeks later did Chekhov reply:

Neither I, nor you, nor all the critics of the world have any solid evidence or the right to negate this type of writing. I do not know who is correct. Homer, Shakespeare, Lope de Vega, and generally speaking, the ancients who were not afraid to rummage through the "manure pile" but who were so more un- wavering in their moral stance than we are? Or, contemporary writers who are prim and proper on paper but so cold in both soul and life? I also do not know who writes in more questionable taste: the Greeks, who were not ashamed to sing of love in its genuinely splendid form, or the readers of Gaboriau, Marlitt, Pierre Bobo [P. D. Boborykin? —I.B.][36] . . .

Your citing of Turgenev and Tolstoy as writers who escaped the "manure pile" does not shed any light on this question. Their fastidiousness does not prove a thing. After all, there existed an entire generation of writers before them who thought that it was dirty and vile not only to feature "men and women villains" in fiction but even to describe peasants and bureaucrats below the rank of titular councillor. . . .

35. Quoted in Vatsuro et al., *Perepiska*, 1:260.
36. Pierre Bobo is indeed Boborykin. See ibid., 1:265.

Literature is artistic when it portrays life as it is. Its purpose is to put forth a truth that is honest and absolute. To narrow the function of literature, to make it so specialized, to have it catch only the seeds [of truth], would be for it as fatal as if one would force Levitan to draw a tree, after having ordered him not to touch the dirty bark and the yellowed foliage. . . .

Chemists believe that nothing is unclean on this earth. The writer must be as objective as the chemist. He must renounce worldly subjectivity. He must also know that manure piles in the landscape play a very respectable role and that evil passions are as innate to life as good ones are.[37]

Fifty years later, after the appearance of my *Dark Allies,* I received similar letters from people like the Kiselyovs,[38] and I responded to them in an approximately similar way. Truly, everything repeats itself.

37. Chekhov to Kiselyova, January 14, 1887, *Pis'ma,* 2:10–11.

38. Regarding Bunin's 1946 *Dark Allies (Temnye allei)*, Mark Aldanov wrote to Bunin on August 2, 1941, "I am terribly grateful to have received a copy of *Dark Allies.* You are a brave man, Ivan Alexeevich! People will scold you for the boldness of several scenes. They will say that it is 'pornography' and that you are holding 'laurels to Lady Chatterley.'" Quoted in A. Zweers, "Perepiska I. A. Bunina s M. A. Aldanovym," *Novyi zhurnal,* no. 150 (1983): 166.

Similarly, about *Dark Allies,* Boris Zaitsev chided Bunin on November 28, 1943, "I have just received your *Dark Allies* . . . and with my well-known eagerness, read it right away. . . . But, old man, I will tell you the truth. . . . All that 'between the legs' stuff, and the pants with the split in them, and references to menstruation and to girls' asses, adds nothing to your stories.

"As you know, I am in no way a prude. . . . I myself have been a great sinner who 'got around' a lot in his time. . . . But literature does not gain anything from such details. . . . I should also add that I am alluding to *aesthetics,* not morals." Quoted in M. Grin, "Pis'ma B. K. Zaitseva I. i V. Buninym," *Novyi zhurnal,* no. 146 (1982): 122 (italics in the original).

Even worse, perhaps, Aldanov and Andrei Sedykh were so distressed by the material in *Dark Allies* that they consulted a lawyer before they published a *Russian* edition of the work in the United States. "Several stories could not be printed," Aldanov told Bunin on March 23, 1945. "If we had done so, we would have been arrested and prosecuted as criminals. Believe me, I am not joking here. Here [in the United States] morality is very strict." Quoted in Zweers, "Perepiska," 171.

Chapter Two

I MET CHEKHOV in Moscow, at the end of [18]95. At that time, we saw each other only in passing, and I would not even bring up these encounters if I had not been able to recall several of his characteristic phrases.

"Do you write a great deal?" he once asked me.

I answered that I had written little.

"What you are doing is wrong," he said, his deep, chesty baritone exuding an almost gloomy air.

"You should work, you know . . . work without stopping . . . your entire life."

Having fallen silent, and without any apparent connection [to what he had just said], Chekhov added, "In my opinion, after one finishes a story, he should cross out the beginning and the end. It is here that we writers lie most of all."

After such fleeting encounters . . . we did not see each other again until the spring of 1899. Having come to Yalta[1] for several days, I one evening met Chekhov walking along the embankment.

"Why have you not come to see me?" he said. "Visit me tomorrow without fail."

"At what time?" I asked.

"In the morning, around eight."

Most likely having noticed the surprise on my face, he explained, "We get up early. And you?"

"So do I," I said.

"Well then come as soon as you get up. We will have some coffee. Do you drink coffee?"

"From time to time."

"Drink it every day. It is a wonderful thing. Whenever I am working, I

---

1. Yalta is in the Crimea, roughly eight hundred miles southwest of Moscow.

take only coffee and broth until evening. Coffee in the morning, broth at midday. Otherwise I do not work well at all."

I thanked him for his invitation. In silence, we first walked along the entire embankment; then we sat on a bench in the square.

"Do you like the sea?" I asked.

"Yes," he answered. "But only when it is completely deserted."

"That is when it is really good," I replied.

"I don't know," he responded, looking off into the distance through the glasses of his pince-nez. Apparently, he was thinking about some personal matter. "As I see it, it is a good thing to be an officer or a young student. . . . To sit somewhere in a place filled with people and to listen to cheerful music."

As he often did, Chekhov first fell silent; then he added without any apparent connection, "It is very difficult to describe the sea. Do you know what I recently read in a student's notebook about the sea? 'The sea was big,' the individual wrote. That was all. I thought it was marvelous."

Yes, Chekhov loved only things that were sincere and organic—so long as they were not vulgar or static. He positively could not stand wind-bags, bookish types, and pharisees, especially those among them who had so entered into their roles that their playacting had become second nature for them. In his own writing, Chekhov almost never talked about himself or his tastes and his views. In fact, his reticence gave rise to enduring views that he was devoid of principles or social awareness.[2] In life, also, Chekhov never made much over his "I"; he very rarely spoke about his likes and dislikes. "I love this" . . . "I cannot stand that"—these were not Chekhovian phrases.

His likes and dislikes, though, were extremely fixed and well defined. Among his likes, it was precisely naturalness that held first place. "The sea was big."[3] For him, with his constant yearning for the most elevated simplicity, along with his repulsion for anything that was mannered and strained, such a phrase seemed to him to be "marvelous." In his words about music

2. In response to one of the most famous charges against Chekhov's alleged indifference to social suffering—an allegation by Pyotr Lavrov, the editor of *Russian Thought* (*Russkaia mysl'*), that Chekhov was a "high priest of unprincipled art" (*zhrets besprintsipnogo pisaniia*)—the usually taciturn Chekhov replied to Lavrov in a letter written on April 10, 1890, that such an accusation was "libel, plain and simple." He continued, "I have never been an unprincipled writer, or what amounts to the same thing, a scoundrel. . . . There is not a single line in my writing of which I am ashamed." (The rift with Lavrov not only was healed but also moved to a close partnership that continued until Chekhov's death.) P. Lavrov, "Vestnik Evropy—fevral', Russkii vestnik—ianvar'," in *Russkaia mysl'*, no. 3 (March 1890): 147; Chekhov to Lavrov, April 10, 1890, *Pis'ma*, 4:56 (see introduction, n. 2).

3. "In my view," Chekhov wrote to his brother Alexander on May 10, 1886, "descriptions of nature must be very brief and have an apropos character. Generalities like 'the setting sun, bathing in the waves of the darkening sea, sheds a light of crimson gold' and so on, or 'the

and the officer, one could discern another characteristic of his personality: his sense of reserve.[4] Undoubtedly, Chekhov's unexpected transition from the sea to the officer was rooted in a secret sadness over his youth, his health. But he loved life and joy; and during the last years of his life, his yearning for happiness, even the most simple and mundane, could often be sensed in his conversation. But only sensed, nothing more.

Within recent times, words have become very cheap. Indeed, both good and foolish words are uttered with remarkable ease and falsity. But it seems that such verbal cheapness truly comes to the fore when people speak of the dead. In recollections about Chekhov, one encounters a great many lies, inaccuracies, superficialities, and on occasion, simple feeblemindedness. For example, people write that Chekhov went to Sakhalin[5] to enhance his reputation as a "serious" individual and that on the way there he caught such a cold that he contracted tuberculosis. They also insist that Chekhov's death was hastened by the staging of *The Cherry Orchard* and that on the eve of its debut, Chekhov was so upset and afraid that the public would not like his play that he raved like a madman all night long.

Such things are complete nonsense. Chekhov went to Sakhalin because he was interested in Sakhalin[6] and because he wanted a change of

---

swallows, skimming the water, chirped merrily,' must be done away with" (Chekhov to Alexander Chekhov, May 10, 1886, *Pis'ma,* 1:242).

Bunin agreed, telling Irina Odoevtseva in 1948, "Chekhov is the only writer who can show the ocean in a drop of water, the Sahara desert in a grain of sand, an entire backdrop in a single phrase. He was occupied with nature constantly. He always carried a small book and wrote his observations in it. How marvelous are his tufted clouds that go along like ghosts in the night." Quoted in I. Odoevtseva, *Na beregakh Seny* (Paris: La Presse Libre, 1983), 349.

4. About his legendary restraint, Chekhov recalled, "As a child, so little affection came my way that now, as an adult, I treat caresses as something unfamiliar and almost beyond my ken. That is why, as much as I would like to, I cannot show fondness for others." Chekhov to Serebrov-Tikhonov, March 7, 1889, *Pis'ma,* 3:173.

5. Sakhalin, an elongated island mass approximately five hundred miles in length, situated in the Pacific just north of Japan, was a Russian penal colony of some ten thousand prisoners.

6. Beyond the motives Bunin cites, there were both negative and positive reasons why Chekhov visited Sakhalin. On the negative side, he was dissatisfied with the direction both his life and his art had taken, and he felt the need to regenerate both. He also was disgusted with the literary politics and infighting in both Moscow and St. Petersburg. On the positive side, Chekhov saw Sakhalin as appealing to both the scientific and literary aspects of his personality: as a doctor, he wished to conduct a scientific study-census of the prisoners on the island; as a writer, he wished to experience Russian reality in all its horror and its depravity.

Chekhov was successful in his quest. His soft-spoken yet direct approach quickly won the confidence of the island's administrators as well as of its prisoners and guards. Within minutes, all three groups talked to him as a confidante and a friend.

Chekhov, though, was quick to show the difficulties on Sakhalin, for example, prisoners who had lost their sense of both morality and reality.

It should also be noted that although Chekhov's account of his trip, *The Island of Sakhalin,* disappointed readers and reviewers who were hoping for a sequel to Dostoevsky's

scene after the death of his brother Nikolai, a talented artist.[7] Also, Chekhov did not contract consumption in Siberia, since, already in December 1884, he was spitting up blood after the "Skopin Affair."[8] Undoubtedly, Chekhov should not have gone to Sakhalin.[9] He should not have undertaken this terribly difficult, almost three-month trip, traveling by post-horse in early spring, encountering cold and rain, going without sleep, and subsisting on the diet of a hermit—the consequence of the savage Siberian roads![10]

As regards Chekhov's distress over *The Cherry Orchard* . . . writers are very sensitive to what people say about them. Many of them have a sensitivity that is shallow, lamentable, and neurasthenic. But such a thing was far from the case with such a great and powerful individual as Chekhov! Who else but he could follow, so courageously, the commands of his heart, not the demands of the mob? Who else but he could so hide the sharp pain that arose in him when stupidity triumphed over reason? People know only one instance when Chekhov was visibly shaken by failure: the evening when *The Seagull* was first staged in Petersburg.[11] But much water had flowed under

---

prison memoir, *Notes from the House of the Dead* (*Zapiski iz mertvogo doma,* 1860–61), his work motivated reformists to investigate conditions on the island and to pursue Chekhov's recommendations for alleviating some of the suffering of the population there.

7. Nikolai Chekhov was a talented artist who often illustrated Anton's stories and who would have had a brilliant career in journalism if he had been stable—and sober. A vagrant who trailed after prostitutes, he often disappeared for days on end only to return home, drunk and vomiting, to sleep off his vodka.

Although Anton was quite fond of Nikolai, he was also appalled by his brother's self-destruction and sought to send him on the right path. "Work constantly day and night," Anton advised Nikolai in March 1886, "Every hour is precious. . . . Smash your vodka carafe" (Chekhov to Nikolai Chekhov, March 1886, *Pis'ma,* 1:225).

The thirty-one-year-old Nikolai died in 1889 of tuberculosis, a disease which, ironically, Chekhov himself diagnosed for his brother.

8. Bunin is referring to the 1884 failure of an important bank in the provincial town of Skopin (150 miles southeast of Moscow), leading to a national scandal as well as to a sensational sixteen-day trial of the bank's executives in St. Petersburg on charges of embezzlement. Here the young Chekhov took it upon himself to serve as a court reporter, covering the entire proceedings of the affair from the act of indictment to the sentences which condemned the guilty parties to exile in Siberia. Realizing that he was only a novice correspondent and unaccustomed to writing like "one possessed," Chekhov came to regret having volunteered for such a difficult undertaking.

"I write about [the scandal] every day," Chekhov complained to Leikin, "and the entire business is unpleasant and burdensome to the highest degree" (Chekhov to Leikin, November 26, 1884, *Pis'ma,* 1:135).

9. Bunin was not alone in his opposition.

10. Chekhov's journey to Sakhalin embraced nearly seven thousand miles, almost half of which had to be covered in what Chekhov himself called a "wicker basket," that is, in a chaise or carriage that was slightly more sophisticated than a cart.

11. At its premiere, *The Seagull* presented problems to everyone concerned. No one, it seemed, could grasp the subtleties of the play. The actors, when they knew their lines, acted

the bridge since that time. Who could know whether he was truly upset [over *The Cherry Orchard*] or not?[12] Even those individuals who were closest to him never knew the full extent of what was going on in the depths of his soul. Furthermore, what can one say about people who were not in Chekhov's group, especially those who were neither sensitive nor bright, people with whom Chekhov was, organically, unable to be open and frank?

As a boy, Chekhov was, in the words of his school friend [Pyotr Sergeenko], a "feeble bumpkin with a moonlike face."[13] Judging by the pictures I have of him, as well as by the stories that his family has told me, I see Chekhov in an-

---

with bombast, not understatement. The audience, filled with jealous writers and critics and eager for the three-act comedy that was to follow, was up for laughter, not tears. It was certainly not in the mood for Chekhov's innovations, for the melds of enthusiasm and absurdity, vulgarity and grief, banality and mystery that inform the work.

The public who attended the debut of *The Seagull* received it with a vengeance. To Chekhov's chagrin, the scanty applause that had ended act 1 of the play moved, by the final scene of act 2, to a deafening hullabaloo. At the most poignant parts of the work, people hissed, guffawed, and laughed; they even turned their back to the stage, engaged in catcalls, or struck up conversations with partners that were so loud that the discourse of the play was inaudible. When the curtain came down, the storm of indignation from spectators drove Chekhov from the theater. Indeed, the failure of the play was to be the most traumatic event of his life.

Reviews of *The Seagull* added insult to injury. "This is not a seagull, but wild game," a critic from the *Exchange News* wrote on October 19, 1896. Another, writing for the *Petersburg Gazette* on the same day, compared it to a German operetta.

Such vituperation was too much for Chekhov. "The moral is," he wrote to his brother Mikhail, that "it is wrong for me to write plays" (Chekhov to Mikhail Pavlovich Chekhov, October 18, 1896, *Pis'ma,* 6:197). Writing on the same day to Suvorin, he added, "*Never again* will I write or put on plays" (Chekhov to Suvorin, October 18, 1896, *Pis'ma,* 6:197; italics in the original).

It should be noted here that the second staging of *The Seagull* was a great success, if only because this time, the public expected drama, not farce.

12. In truth, *The Cherry Orchard* aggrieved Chekhov from beginning to end. Not only was he in the last years of his life when he wrote the play, but he was also under constant—if inhuman—pressure from Olga Knipper, Stanislavsky, and others to finish the work. There were also constant misunderstandings between Chekhov, on one side, and the company and cast, on the other, as to both the content and the form of the piece. A key point of contention was Chekhov's wish to stage *The Cherry Orchard* as a comedy, even a farce, with a certain casualness and lightness of touch, and Stanislavsky's preference for the work as tragedy, with its overtheatricality, naturalistic excesses, and focus on the vanishing life of the gentry, crushed by social and economic change.

Even worse, perhaps, was Chekhov's inability to convince others of his point of view and of his resignation at seeing *The Cherry Orchard* as a work of darkness, not light.

13. It should be noted that Sergeenko was not alone in such a view. As a boy, Chekhov's large, round head was so disproportionate to the size of his body that schoolmates called him "tadpole" and "big head." See P. Sergeenko, "O Chekhove. Vospominaniia," in *Ezhemesiachnye literaturnye i populiarno-nauchnye prilozheniia k zhurnalu Niva na 1904 g. za sentiabr', oktiabr;' noiabr' i dekabr'*, no. 10 (October 1904): 250.

other way. His face was not "moonlike," but simply big, very peaceful and intelligent-looking. Most likely, it was this peacefulness that caused the young Chekhov to be seen as a "bumpkin." But such tranquillity did not mean that Chekhov, even in the last years of his existence, lacked enthusiasm for life. Rather, as I see it, Chekhov's peacefulness was of a special type, that is, it was the inner serenity of a boy whose great talents were maturing, and who showed a gift for precise observation and a rare sense of humor. Indeed, one has to counter his friend's words with the testimony of Chekhov's mother and brothers who insisted that, as a child, "Antosha" was the source of endless stories which forced even the severe Pavel Egorovich to laugh to the point of tears.

Chekhov's tranquillity seemed to wash over him, to bring his innate joy for life to a full flowering. Everyone who knew him at this time spoke about the irresistible enchantment of his happiness, the beauty of his simple, open face and radiant eyes. But with the years, as Chekhov became more insightful and wise in mind and soul, he again took himself in hand. As a youth, he had paid his dues in spontaneous displays of his richly endowed nature; but now, in his severe portraits of life, he stepped forward toward artistic integrity.

It was precisely at this time that I first began meeting with him. In 1895 in Moscow, I saw a middle-aged man, wearing a pince-nez, and simply and elegantly dressed. He was rather tall, very well built, and quite lithe in his movements. He greeted me in a cordial type of way, but also so simply that I—still then a youth[14] who did know his mannerisms—took his simplicity for coldness. Later in Yalta, I saw that Chekhov had changed a great deal. He had gotten thinner; his face had darkened. His entire appearance shone through with the same innate grace as earlier; but this grace was no longer that of a young man but of one who had experienced a great deal in life and who had been ennobled by his encounters. His voice sounded softer.

Generally speaking, though, Chekhov was almost the same person that he had been in Moscow: cordial, but reserved; and speaking in a lively way, but also more curtly and simply [than previously]. During the course of our conversation, he kept thinking about something that was exclusively his own. He also kept challenging his companion to catch the sudden transitions in the hidden stream of his thoughts. His head was slightly raised, since he kept looking at the sea through the glasses of his pince-nez.

On the morning following our meeting on the embankment, I visited him at his dacha. I clearly remember that joyful sunny morning which Chekhov and I spent in his small garden. He was very animated, joked a good deal, and, as he told me, recited the only poem that he had ever written: "Hares and Chinese, a Story for Children."[15]

---

14. Bunin was twenty-five years old at the time.
15. More accurately, the 1887 work is titled "A Fable" ("Basnia").

From that time on, I began to visit Chekhov more and more often, until I became a regular member of the household. Not surprisingly, Chekhov began to treat me differently. He became more spirited and cordial, but his sense of restraint remained. He maintained this reserve not only with me but also with the people who were closest to him. At that time, I eventually became convinced that his reserve did not mean indifference but something that was far greater and more important.

[I remember] the white stone dacha in Autka[16] under a southern sun and a light-blue sky; and its small garden to which Chekhov, in his love for animals, flowers, and trees, gave such attention. [I also remember] his study with its only decorations being two or three pictures by Levitan[17] and a huge half-circular window that looked out on the blue triangle of the sea, as well as on the numerous gardens engulfing the valley about the Uchan-Su River.[18] The hours, days, and sometimes even months that I spent at this dacha—together with my conscious awareness of my closeness to its host who so captivated me with his mind and talent, and even his stern voice and childish smile—will always be for me one of the best memories of my life.

Chekhov loved laughter, but he laughed his dear, infectious laugh only when someone told him something that was truly funny. He himself told the most humorous things without the slightest smile. He adored jokes, hoaxes, and silly sayings. Even in the last years of his life when it seemed that he was getting better, if only for short periods of time, he could not get his fill of such things. . . . One needed only to utter two or three words, and his eyes looked up from his pince-nez in a bright and wily way.

Then there were his letters! How many wonderful jokes does one find in them, but in an absolutely reserved type of way!

"Dear Ivan Alexeevich," Chekhov wrote to me on March 25, 1901, "Allow me to meet you. You must really come. We will have so many types of hors d'oeuvres, and Yalta is experiencing such warm weather now that we have all kinds of flowers! Please, I beg you to come! I have changed my mind about marrying. I simply do not want to do so now; but if you think that you will be bored, I will get married if I have to."[19]

"Dear Ivan Alexeevich," Chekhov wrote in another letter to me on June 30, 1901, "Tomorrow I am going to Yalta, where I will ask you to con-

16. Autka (renamed Chekhovo in 1944) is located two miles west of Yalta.

17. There were actually five paintings by Levitan in Chekhov's study: *Oak and Birch Tree* (*Dub i berezka*, 1884), *The River Istra* (*Reka Istra*, 1884), *The Pull* (*Tiaga*, 1891), Etude (*Etiud*, 1895), and *Haystacks on a Moonlit Night* (*Stoga sena v lunnuyu noch*, 1899). In addition, pictures of Tolstoy, Turgenev, and Grigorovich hung on the walls in the writer's study.

18. The Uchan-Su River is roughly twenty miles from Yalta.

19. Chekhov to Bunin, March 25, 1901, *Pis'ma*, 9:234–35.

gratulate me in writing as regards my lawful marriage. . . . I wish you all the best. Be well. Yours, A. Chekhov, a philistine from Autka."[20]

Did Chekhov's sense of restraint show itself in things that were more important to him and that testified to the rare force of his nature? Who, for example, ever heard him complain? He had many reasons to do so. Having been born into a large family, he had to begin work early and suffered great need as a youth. He also had to toil for little more than pennies, and in circumstances which could have extinguished the most fervid inspiration. He worked in a small little apartment, amid talking and noise; he often wrote at the edge of a table, surrounded not only by his entire family but also by several student-guests.

Chekhov was in need for a long time after that, but no one ever heard him complain about his fate. Such reticence, though, was not due to his retiring disposition or the limited nature of his needs. Although Chekhov was extremely noble and modest in his way of life, he sincerely hated his gray and meager existence. For fifteen years, he was sick with a debilitating disease which eventually led to his death. But did his readers know of his illness, the very same Russian readers who heard so many bitter wails from writers?

Sick people love their privileged position. Almost with delight, the strongest among them torment their loved ones with malicious, bitter, and endless conversations about their illness.[21] But the courage with which Chekhov met his illness and death was truly amazing! Even during those days when he suffered greatly, no one suspected what he was enduring.

"Don't you feel well, Antosha?" his mother or sister used to ask him, when they saw him in a chair with his eyes closed.

"Who, me?" he would answer quietly, opening his eyes, so gentle and clear without his pince-nez. "No, it is nothing. It is just that my head hurts a little."

Chekhov loved literature passionately. He delighted in talking about writers; and rhapsodizing over Maupassant,[22] Flaubert, and Tolstoy was for him a joy. In ecstasy, he often talked about these writers and also about Lermontov's *Taman*.[23]

"I cannot understand," he often said, "how Lermontov, still as a boy,

20. Chekhov to Bunin, June 30, 1901, *Pis'ma*, 10:50.

21. Bunin should know; he was the archetypal hypochondriac.

22. For instance, the character Lysevich in Chekhov's 1894 story "Kingdom of Women Folk" ("Bab'e tsarstvo") exclaims, "Maupassant . . . what a tremendous, colossal, superhuman writer! Every line opens to you a new horizon. . . . What richness of transitions, melodies, and motifs! . . . What irresistible, beautiful, powerful thoughts!" Chekhov, *Sochineniia*, 8:285 (see introduction, n. 4).

23. Mikhail Lermontov's *Taman* appeared in 1840. Bunin also believed that *Taman* was "one of the most splendid pearls in our literature." See Galina Kuznetsova's diary excerpt, written on January 31, 1931, in Kuznetsova, *Grasskii dnevnik*, 207 (see introduction, n. 16).

could write such a thing! If one could write *Taman* and a good vaudeville to boot, one would die a happy man!"

Chekhov's conversations on literature were not at all like the usual professional discourses, namely, discussions that are so unpleasant because they are clannish, narrow, and trifling, or because they focus on exclusively practical or, more often, personal interests. Although Chekhov was primarily a writer, he differed so markedly from the majority of his literary colleagues that the phrase "man of letters" cannot define him in much the same way that it cannot describe Tolstoy. Chekhov conducted discussions on literature only when he knew that his companion loved fiction primarily as art, disinterested and free.

"No writer should read his stories before they are published," he often said. "And the main thing, he should not be forced to listen to any advice. If the writer has made a mistake, if he has talked nonsense, the mistake will be his alone.

"After the high demands that Maupassant placed on his art, it would be difficult to write anything after him, but one must work just the same. We Russians must be particularly bold in our work. There are big dogs and little dogs, but little dogs must not fret over the existence of the big ones. Everyone is obligated to howl in the voice that the Lord God has given him."

Everything that was going on in the literary world was very close to Chekhov's heart. He suffered greatly amid the stupidity and falsehood, affectation and huckstering that now flowered so lavishly in literature.[24] But Chekhov kept such distress above superficial irritation and personal feelings. It is said about almost all deceased writers that they were devoid of pride and that they rejoiced over another's success. And, if I had the slightest doubt regarding Chekhov's pride as a writer, I would not have touched upon this question at all. With all his heart, Chekhov truly rejoiced over any talent. He could not help but do so. Indeed, for him the word "untalented" was the highest form of abuse. He also looked upon his own successes and failures as only he alone could do.

Chekhov wrote for almost twenty-five years, but how many trivial and coarse rebukes of his writing did he have to hear over this time! One of the greatest and most exquisite of all Russian poets, he never spoke in the language of a preacher or an advocate. But given such talent, could one count on the good graces and understanding of the critics in Russia? After all, did they not demand that Levitan "liven up" his landscapes . . . by adding more cows, geese, and feminine figures to his pictures?[25] Of course, Chekhov was

24. Bunin, of course, is referring to works of the decadents and early symbolist writers.

25. Bunin is calling attention to the pensive "mood landscapes" characteristic of Levitan's work.

hardly enamored with the critics, for they poured bile into a soul that had already been poisoned by Russian life. But this bile was only on the surface; it only seemed to be there.

"Yes, Anton Pavlovich, soon we will celebrate your anniversary as a writer!"

"I know these anniversaries. The critics first revile a writer for twenty-five years. Then they give to the poor soul a goose quill made from aluminum; and all day long, they carry on and talk all kinds of nonsense about him, with tears and kisses, to boot!"

More often, though, Chekhov responded to discussions about his glory, or what people had written about him, with two or three words or even a joke.

"Have you read what the critics have written about you, Anton Pavlovich?" one would ask him, having seen an article about the writer somewhere.

But he would only squint his eyes through his pince-nez;[26] and with a crestfallen face, he would answer in a deep-bass voice.

"I humbly thank you for telling me such a thing!" he would say. "The critics will write a thousand lines about another writer, and then, as a postscript, they will add: 'But here is this other writer named Chekhov: he is such a moaner and groaner. . . .' But how am I a moaner and groaner? In what way am I, as my critics call me, a 'gloomy individual' or a 'cold-blooded writer'? After all, 'The Student'[27] is my most favorite story. . . . And for me, the word 'pessimist' is a repulsive one. . . . No, critics are worse than actors. And, as you know, actors lag a full seventy-five years behind everyone else in the development of Russian society."

He often added, "When people take out after you, dear sir, you must remember us sinners a bit more often. Critics are like priests in a seminary: they flay us for the slightest impropriety."

I never saw Chekhov in a vile mood. He became irritated only rarely; and when he did, he got hold of himself in a remarkable way. I also never found him to be cold and aloof. In his own words, he was cold only when he was at work, which he would take up only when the images and ideas of a future piece were becoming absolutely clear to him. At such times, Chekhov worked almost nonstop, without breaks, doggedly pursuing his story to the end.

"A writer should sit down and write only when he feels cold as ice," he once told me.

But, of course, Chekhov's coldness is of a special type. Indeed, do

---

26. Chekhov's habit of screwing up his eyes, throwing back his head, and peering from under the rim of his pince-nez was seen by many people as a supercilious attitude toward others. The truth, though, was that he had a rash on his cornea that had left him practically blind in the right eye.

27. Chekhov wrote "The Student" in 1894.

there exist many other Russian writers whose spiritual sensitivity and forceful perception are more complex than those of Chekhov?

Chekhov was genuine, upright, and charming; he also was a being who was unusually handsome, integrated, and forceful. I have often spoken about Chekhov's composure, precisely because his equanimity seemed to affirm the rare force of his nature. In my view, such poise did not leave him even when he shone brightly with a joie de vivre. Indeed, it was precisely this poise that afforded the youthful Chekhov the potential not to yield to any artistic influence but to begin working boldly, with wild abandon, and at the same time to achieve such unrivaled mastery, "without any contracts with his conscience."

Do you remember the words of the old professor in "A Boring Story"? "I will not say that French writers are talented and intelligent; but they are not as boring as Russian ones, for they possess the rare ability to find that key element of creativity—a sense or feeling of personal freedom."

It was this sense of personal freedom that also characterized Chekhov. Indeed, he did not tolerate situations in which individuals were deprived of such liberty, and he even became sharp and direct when this freedom was impinged on by others.

As everyone knows, Chekhov paid dearly for this "freedom"; but he was not like those who have two souls: one for self, the other for the public. For a long time, the success that Chekhov enjoyed was almost absurdly out of line with his accomplishments. But throughout his life, did he ever make the slightest attempt to increase his popularity? No. He literally looked with pain and repulsion on all the strategies that people now use to achieve success.

"You think that [such success-grabbing individuals] are writers! They are cabbies!" he often said with sorrow.

His unwillingness to put himself forward often bordered on the extreme.

"Scorpion[28] has made a mess of things," Chekhov wrote to me after the first issue of *Northern Flowers*[29] was published. "The people there have shined the spotlight on me, and after I read their advertisement for the work in *Russian News*,[30] I vowed that never again would I have anything to do with scorpions, crocodiles, and hedgehogs."[31]

---

28. Scorpion (Skorpion) was a publishing house founded in Moscow in 1900 to further both European and Russian symbolism. It ceased operations in 1916.

29. *Northern Flowers* (*Severnye tsvety*), published by Scorpion, was an artistic-literary almanac that appeared in five volumes from 1901 to 1905.

30. *Russian News* (*Russkie vedomosti*), one of the most influential newspapers of its time, was published in Moscow from 1863 to 1918.

31. It should be noted that Bunin apologized profusely for Chekhov's unhappiness with the publication. Bunin to Chekhov, April 30, 1901, in Vatsuro et al., *Perepiska*, 3:519 (see introduction, n. 197). Also see Chekhov to Bunin, March 14, 1901, *Pis'ma*, 9:228; Chekhov to Bunin, April 20, 1901, *Pis'ma*, 10:13.

Such an event happened in the winter of 1900. Chekhov had become interested in the activities of the newly organized Scorpion; and, at my insistence, he had given the editors there one of his youthful works, a story entitled, "On the Sea,"[32] to be published in one of their almanacs. Later he often regretted what he had done.

"No, all this new Muscovite art is garbage," he often said. "I remember once seeing a sign in Taganrog that said PROCESSING PLANT FOR ARTIFICIAL MINERAL WATER. Well, this new art is the same thing. As I see it, something is new only if it is talented. And something is talented only if it is new."

Chekhov drew his sense of restraint from the great aristocratic nature of his soul as well as from his constant striving for preciseness with every word he wrote. There will come a time when Chekhov will be understood as he should, when he will be seen not only as an "incomparable" artist and a remarkable master of the word but also as an incomparable poet. When will this time come? Not soon enough, for critics have yet to discern Chekhov's precise and chaste poetry, the full power and tenderness of his writing.

"Hello, dear Ivan Alexeevich!" Chekhov wrote to me on January 8, 1904, when I was in Nice. "Happy New Year! Every new happiness! . . . Give my regards to the dear, warm sun and the quiet sea. Live in complete contentment, and take consolation in that. Do not think about illnesses, and write a bit more often to your friends. . . . Stay happy and well, and do not forget your ill-tempered northern compatriots who suffer from indigestion and depression. I kiss and embrace you. Yours, A. Chekhov."[33]

"Give my regards to the dear, warm sun and the quiet sea. . . ." Rarely did I ever hear such words from him. Very often I rather felt that he was forced to say them, especially in those minutes when he was feeling very ill.

I remember one night in early spring. It was already late, but suddenly I was called to the phone. I picked up the receiver and heard Chekhov's bass voice: "Dear boy, get ahold of a good cabby, and come and get me. Let's take a ride somewhere."

"A ride? At night?" I said in surprise. "What's with you, Anton Pavlovich?"

"I am in love."

"I am very happy to hear that, but it is already after ten. . . . And you might catch cold . . ."

"Young man, stop arguing!"

In ten minutes I was already at Autka. The home where Chekhov was spending the winter, living only with his mother, was, as always, deathly quiet and dark. The only light was the one coming in from the crack of

32. Chekhov wrote "On the Sea" ("V more") in 1883.
33. Chekhov to Bunin, January 8, 1904, *Pis'ma*, 12:10.

23

the door of Evgenia Yakovlevna's room, along with two small candles that burned dimly in Chekhov's study but that were lost in the half-murkiness. As always, my heart ached at the sight of this quiet study where Chekhov passed so many lonely winter evenings, filled, perhaps, with bitter thoughts of that fate which had given him so much but which also had laughed at his life.

He met me on the threshold of his study. "What a night!" he said to me with an unusual tenderness and a somewhat sad joy. "I find it so boring to be home! The only joy I have is when the phones ring, or when Sofia Pavlovna asks me what I am doing, and I say that I am catching mice.[34] Let's go to Orianda.[35] I don't give a damn if I catch cold or not!"

The night was warm and quiet, with a bright moon, light white clouds, and scattered radiant stars in a deep blue sky. The carriage went along softly on the white highway. We were quiet, looking at the shining, matted-gold valley of the sea. We first passed by a forest that had a springlike air, tender, pensive, and beautiful, and that, like a spiderweb, cast delicate, shadowlike designs on the earth. We then came across some darkening clusters of cypress trees that seemed to reach for the radiant stars. We stopped the carriage and walked quietly under these cypresses, past the ruins of a palace shining bluish-white in the moonlight. Chekhov suddenly turned to me and said, "Do you know how long people will continue to read my works? Seven years, that is all."

"Why seven?" I asked.

"Well, then, seven-and-a-half."[36]

"No," I said. "Your poetry will live on long after that, and the longer it lives, the more powerful it will be."

He did not say anything; but when we sat down on a bench and again looked out onto the shining, moonlit sea, he took off his pince-nez, and look-

---

34. Throughout his life, Chekhov loved to catch mice and then to free them on other parts of his property. In his memoirs, Stanislavsky recalls:

> Anton Pavlovich's name day was drawing near, and we had to think about the form of the celebrations, as well as our gifts for him. A knotty problem! I made the rounds of all the old curiosity shops, hoping to come up with something suitable, but with the exception of a length of exquisite, rare embroidery, I found nothing. For want of anything better, we decided to adorn the wreath with it and give it to him as it was.
>
> "I say, that's a lovely thing, but it ought to be in a museum," Chekhov said to me reproachfully when the celebrations were over.
>
> "Tell me what we ought to have given you then, Anton Pavlovich?" I asked.
>
> "A mousetrap," he said gravely, after a pause. (K. S. Stanislavskii, *Moe grazhdanskoe sluzhenie Rossii* [Moscow: Nauka, 1990], 127)

35. Orianda is a town five miles southwest of Yalta.

36. Interestingly, Chekhov told the same thing to Shchepkina-Kupernik, but also added, "But after a certain time, people will begin to read me again and will do so for a long time." Quoted in Shchepkina-Kupernik, "O Chekhove," 232 (see introduction, n. 50).

ing at me with his kind, tired eyes, said, "People are considered poets, my dear sir, only when they use such phrases as 'the finale,' 'the silvery distance,' and 'to battle, to battle, to struggle with darkness!'"[37]

"You are sad today, Anton Pavlovich," I said, looking at his face that was kind, simple, splendid, and slightly pale in the moonlight.

All the time that we had been talking, Chekhov sat with lowered eyes, thoughtfully digging up some small stones with the end of a stick. But when I told him that he looked sad, he cast a playful sidelong glance at me and replied, "It is you who are sad because you wasted money on a cab."

He then added in a serious tone, "No, people will read me for only seven more years, and I have only six more years to live. But don't say a word about this to the reporters in Odessa."[38]

But this time he was mistaken: he lived even fewer years than that.

He died quietly, without suffering, amid the beauty and quiet of a summer dawn, a time of day that he loved deeply. And when he died, an "expression of happiness appeared on his suddenly youthful face."[39]

37. In the first line, Chekhov is quoting tropes from the decadents and early symbolists; in the second, from the proletarian writers, particularly Gorky.

38. Odessa is in Ukraine, some seven hundred miles southwest of Moscow.

39. Bunin is quoting from a letter from Grigory Iollos. The actual citation reads: "an unusually content, almost happy expression on his suddenly youthful face."

Also, in a September 1904 version of these memoirs on Chekhov, Bunin appended a poem by Jacques Delille, a French poet and translator who was popular in Russia in the beginning of the nineteenth century. The 1884 poem, entitled "To a Dead Poet" ("A un poète mort"), reads:

> Moi, je t'envie, au fond du tombeau calme et noir,
> D'être affranchi de vivre et de ne plus savoir
> La honte de penser et l'horreur d'être un homme.
>
> *As for me, I envy you, at the bottom of a tomb, calm and black,*
> *To be free from life and to know no more*
> *The shame of thinking and the horror of being a man.*

Also see "Poslednie minuty A. P. Chekhova: Iz pis'ma G. B. Iollosa," *Russkie vedomosti*, July 9, 1904, 4.

Chapter Three

IN SPRING 1900, I was in Yalta, at the same time actors from the Moscow Art Theater[1] were staging performances. There I also met Mamin-Sibiryak, Gorky, Teleshov, and Kuprin.[2] The actors were putting on four plays: *The Seagull, Uncle Vanya,*[3] Hauptmann's *Lonely Lives,*[4] and Ibsen's *Hedda Gabler.*[5] They played first in Sevastopol,[6] then in Yalta.

Everyone was in an excited and joyous frame of mind. Chekhov was also feeling comparatively well.[7] Early in the morning, the two of us went to the city theater and walked around the stage where people were preparing for the performance in a fervid way. The entire company then headed for Chekhov's place where they usually spent almost all of their free time.

Chekhov was quite enamored with *The Lonely Ones.* He talked about the play a great deal and believed that the Moscow Art Theater should stage similar dramatic pieces.[8]

---

1. The Moscow Art Theater was founded in 1898 by Stanislavsky and Nemirovich-Danchenko; it championed theatrical realism in Russia.

2. Bunin forgets that Sergei Rachmaninoff and Olga Knipper were also there. He also does not note that this was the first time Chekhov's mother, Evgenia, saw her son's plays.

3. Chekhov wrote *The Seagull* in 1896 and *Uncle Vanya* a year later. From all reports, Chekhov so enjoyed the staging of his places in Sevastopol that he became more cordial to Stanislavsky.

4. Gerhard Hauptmann wrote *Lonely Lives* (*Einsame Menschen*) in 1891.

5. Henrik Ibsen's *Hedda Gabler* appeared in 1890. During the performance, Chekhov was off in the dressing rooms of the theater, telling people that he did not regard Ibsen as a dramatist.

6. Sevastopol is in southwestern Crimea, some eight hundred miles south of Moscow.

7. In his memoirs, Stanislavsky offers a less complimentary (and probably more accurate) picture of the writer. "On Sunday," he recalls, "we waited impatiently for the boat from Yalta on which Chekhov was to arrive. At last, we saw him. He was the last to leave his cabin and he looked very pale and haggard. He had a bad cough. His eyes looked sad. They were the eyes of a sick man. But he tried his best to smile at us. I felt like crying. . . . Rather tactlessly, the actors kept asking Chekhov how he was feeling. 'I'm all right,' he replied, 'Never felt better.'" See Stanislavskii, *Moe grazhdanskoe sluzhenie Rossii,* 306–7 (see chap. 2, n. 34).

8. Chekhov shared the dislike of the members of the Moscow Art Theater for the outworn methods of acting—such as theatricality, false pathos, and declamation—that typically accompanied dramatic performances in Russia.

Stanislavsky recalled of these days:

> People came and went. The minute one group finished eating lunch, another group sat down to eat. Maria Pavlovna [Chekhova] was going to pieces, but Olga Leonardovna [Knipper], acting like a faithful friend (or the future mistress of the house), was going about with upturned sleeves and actively helping with the housework.
>
> In one corner of the garden, several groups of people were arguing about literature. They acted like schoolboys, trying to show who could throw a stone the farthest. In another group was I. A. Bunin who, with his unusual talent, was holding forth on something. Chekhov was right alongside him, howling and dying from laughter. When Bunin was in a good mood, no one could amuse Anton Pavlovich like he could.
>
> Gorky with his stories about his wandering life; Mamin-Sibiryak whose unusually bold humor occasionally bordered on buffoonery; Bunin with his graceful jesting; Anton Pavlovich with his unexpected rejoinders; and Moskvin with his precise witticisms [all] made for a unique atmosphere, uniting everyone into a single family of artists. The people there came up with the idea of meeting again in Yalta; they even talked about getting hold of an apartment for such a gathering. In a word, spring, the sea, happiness, youth, poetry, and art—this was the atmosphere in which we found ourselves at that time.[9]

To this, I add, "Who knows what Russians will dream up when they are doing well."

Amid all this hubbub at Chekhov's, I met a lawyer named Ivan Nikolaevich Sakharov. He was well known in Moscow and also was one of those individuals who loved to hang around actors, writers, and artists. He asked me, "Ivan Alexeevich, why don't you leave here?"

"Why?" I asked in surprise.

"Because you must find it difficult to be among such famous people, Gorky, for example."

"Not in the least," I replied dryly. "Gorky and I walk down different paths. I will be an academician . . . and no one knows who will outlive whom."[10]

---

9. Stanislavsky also noted, "Chekhov suddenly looked like a different man. He was transfigured. He reminded me—and I remember that impression very well—of a house which had stood shuttered and locked all winter suddenly opened up in spring so that all its rooms were filled with sunshine. Maria Chekhova also recorded the gaiety of these sessions." See Stanislavskii, *Moe grazhdanskoe sluzhenie Rossii*, 311–12.

10. Gorky died in 1936, Bunin in 1953.

Sakharov smiled a stupid smile, shrugged his shoulders, and left. I continued to visit the theater and the Chekhovs.

After I had been elected as an "honored academician" in 1909, Mr. Sakharov, having met me in the Literary Circle,[11] reminded me, with unrestrained delight, of our conversation in the Crimea.

At the end of 1900, I returned from abroad . . . and immediately headed for Yalta. Anton Pavlovich was not there, since he was spending the winter in Nice. But Maria Pavlovna invited me to live with her until "Anton came home." I agreed. For a while I lived with her; then I lived with Evgenia Yakovlevna.

Now I have learned from Chekhov's letters that Anton Pavlovich was pleased that I had been a guest in his home.

I found life pleasant in this dacha in Autka. There I tried to write and also to make notes about my trip. . . . I also read a great deal and had long conversations with Chekhov's mother.

Sometimes Maria Pavlovna and I talked quite openly. Laughing in a good-natured way, she talked a great deal about Levitan, who used to call her "Ma-Pa." She rendered him quite well: for some reason, Levitan had a slight lisp. Maria Pavlovna also talked about Babkino,[12] where Levitan spent his summers, as well as about his psychological problems.[13] It was also during this time that she told me about Anton Pavlovich's attraction to Lika (Lydia Stakhievna Mizinova). Now, when many things have become clear for me, I know that he had no such feelings for Lydia. She was in love with him, though, and he knew of her feelings for him. But, as he wrote to his sister, Chekhov did not care for her personality. He also thought that she had no sense of taste.[14] So her love for Chekhov was not mutual.[15]

Maria Pavlovna told me that the reason why she never married was be-

11. The Moscow Literary-Artistic Circle (Moskovskii Literaturno-Khudozhestvennyi Kruzhok) was founded in 1898 and continued until a year or so after the revolution.

12. Babkino, near Voskresensk (roughly fifty miles southeast of Moscow), was where the Chekhov family spent their summers between 1885 and 1887.

13. Levitan, a victim of suicidal neurasthenia, vacillated wildly between rapture and depression. (He survived at least one attempt to take his life.) Levitan's love life was equally unstable. The moment he was in the presence of an attractive woman, he fell in love and declared his passion, only to forget about the poor woman the following day. For that reason, Chekhov ended a momentary flirtation between Levitan and his sister, Masha (Maria).

14. For such observations on Chekhov and Mizinova, Bunin is relying on the writer's letter to his sister; see Chekhov to Maria Chekhova, January 9, 1898, *Pis'ma,* 7:149 (see introduction, n. 2).

15. As was the case with Lydia Avilova, Lika Mizinova was the victim of Chekhov's unrequited love. Unlike Avilova, though, Mizinova was single and more lively, forward, and headstrong.

"I am burning the candle of my life at both ends," Mizinova wrote to Chekhov on October 8, 1892. "Come and help me burn it more quickly. . . . You once said you loved immoral women; so you cannot be bored with me." Chekhov, though, kept Lika at arm's length, even ignoring the

cause of her brother. "When I once got a proposal," Maria Pavlovna added, "I told Antosha about it. He congratulated me in a restrained type of way, but I saw from his face that he was very unhappy. . . . So I refused [my suitor]."[16]

In January 1901, I was still living at the Chekhovs' home. I even have a note from that time:

> Winter of 1901, the Crimea, at Chekhov's dacha.
>
> The seagulls are paperlike. They are like seashells or like floats, alongside a rocking ship. The foam is like champagne.
>
> The fissures in the clouds are like some wondrous unearthly country. The cliffs are lime and gray like bird droppings. . . . The noise below, the sunny field of the sea, a dog gives off an empty howl. The sea is grayish-purple, mirrorlike, and rises very high into the sky.
>
> The buckwheat looks up to the clouds.

The first staging of *Three Sisters* was on January 31, and, of course, Maria Pavlovna and "Mamasha," as we all called Evgenia Yakovlevna, were very

---

young woman's desperate cries for help when she found herself abandoned and pregnant in Paris. See Vatsuro et al., *Perepiska*, 2:302–3 (see introduction, n. 197).

16. The story is true. In the summer of 1892, a lively and attractive Ukrainian by the name of Alexander Smagin (later a prototype for Baron Tuzenbach in *Three Sisters*) asked for Maria's hand in marriage. When Maria told Anton of her decision to accept Smagin as a husband, his features hardened into silence.

"I gave [Smagin's proposal] a great deal of thought," Maria later wrote in her memoirs, "But the love and affection I felt for my brother made up my mind for me. I could consent to nothing that would cause him pain, upset his way of life, and deprive him of the creative atmosphere which I always tried to make for him. I informed Smagin of my decision which also caused him suffering." Maria Chekhova, *Iz dalekogo proshlogo* (Moscow: Gosudarstvennoe izdatel'stvo khudozhesvennoi literatury, 1962), 72.

Although Chekhov feigned surprise at Maria's decision ("She is the only girl on earth who does not want to get married," he wrote to Suvorin on October 18, 1892), he was relieved by her refusal. After all, without the discreet, industrious, and self-sacrificing Maria ("She watches over my reputation with the single-minded sternness of a lady-in-waiting, nervous and ambitious," Chekhov wrote), his world would have crumbled irrevocably. Indeed, he was fond of saying that without his sister, the porridge would not boil. See Chekhov to Suvorin, October 18, 1892, *Pis'ma*, 5:117.

It should be noted that this was the third time a man had shown interest in Maria and that not everyone in Chekhov's family was happy with the mysteriously close tie between Maria and Anton. "There is something wrong with your relationship with Maria," Alexander warned his brother. "A single kind word from you, a warm tone of your voice, and she is ready to do your bidding. She is not only afraid of you but also willing to see only your most noble and commendable side" (in a letter circa June 15, 1893, as quoted in Simmons, *Chekhov: A Biography*, 284).

It should also be noted that Smagin, forty years after Maria's refusal of marriage to him, wrote to say that he had never married because Maria had been the one love of his life. See P. Callow, *Chekhov: The Hidden Ground* (Chicago: I. R. Dee, 1998), 205.

nervous [about the production]. Sinani was supposed to have sent a telegram from the theater. So mother and daughter sent their servant, Arseny, off to Sinani's house, with a request by Maria Pavlovna that Arseny phone them from the city.

After about twenty minutes, Arseny reported in an excited voice, "It was a genuinely great success."[17]

In early February of that year, Maria Pavlovna left for Moscow, but I stayed with Mamasha until Anton Pavlovich came home. I enjoyed a strong friendship with Evgenia Yakovlevna, who told me many things about Antosha.

Every word of Evgenia Yakovlevna was filled with adoration [for her son].

As I now see from letters, Anton Pavlovich returned home in the middle of February. By this time, I had moved to the Yalta hotel, where I spent an unpleasant night since a corpse was lying in the room next to me. . . . When Chekhov found out what I had to put up with on that evening, he kept teasing me about having a dead body as my neighbor.

Chekhov insisted that I visit him every day from early morning on. During these days we became especially close, though neither of us crossed some indefinable line. Even though we liked each other a great deal, we related to each other in a reserved type of way. Never have I had a relationship with any other writer as the one I did with Chekhov. There was not a single unpleasantness in our time together.[18] To me he was invariably like an older brother—he was almost eleven years older than I. He was restrained but also tender, courteous, and attentive. At the same time, though, he always loved my company and never showed himself to be my superior. Indeed, I can now say what he often affirmed in letters to close ones: "Bunin has left and I am alone."[19]

During the mornings we first drank this wonderful coffee. Then we sat in a small garden where Chekhov loved to putter amid the flowers or around the fruit trees. We also talked about the village. I kept doing imitations of the gentry and the peasants, along with talking about my life in Poltava[20] and my

17. In truth, the results were mixed, the reception of the premiere of *Three Sisters* moving from a dozen boisterous curtain calls after act 1 to a single halfhearted one after the finale. In fact, it would take several years before critics and the public approved of the play.

18. There was at least one. "Your brother wrote to me," Bunin told Maria Chekhova sometime in 1901, "but he addressed me as 'dear, edifying [*dushespasitel'nyi*] Ivan Alexeevich, Monsieur Bouquichon!' For that 'edifying,' I almost took offense." Quoted in Chekhov, *Pis'ma*, 10:533.

19. Chekhov to O. Knipper, February 23, 1901, *Pis'ma*, 9:209.

20. Poltava is located in Ukraine, approximately 450 miles southwest of Moscow.

attraction to Tolstoyism.[21] Chekhov talked about life in Luka at the estate of the Lintaryovs.[22] We both rhapsodized over Little Russia (which, at that time, was called the Ukraine). We both had visited the Svyatogorsky Monastery[23] and all of the places in Gogol's life. Whenever we were together, Chekhov often had an infectious laugh. He loved to make jokes and to think up all kinds of silly things and absurd nicknames. As soon as he started feeling better, there was no end to all the funny things that he came up with.

Sometimes we thought up stories together. One featured an impoverished despot-bureaucrat. Another was a sentimental tale with heroines named "Irlandia," "Australia," "Neuralgia," and "Hysteria"—all kinds of names in that vein—but with some really good things in it, too. Sometimes I imitated a drunk. I have a favorite picture of Chekhov and me together— I do not remember who took it—where we are sitting in his study. He is in a chair; I am sitting on its arm. He has a smiling face, but mine is dazed and evil-looking—I am doing my "drunkard" imitation.

Other times, I read to him his old stories. At that time, Chekhov was preparing an edition of his works, and I often saw how he, marking up a piece, almost rewrote it anew.

One time, I, for some reason, had begun reading aloud one of Chekhov's oldest things, a story entitled "The Crow."[24]

At first, Anton Pavlovich frowned, but as I continued reading, he became more and more good-humored. Little by little, he began to smile and laugh.

Sometimes we sat quietly, looking through newspapers and journals. We laughed over certain reviews of his stories and even more so about what people wrote about me. At that time, the critics were still afraid to venture an opinion about my work, so they kept trying to find someone whom I supposedly imitated. It so happened that they posited a "Chekhovian mood" in my writing. Chekhov became animated, even upset; he exclaimed with restrained passion, "Oh, this is really so stupid! The same people used to take me to task for the 'Turgenev notes' in my writing! You and I are as alike as a borzoi and a hound. You, for example, are much sharper than I am. You

21. For more on Bunin as a Tolstoyan, see T. Marullo, ed., *The Liberation of Tolstoy: A Tale of Two Writers* (Evanston, Ill.: Northwestern University Press, 2001), 42–50.

22. Luka is situated some 370 miles northwest of Moscow.

23. The Svyatogorsky Dormition Monastery (Sviatogorskii Uspenskii Monastyr') is thought to have been founded as early as the thirteenth century on the northern Donets River in southeast Ukraine. Chekhov's time there, though, was less than fruitful. On one visit, the monastery was packed with fifteen thousand pilgrims, mostly old women. "Till now," Chekhov wrote to his family, "I did not know that there were so many old women in the world, or I should have shot myself long ago." Chekhov to his family, May 11, 1887, *Pis'ma*, 2:82.

24. Chekhov wrote "The Crow" ("Vorona") in 1885.

Bunin and Chekhov, December 1903

would write something like, 'The sea smelled like a watermelon.' . . . That is wonderful, but I would never say such a thing. Now if the subject were a girl student—that would be a different matter."

"What girl student?"

"You remember, the one in the story that we made up. It featured a hot day in the steppe outside of Kharkov,[25] and also this very long train that was going along. . . . You added that this girl student was wearing a leather belt and standing next to the window in a third-class train car. She was pouring some tea from a teapot. A breeze came up and blew the tea into the face of a fat gentleman who had stuck his head out the window."

Another time, around twilight, I was reading "Gusev"[26] in Chekhov's presence and praising him wildly for the piece. But all the time I was telling him

---

25. Kharkov is in eastern Ukraine, approximately four hundred miles southwest of Moscow.
26. Chekhov's "Gusev" appeared in 1890.

how excellent and first-class the work was, he sat there in silence. He had an anxious look on his face when I finished reading the last paragraph of the story: "But above, where the sun was setting, clouds were coming together. One of them looked like a triumphal arc; another, like a lion; and still another, like a pair of scissors." (I thought, "How he loved to compare clouds to objects.") "From behind the clouds there flashed a green ray of light which extended to the very middle of the sky. A little later, this ray took on first golden and then roselike hues. . . . The sky was becoming a tender purple. Looking at the splendid, enchanting heavens, the ocean first frowned, then assumed colors that were tender, joyous, passionate, and difficult for the human tongue to express."

As I was reading, I thought to myself, "Will I ever see such a thing? After all, the Indian Ocean has attracted me since childhood."[27]

Suddenly I heard Chekhov's dry, quiet voice.

"You know that I am getting married."

He then began joking that one should choose a German woman over a Russian one because a German wife would be a better housekeeper and would not allow a baby to crawl through the house or beat a tin washbowl with a spoon.

Of course, I knew of his love affair with Olga Leonardovna Knipper, but I was not sure that it would end in marriage. Being on friendly terms with Olga Leonardovna,[28] I understood that she came from a completely different world than that of Chekhov.[29] I also knew that Maria Pavlovna would find it difficult to have Olga as mistress of the house.[30] Olga Leonardovna was an actress, who would hardly leave the stage; but just the same, many

27. Bunin traveled the Indian Ocean in February 1911.

28. Olga Knipper took a different view of the relationship. "Bunin is a crank [*chudak*]," she wrote to Chekhov on September 30, 1900. Four months later, she continued to her husband, "Bunin has been with me today. His nerves are completely shattered, and he does not know what to do with himself. I am sending him [to you] in Yalta." O. Knipper to Chekhov, September 30 and December 21, 1900, in Derman, *Perepiski Chekhova i Knipper*, 1:202, 239 (see introduction, n. 196).

29. Olga Knipper was the daughter of a German engineer and was educated in art, music, and languages. She claimed this similarity with Chekhov, though: both came from dysfunctional families living a hand-to-mouth existence. When Olga's father died, what Gorky called the "crazy Knipper family"—Olga, her mother, and two rowdy, vodka-loving uncles—were forced to take up residence in a three-room flat which also served as the place for the widowed woman, a teacher at the Moscow Philharmonic Society, to support the family by giving music lessons. See H. Troyat, *Chekhov* (New York: Dutton, 1986), 154, and Simmons, *Chekhov: A Biography*, 475.

30. Needless to say, Maria Chekhova was less than thrilled with her brother's marriage to Knipper. Although she had looked upon the attraction between the two as an infatuation and had even encouraged the relationship, she now felt doubly betrayed by both. Maria not only was shocked by her brother's sudden foray into marriage—"odious" and "shocking," she called it—

things in Chekhov's household would have to change. There arose many quarrels between sister and wife.[31] Furthermore, such unpleasantries had to have affected the health of Anton Pavlovich, who during such confrontations suffered greatly first for one, then for the other, and finally for both of them. At such times, I often thought, "This is suicide! This is worse than Sakhalin!" But of course I did not say anything.[32]

Chekhov ate little for lunch and dinner. When he was finished, he almost always rose from the table and went back and forth through the dining room, stopping at where a guest was sitting and earnestly treating him to a joke or witticism. He would also stop where his mother was and, picking up a knife and fork, begin to cut her meat ever so carefully, always in silence and with a smile.

As I gradually came to know Chekhov's life, I began to understand the nature of his diverse experiences and to compare them with my own. I began to understand that, compared to him, I was a boy, a pup. After all, before he had reached the age of thirty, he had written "A Boring Story," "Typhus," and other stories in which he had expressed episodes from his life in writing. . . .

---

but also shaken by the changes she knew the union would bring to the household. See Troyat, 266, and Simmons, 533.

Although Chekhov sought to reassure his sister that "everything will remain as before," Maria knew that he had given his heart to another and that she would now be a distant second in his life and work. (Mercifully, she rejected Anton's request to join the married couple on their honeymoon.)

31. Such misunderstandings were understandable, even though mother, sister, and wife all treated Chekhov like a child. Maria and Evgenia did not dare to criticize the writer's bachelor-like ways. They had allowed him to be slovenly in his habits and, if he wished, even to go without meals and other necessities.

Olga's Germanic taste for law and order, though, quickly put an end to the coddling and chaos. With almost maternal authority, she made Chekhov attend to his personal hygiene and appearance, as well as to have him partake of special diets.

Understandably, there were frequent blowups in the war of Evgenia, Maria, and Olga for Chekhov's body and soul. Mother and sister saw Olga as a troublemaker and intruder; Olga threatened to take her husband from them. They proclaimed an uneasy truce only when Anton sought to make peace, if only because such wrangling worsened his already weakened state.

32. The union of Chekhov and Olga Knipper (eleven years his junior) was indeed fraught with complexity. Doubtless, the two loved each other deeply, but the demands of Olga's career and the exigencies of Anton's health demanded that the two live almost separate lives.

As a result, they had no choice but to conduct their marriage by correspondence. Their letters were filled with sadness and affection, loneliness and languor, bitterness and regret, along with the most intimate details of their quasi-independent lives.

In this regard, Chekhov was the nobler of the two. He never made an issue of her career, refusing to tie a young, vibrant woman to the vicissitudes of his sickbed. Chekhov, however,

I never saw Chekhov in a robe. He always dressed neatly and precisely. He had a pedantic love for order—a love that was passed on to him in much the same way that persistence and edification are bequeathed from one generation to the next.

Along the shores of the Black Sea there worked many Turks and people from the Caucasus. Knowing the suspicion and ill will that Russians harbor toward foreigners, Chekhov never let pass an opportunity to say how much he admired what honest, hardworking people these groups were.[33]

His rooms were remarkably neat; his bedroom was like that of a girl.[34] No matter how weak he was, he did not allow himself the slightest indulgence in his dress.

His arms were big, ascetic-looking, and pleasant.

Even during dinner Chekhov was precise and sparing with words. . . . He spoke wonderfully; everything that he said was clear, correct, with a personal

---

could also be cruelly insensitive, engaging his wife in trivia but jealously keeping his inner and literary sides to himself or as worlds to be shared with Tolstoy, Gorky, and Bunin.

Olga was also not above hitting below the belt. Inquiries about his health and laments over their separation were the prelude to strident objections to being treated like a doll, endless demands to write stories and plays, as well as breathless remarks on rehearsals, performances, concerts, suppers, and balls in which she was the center of attention.

In Olga's defense, though, it should be noted that the problems that other women had with Chekhov—affection, commitment, and the like—were also hers. Indeed, her letters of complaint to the writer could have been written by Avilova, Mizinova, or any other woman in Chekhov's life. "Sometimes I feel myself superfluous," she wrote to her husband on August 28, 1902. "I think that you need me only as an agreeable woman, and that as a human being I am . . . a stranger to you." Quoted in Derman, *Perepiski Chekhov i Knipper,* 2:470–71.

33. In his memoirs, Kuprin recalls, "Chekhov was disembarking from the Sevastopol steamer at Yalta. A Tatar, eager to shoulder the writer's luggage, jumped ahead of the other porters and stumbled against a ship's officer. The man struck the Tatar in the face and ordered him back. Chekhov, waiting, was visibly upset. . . . Quietly, he said to the officer, 'Aren't you ashamed?'" See Kuprin, "A. P. Chekhov," 136–37 (see introduction, n. 68).

34. Others called attention to Chekhov's "feminine" side. "What a nice, charming man," Tolstoy confessed to Gorky, "so modest and gentle, just like a young girl, and he walks like a young girl" (Baboreko, "Chekhov i Bunin," 406; see introduction, n. 222). It should be noted here, though, that Bunin often protested the "maidenly" features that critics discerned in Chekhov's personality and writing. "Chekhov was an individual who was firm and unyielding in many things," Bunin told Pusheshnikov in October 1911, "but he is always drawn as feminine, tender, helpless, and sickening-sweet" (Gor'kii, "Lev Tolstoi," *Polnoe sobranie sochinenii,* 16:300; see introduction, n. 22).

Similarly, Bunin wrote to Georgy Adamovich on July 16, 1947, "Consider some of the nonsense that Gorky says about Tolstoy. . . . How could such an 'insightful' individual as Tolstoy not

touch. When Chekhov talked, he did not sound like a writer. Metaphors and epithets were rare [in his speech] and, more often than not, quite ordinary. He never vaunted turns of phrase, nor did he ever delight in a successfully uttered word.

People of various social strata gathered at Chekhov's place, but he was at home with everyone. He did not have any pretenses; he did not offend anyone's pride; he never felt extraneous or forgotten.

[I recall] a winter day in the Crimea, gray and cool, with thick, sleepy clouds over the Yaila.[35] Chekhov's home was quiet, other than for the regular ticking of the clock in Evgenia Yakovlevna's room. Chekhov was without his pince-nez, sitting at the desk in his study, and jotting down something in a slow and careful manner. He got up, put on his coat, hat, and short leather galoshes, and headed to where he had set a mousetrap. He returned, holding a live mouse by the tip of its tail. He next went out onto the porch and slowly through the garden right up to the gate, behind which lay a Tatar cemetery on a stony hill. He carefully threw the mouse there, and attentively looking at the small young trees, he headed for the small bench in the middle of the garden. Behind him ran a crane and two small dogs. Having sat down, he carefully used his small cane to play with one of the dogs, who fell on its back by his legs. He burst out laughing: fleas were crawling along the animal's rose-colored stomach. Then, leaning against the bench, he looked

---

see that Chekhov walked like the son of a strict shopkeeper, that he was tall and broad-shouldered, that he was always somewhat severe, extremely reserved, but never shy. In no way was Chekhov [anything else]."

On a roll, Bunin continued:

Gorky also made up stories regarding Chekhov's "sereneness," his futile "sadness." Shedding actorlike tears from his eyes—he was a master of such things!—Gorky once said something about his rival, Chekhov, that went like this: "One sometimes looks at Chekhov and thinks that he should *take the unhappy man by the hand* and carry him off somewhere far from all the vulgarity that surrounds him." Imagine Gorky or even I doing such a thing! Imagine Chekhov letting us do it!

After all, it was not for nothing that Gorky wrote about Chekhov and me in 1913, "I highly recommend Chekhov and Bunin to your attention. Both men have a wonderful sense for everyday things and can depict them splendidly." You see how easy it is for him to do such a thing. Even as he praises us, saying anything that comes into his head, he also digs our graves: Chekhov and Bunin, if you please, are good only for "feeling *everyday things*," while at the same time, Gorky is an "eagle," a "stormy herald," and the like (A. Zweers, "Pis'ma I. Bunina k G. Adamovichu," *Novyi zhurnal*, no. 110 [1973]: 162, italics in the original).

35. The Yaila-Dagh is a mountain range in the southern Crimea.

off into the distance, to the Yaila. Having lifted his head, he thought of something. He sat like that for an hour, an hour and a half.

In a letter to O. L. Knipper, dated February 20, Chekhov wrote, "Bunin is
here [in Odessa] and, fortunately, he visits me every day." In a missive to her
three days later, he continued, "Bunin was here, but now he is gone. I am
alone."

[Several months later] Chekhov kept insisting in the presence of Olga
Leonardovna that I spent all my time at his place.

I often left there at night, but not before he told me, "Come by tomorrow, a bit earlier."

Chekhov pronounced certain letters with a lisp. His voice was somewhat dry, and he often talked without any intonation, as if he were muttering.
Sometimes it was difficult to grasp that he was talking in a serious manner.

Every now and then, I refused to visit Chekhov. Whenever I did so, he
took off his pince-nez, put his hands on his heart, and with a barely percepti-
ble smile on his pale lips, he repeated in a clear, distinct way, "But I very much
want you to come, Mister Marquis Bouquichon! If you find it boring to be with
an old forgotten writer, go sit with Masha, with Mamasha who is in love with
you, and with Knipshits the Hungarian. . . . We will talk about literature."

We three—Maria Pavlovna, Anton Pavlovich, and I—once went to
Suuk-Su,[36] where we had a wonderful lunch. I wanted to pay, but Chekhov
said that we would settle accounts at home and that he would give me a bill.
He gave me this absurd invoice:

Bill for Mister Bouquichon (the French Marquis and Deputy)
Money has been laid out for you for the following:

1 front seat in a carriage	5 rubles
5 fish *à la femme au naturel*	1 ruble, 50 kopecks
1 bottle of wine *extra sec*	2 rubles, 7 kopecks
4 shots of vodka	1 ruble, 20 kopecks
1 sirloin	2 rubles
2 lamb kebabs	2 rubles
2 lamb chops	2 rubles
Salad "Tire-bouchon"	1 ruble
Coffee	2 rubles

36. Suuk-Su, located near Gurzuf in the Crimea ten miles northeast of Yalta, is a medieval
burial ground dating back to somewhere between the sixth and tenth centuries. The ethnic origins of the human remains there are still a matter of debate. Some scholars traced the deceased
to the Goths, others to the Sarmatian and Alan populations of the Tauride.

Sundries	11 rubles
Total	27 rubles, 75 kopecks

Respectfully yours,
Your hosts, Anton and Maria Chekhov [37]

He began calling me Bouquichon because, in a newspaper, he once saw a portrait of some French marquis who looked like me.

On April 20, I received this advertisement and an unhappy letter from him:

A New Story
by A. P. Chekhov
"Northern Flowers"
Almanac of the Scorpion Publishing House
Price: 1 ruble, 50 kopecks

[Chekhov wrote,] "In the first place, I did not write a story entitled 'Northern Flowers.' In the second place, why did you ever introduce me to this group, my dear Ivan Alexeevich? Why?"

In a letter dated April 22, he was already writing to Knipper about the subject of marriage. He ended his missive by saying, "There are times when I am seized by the most powerful desire to write a four-act vaudeville or comedy for the Moscow Art Theater. If nothing prevents me from doing so, I will eventually write such a piece, though I will submit it no earlier than the end of 1903." (He never thought of *The Cherry Orchard* as drama.)

In a letter to Knipper, written on April 26, 1901, Chekhov continued, "If you will give me your word that not a single soul in Moscow will know about our wedding before it comes to pass, I will marry you on the day of my arrival there. For some reason, I very much fear a wedding ceremony, all the well-wishing, and even the champagne one has to carry in his hand and the vague smile that one has to wear on his face. After we leave the church, I would like to head not for home but straight to Zvenigorod.[38] Or perhaps we could even get married there."[39]

How well I understand his feelings in the matter![40]

In Moscow Chekhov saw Doctor Shchurovsky, who diagnosed "dullness on the left and the right; also on the right a sizable lump under the shoulder

---

37. Chekhov to Bunin, early April 1901, *Pis'ma*, 10:10. The total is actually 30 rubles, 40 kopecks.
38. Zvenigorod is located thirty miles west of Moscow.
39. Chekhov to O. Knipper, April 26, 1901, *Pis'ma*, 10:17.
40. Bunin had three mates in life: a union (most likely common-law) with Varvara Pashchenko from 1891 to 1894; a marriage to Anna Tsakni in 1898, which failed after eighteen months; and

blade. Immediately go and drink the *koumiss* in the Ufa Region,[41] and if you cannot bear such a thing, go to Switzerland."

On May 25 Anton Pavlovich wrote to his mother, "Dear Mamam, I ask your blessing for my upcoming marriage. I am leaving to drink the *koumiss*. . . . I am feeling better. Anton."[42]

The wedding took place in secret. I do not know who the witnesses were.[43]

How Anton Pavlovich shortened his life, living by the sea! . . . If one follows the course of his health in his letters, one sees that he was always worse in Yalta than anywhere else.[44] Not a single doctor ever sent him to the snows, to Switzerland! Shchurovsky was the only one who considered it, but only if the *"koumiss* did not help."[45]

In August I received a letter from Anton Pavlovich in which . . . he joked, "I greatly look forward to your coming. From September 1st on, I will be sitting, say at night at the pier, waiting for your boat to arrive. . . . Come do not

---

a second common-law arrangement with Vera Muromtseva-Bunina in 1907, which the two legalized in 1922 in France.

41. Ufa is in the northwestern Urals, about a thousand miles east of Moscow.

42. Chekhov to Evgenia Chekhova, May 25, 1901, *Pis'ma*, 10:32.

43. Chekhov was so determined to avoid a public marriage that he conferred with Vishnevsky, a member of the Moscow Art Theater, to arrange, on the day of the writer's wedding, a dinner for family and friends. While the group waited patiently for Anton and Olga to appear, the couple were married in a small church on the outskirts of Moscow. The only people present were the four witnesses: for Olga, her brother, Volodia, and an uncle; for Anton, two of Volodia's student friends. It should also be noted that only hours before his marriage, Chekhov had met his brother Ivan but did not tell him of his plans.

After the ceremony, the newlyweds paid a quick visit to Olga's mother and then boarded the train for a visit to Gorky who, for his part in the March 1901 riots in St. Petersburg against the conscription of students into the army, was under house arrest in Nizhnyi Novgorod. Immediately before leaving Moscow, though, Chekhov sent two telegrams: one to Vishnevsky to announce his marriage to the guests at the restaurant, the other to his mother as quoted in the text.

44. It should also be noted that Chekhov was often bored and lonely in Yalta. "I am bored in Yalta," Chekhov wrote to Serebrov-Tikhonov on January 5, 1899. "I have turned into a philistine, and I have a feeling that it will not be long before I will set up house with a pock-marked peasant woman who will beat me on weekdays and pity me on holidays. We writers have no business living in the provinces. . . . Yalta differs only slightly from holes like Elets. Here even the bacilli sleep" (Chekhov to Serebrov-Tikhonov, January 5, 1899, *Pis'ma*, 8:16). Elets was the site of one of Bunin's childhood homes, approximately two hundred miles south of Moscow.

45. It did. For the first time since childhood, Anton put on weight. By mid-June, he was twelve pounds heavier, the reasons being that *koumiss* is easily digestible and also raises the body's defenses against tuberculosis, encouraging in the stomach the growth of benign flora at

disappoint me. We will live for a while in Odessa; then, if you wish, we will go together to Moscow."

On September 8, Anton Pavlovich wrote to his wife, "Now I am healthy. Bunin comes to visit me every day."

We engaged in endless conversations.

Anton Pavlovich kept telling me about the *koumiss* and where he had gotten well. He also told me that when he returned to Yalta, he again "had gotten sick and began coughing, and in July, even started spitting up blood." He raved about the steppe, the horses, and the natives [in Aksyonovo].[46] The lackluster public and the fact that the city was without any modern conveniences were the only things that bothered him. He thought that *koumiss* tasted like *kvas*[47] and that it was tolerable, even though he got quite tired of it.

Chekhov kept complaining about the newspaper, *Courier*,[48] [that] "almost every issue had all kinds of lying and vulgarities about him."

As I have now learned from a letter to Knipper, Chekhov wrote about me on the day following my arrival there: "Bunin is full of joie de vivre."[49] Anton Pavlovich almost always had an exciting effect on me.

[In Yalta] Chekhov felt compelled to visit Lev Nikolaevich Tolstoy.[50]

When he returned, I was already at his place in Autka. I greedily listened to his stories about Tolstoy. As always, he went on and on about the clarity of Tolstoy's mind. He also told me: "Do you know what especially intrigues me about Tolstoy? His suspicion of all us writers. He sometimes praises Maupassant, Kuprin, Semyonov, and me.[51] . . . Why? Because he re-

---

the expense of tubercular bacilli. It should also be noted that the beverage made him drowsy, drunk, and lascivious.

46. The little station of Aksyonovo was the site of a sanatorium about eighty miles southwest of Ufa.

47. *Kvas* is a fermented drink, resembling sour beer, and made from rye, barley, and the like.

48. *Courier* (*Kur'er*) was a daily newspaper published in Moscow from 1897 to 1904.

49. Chekhov to O. Knipper, September 6, 1901, *Pis'ma*, 10:73.

50. At the time, Tolstoy was recovering from an attack of malaria at the estate of Countess Sofya Panina, at Gaspra, about twenty miles southwest of Yalta.

51. For instance, Tolstoy believed that Guy de Maupassant was one of the best writers of the age because of the writer's talent for portraying the difficulties between the sexes. See his 1894 article "Istoriia pisaniia i pechataniia predisloviia k sochineniiam giudi de mopassana," in L. Tolstoi, *Polnoe sobranenie sochinenii v devianosta tomakh,* 90 vols. (Moscow: Gosudarstvennoe izdatel'stvo khudozhestvennoi literatury, 1930–58), 30:487–508, hereafter cited as *Polnoe sobranenie sochinenii* with volume and page number.

gards us as children. For Tolstoy, our stories, tales, and novels are child's play. That is why he puts Maupassant and Semyonov in the same heap. Shakespeare, though, is an entirely different matter. Shakespeare irritates Tolstoy because Shakespeare does not write like he does."

[Tolstoy's son] Ilya L'vovich Tolstoy often told me in 1912 that writers in the family home were regarded "like this"—he bent down and raised his hand only as high as the bottom of the couch. Whenever he told me such things, I recalled Chekhov's words.

It always seemed to me that although Chekhov had a high standing in literature, even his own special place, he never took stock of his worth.

Having read the ending of Gorky's *The Three of Them*,[52] Chekhov wrote, "There is something remarkably barbaric [about the piece]. If Gorky had not written the thing, no one would have read it."[53]

On December 10, Chekhov again began to spit up blood, a condition that lasted for ten days. Of course, Evgenia Yakovlevna found it difficult to look after both the house and her patient, especially since Chekhov would not let her out of his sight. His affliction was, in part, caused by his distress over Tolstoy who had come to visit his daughter in Yalta and had taken ill.

Thank God, Maria Pavlovna arrived at her brother's for Christmas. Attending to her brother was for her as natural as eating—she was a superb caretaker.

On January 15, 1902, I received a letter from Anton Pavlovich. Along with greetings for the New Year . . . he said, "Have I written to you about [your story] 'The Pines'? It is very new, and very fresh, and very good; only it is way too dense, like condensed broth."[54]

In that January when Tolstoy had taken ill, Anton Pavlovich very much feared for the fate of the great writer. Al'tshuller, who was treating Tolstoy, kept Chekhov abreast of the writer's illness.

On February 7, Tolstoy was in a particularly bad way. His heart was

---

52. Gorky's novel *The Three of Them* (*Troe*) appeared in 1901.

53. Chekhov to O. Knipper, December 7, 1901, *Pis'ma*, 10:133.

54. Chekhov to Bunin, January 15, 1902, *Pis'ma*, 12:84. Bunin wrote "The Pines" ("Sosny") in 1901. Similarly, Chekhov wrote to Alexander Amfiteatrov, "I have truly just read a wonderful story, Bunin's 'Black Earth' ['Chernozem']. In it were places where I could utter surprise." Chekhov to Amfiteatrov, April 13, 1901, *Pis'ma*, vol. 10:169.

functioning poorly. Chekhov was very upset, saying that Tolstoy "would not make it."[55]

During this same period also, Anton Pavlovich was upset that Gorky still had not been elected as an academician.[56] He kept asking Kondakov and Korolenko [for information], even though hardly anyone was surprised at Gorky's [failure to enter the academy]. After all, he was on trial! Most likely, also, Chekhov was unaware of the privileges that an academician had. For example, he did not know that an honored academician could travel to any city he wanted and that, at any time during his stay there, he could demand a hall and deliver a lecture for the purposes of enlightenment, without any censorship whatsoever.[57]

Can one even imagine how Gorky would have exploited such a privilege? After all, Kuprin was never named an honored academician, even though his name had been put forth several times. The reason for this was simple: Kuprin was too fond of wine. Also, people feared that he, too, might abuse the privilege of speaking wherever and on whatever he liked.[58]

Returning to the issue of Gorky's election as an honored academician, I wish to make it clear that Gorky lacked academic credentials[59] and that he

55. "I fear Tolstoy's death," Chekhov wrote to Men'shikov on January 28, 1900:

His death would leave a large empty space in my life for three reasons. First, I have loved no man as I have loved him. . . . Second, when literature has a Tolstoy, it is easy and gratifying to be a writer. Even if you believe that you have never accomplished anything and are still not accomplishing anything, you do not feel so bad because Tolstoy accomplishes enough for everyone. His activities provide justification for the hopes and aspirations that are usually placed on literature.

Third, Tolstoy stands above us. His authority is enormous. As long as he is alive, bad taste in literature, all vulgarity in its brazen-faced or lachrymose varieties, all bristly or resentful vanity will remain far in the background. His moral authority alone is enough to keep what we think of as literary trends and schools to a minimum. Indeed, if it were not for Tolstoy, literature would be an unfathomable jungle or a flock without a shepherd." (Chekhov to Men'shikov, January 28, 1900, *Pis'ma,* 9:29–30)

56. What happened was this: Gorky had indeed been elected to the literary section of the Academy of Sciences in December 1901, but the fact that he had just been released from prison and also was under police surveillance at the time moved Nicholas II to insist that the electors rescind the distinction. Chekhov, of course, was so distressed by the move that he resigned from the academy.

57. Bunin fails to note that an honored academician also enjoyed exemptions from censorship, arrest, and inspection by customs officials.

58. Bunin's claim of Kuprin's love of wine is true. Indeed, it was a failing that became even more pronounced (and tragic) in the writer's years as an émigré. Also, the fact that Kuprin had attacked capitalist-style bosses in his 1896 novella *Molokh* as well as army officers in his 1905 work *The Duel* (*Poedinok*) did not endear him to conservatives who feared that he would be a "loose cannon" at public lectures and the like.

59. Bunin was one to talk; neither man went to the university.

was being considered [for the honor] only because, at the beginning of the century, he was so abnormally different from other Russian intellectuals.[60]

One could erect a monument in Gorky's honor; one could praise him in all kinds of ways; but to elect him as an academician!

One should also note that when Chekhov, being a wise and sober individual, sent his list of candidates for honored academician to A. N. Veselovsky, he did not include Gorky among his choices. And when Gorky learned of Chekhov's omission, he became very upset.[61] Such were the times! Further, the reason why Anton Pavlovich refused to nominate Gorky was weak. He wrote:

> The newspapers had published an article saying that in light of Gorky's being subject to civic action[62] . . . the elections [of honored academicians] had to be deemed invalid. Further, it was clear that since the Academy of Sciences typically notified [new academicians of this honor], and that since I was a member of this group, such a notification also came forth from me. I heartily congratulated the winners, even though I had acknowledged the elections as invalid. Such a contradiction did not enter into my consciousness, nor was I later able to reconcile it with my conscience.

Chekhov requested to resign as an honored academician in a letter to Veselovsky on August 25, 1902. He had fretted over his decision for several months, writing to Kondakov and Korolenko, who had also "requested him to relinquish this title."

In spring I went to Yalta. Tolstoy had gotten better, and while I was there, Chekhov wished to pay him a visit. He was greatly agitated. He kept changing his trousers, constantly making jokes, but also strenuously trying to repress his nervousness.

"I am afraid of Tolstoy. Just think: It was he, after all, who wrote how Anna [Karenina][63] felt and saw how her eyes shone in the darkness." As if rejoicing that Tolstoy had taken ill, he added laughingly, "I am being very serious here. I really am afraid of him."

For almost an hour, Chekhov could not decide which pants he would wear to see Tolstoy. Having taken off his pince-nez, he looked younger. As was his custom, he kept mixing serious and silly things, coming out of the bedroom with different pairs of pants.

60. Bunin is referring to Gorky's status as a *samouchka*, or "self-taught individual."

61. There is no evidence for Bunin's assertion here.

62. In 1901, Gorky was arrested for alleged revolutionary activities and confined to a prison in Nizhnyi Novgorod. With the intercession of Tolstoy, though, he was released a month later.

63. Throughout his life, Chekhov expressed nothing but affection for Tolstoy's "dear, sweet Anna." See Chekhov to his family, March 10, 1887, *Pis'ma*, 2:35.

"No, these are obscenely narrow! Tolstoy will think that I am a hack!"

He went to put on the other pair and again came out, laughing, "These are as wide as the Black Sea! Tolstoy will think that I am a dandy!"[64]

Having returned [from visiting Tolstoy], Chekhov said, "You know, it is incredible, a miracle. Here is this old man lying in bed. Physically, he is barely alive and pale as a ghost. But intellectually, he is not just a genius, but a super-genius!"

"When Tolstoy dies, everything will go to the devil," he often said.

"Literature, too?"

"Literature, too."[65]

But here he was mistaken, for literature had already begun "to turn to dust" even during Tolstoy's life.[66]

Chekhov often said, "What kind of dramatists are we! The single, genuine dramatist is Naidyonov. No matter what he does, he is a born playwright; he has the most dramatic spring inside him. He should write ten more plays. Even if nine of them should fail, the tenth will be such a success that one will cry out only in joy and surprise!"

Having fallen silent, he broke out into merry laughter, "You know, not long ago I was at Tolstoy's place in Gaspra. He was still confined to bed, but he talked about everything, including me. Finally, I got up and said farewell. But he held me by the hand and said, 'Kiss me.' When I went over to him to do so, he suddenly whispered into my ear with a lively, old man's patter: 'But just the same I cannot stand your plays. Shakespeare was a wretched writer,[67] but you are still worse!'"[68]

Sometimes, during the evenings, guests gathered [at Chekhov's house] for dinner . . . and I was sometimes asked to read one or another of Chekhov's stories. About such readings Teleshov recalled, "At first, Anton Pavlovich

---

64. In truth, Chekhov had little cause to worry about Tolstoy's opinion of him. Sergeenko recalled, "In Tolstoy's house, no one Russian writer was read so often and with so much pleasure as Chekhov" (Sergeenko, "O Chekhove," 250–51; see chap. 2, n. 13). In fact, Tolstoy and Chekhov so relished each other's company that they even planned to visit the United States together. See Chekhov to Ilya Repin, January 23, 1893, *Pis'ma*, 5:158.

65. It should be noted that émigré critics said the same thing about Bunin about his eventual parting from this life.

66. Bunin is, of course, referring to the rise of modernism in Russian literature and art.

67. For more on Tolstoy's animosity toward Shakespeare, see his article from 1903 to 1904, "O Shekspire i o drame," in Tolstoi, *Polnoe sobranie sochinenii,* 35:216–75.

68. Tolstoy particularly criticized Chekhov's plays both for what he saw as their static quality and for their indifference to social and moral issues. "Where is the drama?" he asked Alexander

frowned, for he found it difficult to listen to one of his own pieces. But then he unwittingly began to smile, and as Bunin continued reading, he shook from laughter in his chair. Then he would fall silent and try to get ahold of himself."

Having once listened to one of his own "fragmented" stories, Anton Pavlovich said, "Now you all know how to write good stories. Everyone has gotten used to such a thing. I was the one who opened the way to the short story, but everyone still scolds me for doing so. . . .

"People want me to write a novel; otherwise they feel that I am not a writer."

Everyone was delighted when Tolstoy got well. In a word, the mood was ecstatic.

I often have the feeling that whenever I render several of Chekhov's judgments and opinions, many people think that I am actually giving my own. That is why I find it very pleasant to read Serebrov-Tikhonov's memoirs,[69] since he affirms many of the things that Anton Pavlovich said to me. Serebrov wrote:

> One evening Chekhov invited me for tea on the terrace. We discussed Gorky in a free and easy way. I know that Chekhov loved and esteemed Gorky[70] and that he did not stint on praise for the author of "The Stormy Petrel."
>
> "Excuse me . . . but I do not understand," Chekhov interrupted me with the somewhat distressed courtesy of someone whose foot had just been stepped upon. "I know that all of you like Gorky's 'The Stormy Petrel' and his 'Song About a Falcon.'[71] . . . I also know that you will tell me it is because these pieces have politics in them! But what kind of politics? [When someone says,] 'Forward without doubt and fear!'—such a thing is not politics. After all, does anyone know where this 'forward' leads to? If one is called 'forward,' he has to be shown a goal, a road; he also has to be shown the means of get-

---

Sanin. "What does it consist in? It does not go anywhere!" Sanin to Chekhov, March 12, 1900, in "Tolstoi o Chekhove: Neizvestnye vyskazyvaniia," *Literaturnoe nasledstvo,* 873.

Chekhov, though, took Tolstoy's criticism in stride. Pyotr Gnedich reports in his memoirs that when Chekhov told him about Tolstoy's dislike of Chekhov's plays, he "threw back his head and roared so loudly that his pince-nez popped off his nose." P. Gnedich, "Iz zapisnoi knizhki," *L. N. Tolstoi v vospominaniiakh sovremennikov,* vol. 1 (Moscow: Gosudarstvennoe izdatel'stvo khudozhestvennoi literatury, 1955), 457–58.

69. Bunin is reading from Serebrov-Tikhonov, "O Chekhove," in Kotov, *A. P. Chekhov,* 291–308 (see preface, n. 3).

70. In Gorky, Chekhov particularly liked the writer's spontaneity, fierce idealism, and inner goodness. "Gorky looks like a tramp from the outside," Chekhov observed, "but inside, he is quite elegant." Chekhov to Avilova, March 23, 1899, *Pis'ma,* 8:134.

71. Gorky's "The Song About a Falcon" ("Pesnia o sokole"), appeared in 1894, and "The Song About a Stormy Petrel" ("Pesnia o burevestnike") appeared in 1901.

ting there. In politics, one gets nowhere merely with the 'passions of the brave.'"

I was so amazed by what I had just heard that I burned my tongue when I sipped my tea.

"The sea laughed," Chekhov continued, nervously twisting the cord about his pince-nez. "You, of course, are in ecstasy [over such a phrase]! . . . You come across 'the sea laughed' and stop reading. You think that you have stopped because such a phrase is artful and good. But how could you possibly think such a thing! You have stopped because you immediately did not understand how such a thing could happen. Here is the sea—and suddenly it laughs? . . . The sea neither laughs nor cries. It makes noises, it splashes, it sparkles. . . . Look at anything in Tolstoy: The sun rises, the sun sets. . . . Birds sing. . . . No one sobs, no one laughs. After all, the key thing is simplicity."

"You also cite from [Gorky's] *Foma Gordeev*,"[72] Chekhov continued, wrinkling the crow's-feet under his eyes. "Again the entire work is unsuccessful! It talks only about one thing, it is built only about one hero. . . . And all the characters are woefully the same. . . . Only the gentry can write novels. People of our caste . . . petit bourgeois and the like—do not have the talent for such things. . . . If someone asks us to build a birdhouse, this is something that we can do! Not long ago I saw one that had three stories and twelve windows!"

"But to write a novel, one has to understand the laws of equilibrium and symmetry. A novel is a palace, and for the reader to feel at home in it, he must not see it as a museum, nor must he be surprised or bored in it. Sometimes the reader must take a break from both the hero and the author. He should be given a landscape, something humorous, new characters or turns of events. . . . How many times have I said such things to Gorky, but he does not listen. . . . He should call himself 'Proud One,'[73] not Gorky."[74]

I could see that I was not getting anywhere with Gorky. So I tried to change the topic by bringing up the [Moscow] Art Theater.

"It is nothing special," Chekhov said, putting a damper on my enthusiasm. "It is a theater just like any other.[75] But Mosvkin—now there is a talented

---

72. Gorky wrote *Foma Gordeev* in 1899.

73. Chekhov is playing with Gorky's name: compare the Russian words for "proud" (*gordyi*) and "bitter" (*gor'kii*). Generally speaking, Chekhov valued Gorky for his personality, not his prose: "The time will come when Gorky's works will be forgotten, but he himself will remain in people's memories for a thousand years" (Chekhov to Alexander Yuzhin-Sumbatov, February 26, 1903, *Pis'ma*, 11:164).

74. It should also be noted that Chekhov had little use for Gorky's famed peasant blouses: "I cannot get used to them, any more than I can grow accustomed to a court chamberlain's uniform." Chekhov to O. Knipper, November 17, 1901, *Pis'ma*, 10:117.

75. Serebrov-Tikhonov's claim is not in sync with other comments by Chekhov on the Moscow Art Theater. Chekhov once wrote to Nemirovich-Danchenko, "[The Moscow Art

artist for you. There is no one else like him in the world. I remember how the Alexander Theater [76] staged my *Seagull*. With a prompter in the wings, no less."

Like a drowning man grasping at straws, I again changed the topic, this time to the "decadents"[77] who were being considered as a new trend in literature.

"There are no such things as decadents, nor did they ever exist," Chekhov shot back mercilessly. "Where did you get that idea from? . . . France has Maupassant, and here in Russia I was the one who began writing short stories. That is all the new direction in literature we have had. . . . They are not decadents but hooligans! They sell rotten goods. . . . [They espouse] mysticism and all kinds of devil stuff! They concoct all kinds of things for their amusement. Their legs are not pale but as hairy as everyone else's.[78]

"For instance, what kind of writer is Leonid Andreev? He is simply a legal clerk who loves to talk.

"Decadents are students who pass themselves off as heroes so that they go after the ladies more easily."

"We Russians are such a lazy bunch," Chekhov said. "Even our nature strikes us as lazy. We only have to look at this little river before us, and it seems too lazy to move! It can barely make it round the bend, and all from laziness. All our celebrated 'psychology,' all our *dostoevshchina* is tied up with our indolence. We are too lazy to work; that is why we make up things as we go along."[79]

[Chekhov told Serebrov-Tikhonov] during tea on the terrace, "I am often reproached—even Tolstoy used to rebuke me—for writing about trifles and for not having any positive heroes in my stories, for example, revolutionar-

---

Theater] is the only theater I love. . . . If I lived in Moscow, I would try and join the staff if only as a watchman, so I could help in my own small way and keep you, if possible, from losing your enthusiasm for so dear an institution" (Chekhov to Nemirovich-Danchenko, November 24, 1899, *Pis'ma*, 8:309).

76. The prestigious Alexander Theater (Aleksandrinskii teatr), home to Russia's oldest theater company, was built in St. Petersburg in 1832.

77. "Decadence" was a literary current which flourished in Russia in the fin de siècle and emphasized aestheticism, sensationalism, and religious and sexual perversity.

78. Chekhov is referring to Valery Bryusov's one-line poem, "O, cover your pale legs . . ." (*O, zakroi svoi blednyi nogi . . .*, 1895).

79. Bunin agreed. See his 1919 articles in the newspaper *Southern Word* (*Iuzhnoe slovo*), as quoted in *Skorb' zemli rodnoi: Sbornik statei 1919 goda* (New York: Narodnoi gruppy, 1920), 44–50; B. Lipin, "Bunin v 'Iuzhnom slove,'" *Zvezda*, no. 9 (1993): 125–41; and P. Shirmakov, "Vozrashenie Bunina," *Svetskaia priroda i chelovek*, no. 3, (1991): 62–66. These pieces have been translated in the coda to T. Marullo, *Cursed Days: Ivan Bunin; A Diary of a Revolution* (Chicago: Ivan R. Dee, 1998), 213–56.

ies, Alexander the Greats, or, as in Leskov, simple honest policemen. . . . But where would I get such people for my works?

"Life in our country is provincial, the cities are feeble, the villages are poor, and the folk is ragged. . . . In our youth, all of us twitter and chirp; but by the time we reach our forties, we are already old men who begin to think about death. . . . What kind of heroes are we?! . . .

"You tell me that people cry at my plays. . . . But you are not the only one who does. . . . After all, I did not write them to make people cry; it was Stanislavsky who made them so worthy of pity. I wanted something different. . . . I wanted only to tell people in an honest way, 'Look at yourselves, look at how boring and impoverished your lives are!' . . . I wanted that people understand such a thing and that, once they did so, they would invariably create a different and better life for themselves. . . .

"I do not envision such a new life, but I know that it will be completely different from the one that exists now. . . . And until such a new life comes into being, I will tell people again and again: 'Understand how poorly and dully you are living!' Now is that something to cry over?"

Getting up from the table, Chekhov concluded: "Time to go to bed. . . . A storm is coming."

And it was during the storm that his throat started to bleed.

On October 26, I received a postcard from Chekhov which he did not sign but which said, "Dear Jean! Cover your pale legs!"

In a letter, written on December 20, he wrote to his wife, "I keep thinking that you need a son who could occupy your time and fill your life. You will have a son or a daughter, believe me, dear one; only you will have to wait a bit and return to normal after your illness. I am neither lying to you nor hiding the slightest thing from you. On my honor, I am only telling you what the doctors told me."

At that time I was still living in Moscow and occasionally dropped in on Olga Leonardovna. I sometimes found her in tears. She was going through a difficult time, but she never complained.[80]

In a joking type of way, Chekhov kept pestering that I include him in my memoirs. . . . I sometimes objected, saying that he should write about me,

---

80. Bunin is mistaken here. During this time, Chekhov and Olga Knipper had been apart for five months, the longest separation to date in their marriage. Olga's letters to her husband were particularly charged with self-pity and regret, to the effect that she was a bad wife, she should quit the theater, she wanted a child, she wanted meaning in her life.

Knipper's distress was enduring. For instance, on October 5, 1903, she wrote to her

but he kept assuring me that I would live to be a hundred, that I was "hale and hearty" and other things in that vein. Finally, I said:

[In my memoirs] I will, first of all, write about how I met you in Moscow. It was in December 1895. I did not know that you had come to Moscow; but we were together [in a restaurant] with some poet. . . . We were drinking red wine and listening to a car outside. The poet kept reading his verse, getting more and more excited by what he had written. We left there very late, but the poet had gotten so carried away by his work that he continued to read his poems on the staircase. He even kept reading as he began looking for his coat and scarf. The porter said to him in a helpful way, "Allow me, sir, to find your coat for you."

"What do you mean, you scoundrel, that you will help me find my coat? Do you think I will take something that does not belong to me?"

"Exactly so, sir, you have somebody else's coat right now."

"Keep still, you scoundrel, this is my coat!"

"No it's not, sir, it is not your coat!"

"Then tell me this very minute, whose coat is it?"

"It belongs to Anton Pavlovich Chekhov."

"You're lying. For that I will kill you right on the spot!"

"Do what you have to do, but the coat still belongs to Anton Pavlovich Chekhov."

"Does that mean that he is here?"

"He has been here all along."

[When we learned that you were present] we almost threw ourselves at you at three o'clock in the morning. But, fortunately, we got hold of ourselves and came to your place the very next day. The first time we tried to visit you, you were not there. We saw only your room which the maid was straightening up, and one of your manuscripts on the table. It was the introduction to "A Woman's Kingdom."[81]

[Chekhov asked,] "Who was the poet? Of course, I'm guessing it was

---

husband, "I simply do not know what to write to you. I know that you are ill and that I am just a nobody who comes, lives with you for a while, and then goes away. My entire life is such a piece of horrible hypocrisy that I do not know what to do. . . . I keep accusing myself, and I feel that it is all my fault. I do not seem to be able to cope with life." O. Knipper-Chekhova, *Vospominaniia i stat'i: perepiska s A. P. Chekhovym (1902–1904)*, vol. 1 (Moscow: Iskusstvo, 1972), 291–92.

Such angst, though, did not stop Olga from attending rounds of parties, skiing, and the like, as well as from seeking the attention of Vishnevsky and other admirers. Rumors were rife throughout Moscow that the Chekhovs were on the brink of divorce.

81. Bunin is mistaken as to the piece, the aforementioned citation more accurately describing "House with a Balcony: The Story of an Artist."

Balmont.[82] And how did you know which manuscript was lying on the table? Did you take a peek at it?"

"Forgive me, dear one, I could not restrain myself."

"But what a pity that you did not stop by at night. It would have been very nice to go off somewhere suddenly. I love restaurants."

Chekhov truly loved restaurants. He always invited all his friends to have lunch or dinner with him somewhere. It also gave him great pleasure to be the host. He admired my knowledge of wines, as well as my love for hors d'oeuvres and refined dishes. Evgenia Yakovlevna likewise valued my knowledge of good food and drink, though she herself was a great master in culinary arts and also loved to entertain.

As regards my ties to writers, my relationship with Chekhov was a highly singular one. With someone in my own study, I could be completely silent for hours on end. But with Chekhov, I sometimes spent entire mornings in conversation with him.

Sometimes it seemed that I was disturbing Chekhov. So in the evening, when we said good-bye, I made up excuses, saying that I had to go somewhere [on the following day]. In such instances, he invited me back in a touchingly insistent way, joking that he, as an old writer, would not bore me.

In the beginning of December, Anton Pavlovich arrived in Moscow. . . . I visited him every evening, sometimes staying with him until three or four o'clock in the morning, that is, until Olga Leonardovna returned home.

More often than not, she was leaving for the theater, but sometimes she was heading to some charity concert. She would be escorted by Nemirovich[-Danchenko], who wore tails and smelled of cigars and eau de cologne. After she had gotten ready for the evening, she—beautiful, young, and perfumed—would go up to her husband and say, "Don't be bored without me, Dusik. After all, you always love when Bouquichonchik is here." Then, turning to me, she would say, "Good-bye, dear." I would kiss her hand, and she and Nemirovich[-Danchenko] would leave. Chekhov would not let me go until she returned. These vigils were especially dear to me.[83]

---

82. Chekhov first met Balmont in Yalta in 1898.

83. Bunin also told Bakhrakh:

> One time around evening—it was during one of his last visits to Moscow—I dropped by to see Chekhov. Sad and sitting home alone, he was truly happy to see me. We talked for a long time. It was getting late, and I tried to leave several times, but Anton Pavlovich would not let me go.

He sometimes was very hard on himself. [During such moments] I tried to distract him, to talk about myself or to ask him about his family. He talked a great deal about his brothers, Nikolai and especially Alexander, whom he thought of highly but worried about without end. Alexander sometimes took to drink, the problem being, as Chekhov explained, that he was greatly gifted but had done nothing with his talents.[84]

I once asked Anton Pavlovich, "Does it bother your brother that you, as a writer, have pushed him into the shadows?"

Smiling his pleasant smile, he answered, "Not at all. Alexander writes every now and then to earn some extra money. But I do not know what interests him more: literature, philosophy, science, or poultry breeding. He has a talent for so many things that he cannot focus on anything. . . . But then there is my brother Mikhail, who had a job in a finance department but who left that position to work in Suvorin's book trade. He tries his hand at stories, but he does not have the talent to be a genuine writer. Our family

---

"Stay a little longer," he said, "and share the silence with me."

I sensed that he did not like to be alone. And so I stayed. Around three in the morning, the doorbell rang, and in flew Olga Leonardovna, all perfumed, merry, and twittering.

"Dusin'ka," she said. "So you are not alone. How very nice."

She put out something to eat and with an appetite, began tearing into a cold chicken. Chekhov looked at her almost with hatred. (A. Bakrakh, "Razgovory s Buninym," *Smena*, nos. 4–6 [1964], 110)

Olga Knipper could be even more insensitive with Chekhov. Her letters to the writer were often filled with comments regarding dalliances—real or imagined—not only with Nemirovich-Danchenko but also with Stanislavsky, Vishnevsky, and other men of the Russian stage. "I flirted with Konstantin Sergeevich [Stanislavsky]," Olga wrote to Chekhov on January 11, 1902. "Are you upset? Then—horror of horrors—we went to a cabaret" (Knipper to Chekhov, January 11, 1902, in Derman, *Perepiski Chekhova i Knipper*, 2:231).

Chekhov did not take Olga's bait, though. Even though he knew—and saw—how Nemirovich-Danchenko and Vishnevsky had been attending to his wife, he exacerbated the tension in his marriage by refusing to question or oppose Olga's popularity with the men of the Russian stage. Instead, he answered her taunts in a characteristic way: with a joke. "Obviously Vishnevsky is counting on you to become a widow," Chekhov wrote to his wife. "But tell him that to spite him I am going to leave a will forbidding you to marry again" (Chekhov to O. Knipper, May 2, 1901, *Pis'ma*, 10:357).

It should also be noted that some of Chekhov's biographers—Rayfield, for one—believe that it was Nemirovich-Danchenko, not Chekhov, who may well have fathered Olga's miscarried child. Conception for the infant, he insists, took place when "Olga and Anton were eight hundred miles apart." Rayfield, *Chekhov: A Life*, 557 (see introduction, n. 230).

84. Alexander Chekhov was a gifted, well-read, and ambitious writer and linguist. Like his brother Nikolai, though, he was also erratic and stubborn, irritable and irresolute. He was also a pathologically sensitive man who always turned good fortune into adversity and who, when drunk, became violent and vulgar with family and friends. In time, though, Alexander led enough of a stable life to attend to Chekhov's many needs, particularly the details of publishing his brother's works.

does not have the ambition that today's writers have. But all of us love the things that engage us."

Anton Pavlovich often asked me about the first staging of Gorky's play *The Lower Depths*[85] as well as about the subsequent dinner that cost eight hundred rubles. He also wanted to know what was served for such a price.

I, imitating Gorky, answered, "Some fish for the first course and something else besides, the devil knows what, perhaps horse."

Chekhov laughed heartily. He took special delight in the remark of Professor Klyuchevsky, who was also at the affair. Klyuchevsky was cool, calm, steadfast, modest, serenely happy, and dressed in a buttoned-down jacket. He responded to Gorky's remark by inclining his head slightly to the side and, looking askance with knowing eyes and glasses that shone brightly in the light, said quietly to those of us alongside him, "Horse! Such a thing would be grand in size, but I would be a bit offended. After all, why a horse precisely? Are we cabbies or something?"

What did Chekhov think about death? Many times, and in a way that was painstaking and firm, he said that immortality, life after death in whatever form, was complete nonsense.

"It is superstition. And any kind of superstition is a terrible thing. One must think boldly and clearly. Sometime we will talk about such a thing in a substantial way. I can prove to you that, just as surely as two plus two equals four, the notion of immortality is absurd."

But then there were times when he affirmed just the opposite in an even more steadfast way: "There is no way that we merely disappear after death. Immortality is a fact. Just you wait, I will prove such a thing to you."

In the last period of his life, Chekhov dreamed aloud, saying, "How I would love to be a wanderer, a pilgrim, to go to sacred places, to settle in a monastery in a forest, to sit on a bench by some monastery gates alongside a lake during a summer evening."

Chekhov's [story] "The Archbishop" passed unnoticed, but not so his *Cherry Orchard*, with its big paper flowers[86] so incredibly thick and white behind

85. Gorky wrote *The Lower Depths* (*Na dne*) in 1902. It should be noted here that Chekhov liked the play. "Your work is new and undoubtedly fine," he told Gorky. "The second act is very good, the very best, the most powerful, and when I read it, especially the end, I almost leapt with joy" (Chekhov to Gorky, July 29, 1902, *Pis'ma*, 11:12).

86. Here Bunin echoes Chekhov's own quarrel with Stanislavsky's penchant for lavish effects (real and otherwise) with which he staged the writer's plays. Drama, Chekhov believed, should be a minimalist affair, with the emphasis being on the internals, characters and acting, not the

the windows of the estate onstage. Who knows what would have been the course of his fame, if it had not been for his story "The Peasants"[87] and the [Moscow] Art Theater!

Chekhov kept giving me advice regarding my health, and, as always, insisting that I would live to a ripe old age since I was a "hale and hearty young man." He also kept persuading me, for the umpteenth time, to write on a daily basis, to quit being a "dilettante," and to assume a "professional" attitude toward writing.

At the time, I did not know that this would be our last meeting.

Olga Leonardovna usually returned home about four in the morning, and sometimes in compete daylight, reeking of wine and perfume.

"Why aren't you asleep, Dusya?" she would ask. "You're going to get sick again. And you're still here, too, Bouquichonchik. I'm sure he wasn't bored with you being here!"

I quickly rose and left.

The Cherry Orchard premiered on his name day.[88] The people at the theater had arranged a celebration in his honor which, of course, tired him greatly. Chekhov could not tolerate any gathering of this type; he hated being the center of attention. I can well imagine how many vulgar things he had to listen to [at such affairs].[89]

In a letter to his sister written on May 21, Chekhov wrote that "the other day, for no particular reason, I was stricken with pleurisy. . . . But no matter what happens, I have ordered two tickets for June 2 for the Black Forest."

I have always wondered why Chekhov went abroad in such a condition. Teleshov said, "He went there to die." So that means that Chekhov understood the seriousness of his situation. Also, the thought has sometimes

---

externals of stage sights and sounds. "The stage is art and reflects the quintessence of life," Chekhov told Stanislavsky. "So you must not introduce anything on stage that is not essential" (quoted in K. Stanislavsky, *Sobranie socheninenii v vos'mi tomakh*, vol. 7 [Moscow: Iskusstvo, 1960], 126).

With pointed reference to Stanislavsky, Chekhov once announced his intention to write a play with this beginning: "'What fine quiet,' the chief person of my play will say, 'How wonderful! We hear no birds, no cuckoos, no owls, no clocks, no sleigh bells, no crickets'" (ibid).

87. Chekhov wrote "The Peasants" ("Muzhiki") in 1897.

88. That is, on the day of his christening: January 17, 1860. (Chekhov was born the day before.)

89. The situation was worse than Bunin described. When after the third act of *The Cherry Orchard* the weak, coughing, and unsuspecting Chekhov was called not only to the theater but also out onto the stage, he aroused such sympathy from the audience that people demanded he be seated to face the endless ordeal of speeches and applause.

occurred to me that perhaps Chekhov did not want his family to be present at his death and that he wanted to spare everyone all kinds of burdensome impressions. So he did not object [to going abroad]. Of course, like most people stricken with consumption, he periodically hoped that he would get well. Even more remarkable was that when he was in Moscow, he started writing to his sister in a more tender way.

In his last letter to me, which was written in mid-June and which has not been included in any collection of his letters, he wrote, "I do not feel badly and have ordered a white suit."

On July 4, 1904, I rode out to the post office in the village. After I had gotten various letters and newspapers there, I headed to the blacksmith's to have my horse reshod. It was a hot and sultry day in the steppe. The sky gave off a matted light; a hot southern wind was blowing. Sitting on the threshold of the blacksmith's hut, I opened the newspaper—and suddenly it was if an icy razor had slashed my heart.[90]

A cold had hastened Chekhov's death. After he had arrived in Moscow from Yalta, he went to the baths; but after finishing there, he got dressed and went out too quickly. He had met Sergeenko in the dressing room and had run away from him, from his persistent and chattering nature.

This was the very same Sergeenko who had tired out Tolstoy many years before (when Sergeenko was writing his *How Tolstoy Lives and Works*)[91] and whom Chekhov, seizing upon the man's thin, tall figure and his invariable black suit and hair, used to call "a hearse on legs."[92]

90. Bunin, though, did not attend Chekhov's funeral in Moscow, the pneumonia of his eighty-year-old mother, Lyudmilla, keeping him at the family estate in Oryol. "My especially dear friend," Bunin wrote to Maria on July 9, 1904, "I have been literally struck by lightning. . . . But I want you to understand that through all your trials and tribulations at this time, I share with you with indescribable grief" (Chekhova, *Iz dalekogo proshlogo*, 241).

91. Sergeenko published *How Count Tolstoy Lives and Works* (*Kak zhivet i rabotaet graf L. N. Tolstoi*) in Moscow in 1898.

92. Bunin fails to mention that the self-centered and jabbering, volatile and vacuous Sergeenko had been Chekhov's classmate at the gymnasium in Taganrog.

Chapter Four

THE [MOSCOW] ART THEATER celebrated the fiftieth anniversary of Anton Pavlovich's birth with a literary matinee in which I recalled my memories of the writer.

The theater was filled to overflowing. In a specially marked theater box sat Chekhov's relatives: his mother, his sister, and Ivan Pavlovich with his family. Most likely, Chekhov's other brothers were present, but I do not recall them.

My address called forth genuine cries of delight from the audience, because when I enacted my conversations with Chekhov, I did so by using his own words, voice, and intonation. His family was profoundly affected; his mother and sister were crying.[1]

Several days later, Stanislavsky and Nemirovich[-Danchenko] paid me a visit and suggested that I join their troupe.

Immediately after the matinee, we were invited to Maria Pavlovna's home. . . . Present was the son of Alexander Pavlovich, Mikhail, a young stu-

1. The evening "in memory of Chekhov" was held at the Moscow Art Theater on January 17, 1910. Even at this time, though, Bunin believed that Chekhov had been misinterpreted by readers and reviewers. "Chekhov is greatly valued but poorly understood," Bunin told his listeners. "He is seen as a gloomy individual who wrote about gloomy people. . . . Also, his plays are what they are because of the dark and savage land in which he was born. Such is our life" (Baboreko, "Chekhov i Bunin," 401; see introduction, n. 222).

Reviewers of the event agree with Bunin as to the warm reception of his talk. A reporter from the newspaper *Speech* (*Rech'*) noted on January 19, 1910, "Bunin's talk, delivered in a splendid . . . in a genuine and moving way, made a huge impression on the audience. People broke out into loud laughter when Bunin told humorous anecdotes about the writer. They also held their breath or gasped in amazement when Bunin assumed Chekhov's mournful, noble, and splendid face."

There were several reservations, however, such as Bunin's noting of Chekhov's dislike of the modernists, as well as his inability to "keep himself in the background when he talked about the writer" ("Pamiati A. P. Chekhova," *Russkoe slovo*, February 19, 1910, 3).

It should also be noted that on the following day, Bunin participated in a "Chekhov morning" (*Chekhovksoe utro*) at the University of Moscow in which he acquainted representatives of both the intellectual and aesthetic worlds with his memories of the writer.

M. Semenov et al., *Chekhovskii iubileinyi sbornik* (Moscow: Tipografiia I. D. Sytina, 1910), 523.

dent at the school for the Moscow Art Theater, who impressed us with his talent for gesture; and the son of Ivan Pavlovich, Volodia, a student, who, when he took his leave, kept rearranging people's hats in such a comical way that we who were looking at them from the dining room were greatly amused.

Someone said, "But this is exactly what Chekhov would have done! There is a new generation afoot!"

In the five years after Chekhov's death, Evgenia Yakovlevna had aged a great deal. But [at the matinee] we were overjoyed to see each other, acting as though we were family. She always did love me. She began saying nasty things about Yalta, but she also remembered her time in the region around Moscow with delight.

"It is better around Moscow," she said. "Here one can pick mushrooms, there are plenty of them around, but [in Yalta] . . . one has only the sea."

Her simplicity was absolutely charming.

"Literary hypocrisy is the worst hypocrisy of all," Chekhov once told me.[2]

Chekhov said it well when he wrote to Gorky, "You have way too much description [in your writing]. . . . Readers would have no problem if I would write, 'The man sat down on the grass.' . . . But they would be dazed if I said, 'An erect, average-sized, and narrow-chested man with a reddish beard sat down on the green grass still untrammeled by passersby. He did so shyly and noiselessly, looking around with a frightened air.'"[3]

Chekhov said, "A writer has to train himself to be an observer, tireless and sharp-eyed. . . . He must do so until it becomes a habit . . . as if it were second nature to him."

He was the same with everyone, no matter what rank the individual held.

He grew to love Vsevolod Garshin with his whole soul, despite the fact that their friendship was short. (Garshin committed suicide in spring 1888.)[4]

There was something Mongol-like about Chekhov's mother, [about] Nikolai, and about the writer himself.

2. Chekhov wrote the same thing to Suvorin—about Merezhkovsky! See Chekhov to Suvorin, February 5, 1893, *Pis'ma*, 5:163 (see introduction, n. 2).

3. See Chekhov to Gorky, September 3, 1899, *Pis'ma*, 8:258–59. In another letter to Gorky, Chekhov also objected to what he saw as the "monotonous . . . languor, murmuring, and plushness" of Gorky's descriptions (Chekhov to Gorky, December 3, 1898, *Pis'ma*, 7:352). In fact, Chekhov was often so annoyed by the "disgusting nonsense" that Gorky wrote that he threatened to give up reading Gorky altogether (Chekhov to Avilova, March 9, 1899, 8:121–22).

4. The psychotic thirty-three-year-old Garshin ended his life on April 5, 1888, by throwing

The portraits of his grandfather, grandmother, father, and uncles are those of peasants. The women are Mongols with wide cheekbones and mouths without lips. Chekhov's grandfather, grandmother, mother, father, and uncle were all peasants with wide cheekbones. I find it simply terrible to look at them, especially given the fact that I have lived in Europe for more than thirty years. The uncle's lower jaw is strikingly coarse. The father is more pleasant-looking, but his lower jaw is almost like that of the uncle.

Chekhov once asked me (unexpectedly, as often was his custom), "Do you know what happened to me once?"

Having looked at me over his shoulder for some time, he burst out laughing, "For some reason, I was climbing the main staircase of the Nobility Club in Moscow;[5] and alongside a mirror, with his back toward to me, was Yuzhin-Sumbatov. He was holding Potapenko by the button of his jacket and telling him, insistently, through his teeth, 'You must understand that you are now the number one writer in Russia.' . . . Suddenly Yuzhin-Sumbatov saw me in the mirror. Blushing, he quickly added, pointing to me over his shoulder, 'He, too.'"

Chekhov's notebook[6] includes several things that I heard from him personally. For example, he often asked me (each time forgetting that he had already done so and laughing with all his heart), "Listen, do you know that type of lady who, when you look at her, always seems to have gills under her bodice?"

He often said, "In nature, a repulsive caterpillar gives way to a charming butterfly; but with people, it is just the reverse: a lovely butterfly becomes a repulsive caterpillar."

"It is a terrible thing to dine daily with a person who stutters and talks rubbish."

"When a talentless actress eats a partridge, I feel sorry for the partridge because it was a hundred times more clever and talented than the actress."

He also sometimes said, "A writer must be a pauper. He must be in such a situation because he knows that he will die from hunger if he succumbs to laziness and does not write. Writers should be placed under arrest, put in cells, and whipped and beaten to make them write. . . . Oh, I am so very grateful for my fate, that I was so poor in my youth!"

---

himself down a staircase. The admiration was mutual. "Garshin is simply in raptures over your *Steppe*," Pleshcheev wrote to Chekhov on March 10, 1888. "I met him at the house of some friends and he made me read aloud several passages [from it]." See Vatsuro et al., *Perepiska*, 1:472 (see introduction, n. 197).

5. The Russian Nobility Club (Rossiskoe blagorodnoe sobranie) was founded in 1782.

6. Chekhov wrote his *Notebooks* (*Zapisnye knizhki*) between 1891 and 1904.

How he admired Davydova!

[Chekhov said,] "Mamin-Sibiryak sometimes asked Davydova, 'Alexandra Arkadievna, I do not have a kopeck to my name. Give me at least fifty rubles as an advance.' She always replied, 'You might as well die, my dear, for I will not give you the money. But I will change my mind only if you agree that I can lock you up immediately in a room in a castle; send you ink, pens, paper, and three bottles of beer; and let you out only when you knock on the door and tell me that you have finished a story.'"

But regarding a writer's finances, Chekhov sometimes said just the opposite: "A writer must be fabulously rich, so rich that, anytime he wishes, he can travel around the world in his yacht; arrange an expedition to the sources of the Nile, the South Pole, Tibet, and Arabia; and buy himself all of the Caucasus or the Himalayas. . . . Tolstoy says that the individual needs only six feet of land.[7] That is rubbish. A dead man needs six feet of land, but a living one needs the entire earth. Especially if that person is a writer."

He wrote this remarkable line in his notebook: "I will lie in the grave alone, just as I have lived alone throughout my life."

Chekhov once went with a small group of his close friends to Alupka.[8] One morning he was having breakfast in a restaurant and was in a merry and joking mood. Suddenly there arose from behind a neighboring table a gentleman with a glass in his hand.

"Gentlemen!" he said. "I propose a toast to someone who is honoring us with his presence, Anton Pavlovich, the pride of our literature, the singer of somber sentiments."

Chekhov turned pale, got up, and left.

When I visited Chekhov, we sometimes spent the entire morning in his study in silence, looking through newspapers, of which he had a great many. He would say, "Let's read the paper and dig up something from a provincial chronicle to use in a drama or a vaudeville."

Sometimes he suddenly put down the paper, took off his pince-nez, and laughed in a lighthearted way.

---

7. Chekhov is referring to Tolstoy's 1886 essay "How Much Land Does a Man Need?" ("Mnogo li cheloveku zemli nuzhno?").

Consider a similar quote from the character Ivan Ivanych in Chekhov's 1898 story "Gooseberries" ("Kryzhovnik"): "Man does not need six feet of earth, not a farm, but the entire globe, all of nature, [places in which] he will have room for the full play of all the capabilities and peculiarities of his free spirit." Chekhov, *Sochineniia*, 10:58 (see introduction, n. 4).

8. Alupka is located on the southernmost tip of the Crimea, roughly eight hundred miles south of Moscow.

[I asked,] "Is it something that you read?"

"A merchant named Babkin from Samara[9] has left his entire fortune to build a monument of Hegel," he answered in a thin voice, still laughing.

"You have to be joking."

"Cross my heart, I am telling you the truth. To Hegel, no less." . . . "You have gentry blood in you. Peasants and merchants go to hell very quickly. Read my story, 'Three Years.'[10] Moreover, you are an extremely healthy individual, even though you are as thin as a borzoi. Take some medicine to stimulate your appetite, and you will live to be a hundred. I will prescribe some stuff for you today. I am a doctor, after all. . . . But whatever you do, do not write in your memoirs that I was 'an individual of crystal purity, a respectable talent.'"[11]

"People have written the exact same thing about me," I said.

He began to laugh loudly, with that intense type of pleasure which he showed whenever he particularly liked something.

"Wait a minute," he said. "Was that Korolenko who wrote that about you?"

"Not Korolenko, but Zlatovratsky," I replied. "It was about one of my first stories. He wrote that my piece would do honor to a more prominent talent."

Chekhov laughed so hard that his head fell on his knees. He then put on his pince-nez and, looking at me with a direct and cheerful air, said, "All the same, it is better than what they wrote about me."

After having fallen silent for a while, he continued, "It is absolutely essential that Korolenko cheat on his wife if that would make him a better writer. Otherwise he is way too noble to do so. Do you remember when you told me how Korolenko was moved to tears by the poems of some Verbov or Vetkov in *Russian Wealth*?[12] Apparently, this Verbov-Vetkov had written about how some 'reactionary wolves' had surrounded a bard—some poet of the people who had been caught in a terrible storm in a field—and how this bard supposedly touched the strings of his lyre so loudly that the wolves ran away in fear. Were you telling me the truth when you told me about such a thing?"[13]

"I give you my word that it is true."

9. Samara is located five hundred miles southeast of Moscow.

10. Chekhov's "Three Years" ("Tri goda") appeared in 1895.

11. Bunin is paraphrasing Nikolai Zlatovratsky's less-than-enthusiastic review of his 1901 anthology, *To the Edge of the World and Other Stories* (*Na krai sveta i drugie rasskazy*), in *Zhurnal dlia vsekh*, no. 12 (1901): 1534.

12. *Russian Wealth* (*Russkoe bogatstvo*) was a scientific, literary, and political journal that was published first in Moscow and then in St. Petersburg between 1876 and 1918.

13. The poets in question are A. M. Verbov and N. Viedkov, individuals who are now so obscure that they do not appear in bibliographical indexes and the like. The poem in question, though, is Viedkov's 1899 piece entitled "Waiting for Morning" ("V ozhidanii utra").

"Oh, by the way, do you know that all the coachmen in Perm[14] look like Dobrolyubov?"

"You do not like Dobrolyubov?"

"No, I like him. [Men of his generation] were all decent people. Not like that Skabichevsky who once wrote that since I did not have 'the divine spark' [to write], I would die under some fence from drinking."[15]

"You know," I said, "Skabichevsky once told me that he had never seen how rye grows and that he had never spoken to a peasant."

"That is precisely the point. And throughout his life, he wrote about the people and stories of folk life."

Chekhov once became unusually happy when I told him that our village vicar, at an affair celebrating the name day of my father, had eaten two pounds of caviar, right down to the very last grain. Chekhov used the story to begin his work "In the Ravine."

He loved to repeat that if someone does not work and live in an artistic atmosphere, he could be Solomon himself but would always feel empty and talentless.

Sometimes Chekhov took a notebook from his desk and, raising his face so that his pince-nez sparkled in the light, waved it in the air: "I have one hundred story plots here! Yes, my dear sir, exactly one hundred plots! Not like you young whippersnappers! Some workers you are! If you want, I will sell you a couple!"

Sometimes Chekhov loved to go for evening walks. One time we were returning from such a stroll very late at night. He was very tired and could barely put one foot in front of the other. (In the preceding days, he had covered many handkerchiefs with blood.) Chekhov had closed his eyes and was silent. We were going past the balcony behind a well-lit screen with womanly silhouettes when suddenly he opened his eyes and said in a very loud voice, "Have you heard? Something terrible has happened! Bunin has been murdered! In Autka, in the home of a Tatar woman!"

14. Perm is located seven hundred miles northwest of Moscow.

15. The occasion for such a remark was a review of Chekhov's anthology *Motley Stories* (*Pestrye rasskazy*) in which the critic, Alexander Skabichevsky, also compared Chekhov to a "squeezed out lemon rotting under a gate" (A. M. Skabichevskii, "Novye knigi: 'Pestrye rasskazy,'" *Severnyi vestnik*, no. 6 [1886]: 124).

Chekhov never forgot Skabichevsky's remarks. Toward the end of his life, he told Gorky, "I have read criticisms of my stories for twenty-five years, and I do not recall a single remark of any value, nor have I heard a piece of good advice. Skabichevsky, though, made an impression on me, when he wrote that I would die drunk in a ditch." Quoted in Gor'kii, "A. P. Chekhov," *Polnoe sobranie sochinenii*, 6:52 (see introduction, n. 17).

Bewildered, I stopped dead in my tracks, but he whispered quietly, "Not a word to anyone! Tomorrow all of Yalta will be talking about Bunin's murder!"

A writer once complained, "I could cry with shame when I think about how poorly and weakly I started off as a writer!"

"What are you moaning about?" Chekhov exclaimed. "It is wonderful to start off writing poorly! You have to understand that if a beginning writer does everything perfectly, he is ruined, he is lost before he has even begun!"

Then, with passion, he began to argue that only gifted people mature quickly and early but that such individuals are unoriginal and devoid of talent. Gifted people, he continued, can adapt to circumstances and "live in a lighthearted manner," but a true talent suffers torment in seeking to come to the fore.

Chapter Five

ONE TIME WHEN Chekhov was reading the paper, he raised his face and slowly, without any intonation, said, "People always say the same thing: it is Korolenko and Chekhov, Potapenko and Chekhov, Gorky and Chekhov."[1]

"For every one intelligent individual, there are a thousand stupid ones; and, for just one intelligent word, there are a thousand stupid ones. And it

1. Bunin objected to other pairings as well. He wrote a long (and here edited) letter to Boris Zaitsev on July 18, 1947:

> In your feuilleton, you write that Chekhov and Gorky are as much a "pair" as Corneille and Racine, Voltaire and Rousseau, Schiller and Goethe, Pushkin and Lermontov, Tolstoy and Dostoevsky. . . . If I were Sagaidachnyi and you were my Tatar captive, I would impale you on a stake for what you said!
>
> So *calmly* do you cite Gorky's first letter to Chekhov [in late November 1898]: "I want to write *something* to you, Anton Pavlovich. I love you so selflessly, sincerely, *from the bottoms of my toenails.* . . . Oh, *God damn it,* I grasp your hand not only as an artist, but also as the sincere but sad individual you must be. Am I right in thinking so? Your talent is a spirit that is clean and clear; but it is also one that is entangled in the ties of this earth, the base ties of everyday life. . . . But let the artist in you cry out to the heavens, and may his sobs be heard everywhere. . . . Do not let me offend you, for I am a very absurd and vulgar person, and my soul is so incurably sick, *as must be the soul of any thinking person.*"
>
> Do we not have a genuine Schiller here? But what you say about Chekhov is good. You add in an uncertain, questioning tone: "Did such a letter not *grate upon* Chekhov's nerves, if not the least little bit?" To tell you the truth, such a missive would make a pig sick! You then go on to say: "After all, how many times did Chekhov praise Gorky in letters not only to Gorky himself, but also to [Gorky's] wife. He praised Gorky even more than Tolstoy did."
>
> I never expected that you could be so gullible! . . . When I was with Chekhov, I would hear such guffaws and censure so many times that to this day that I still marvel whenever I read his laudatory letters to Gorky!
>
> I am already quite tired of writing this letter, but I cannot help but add several more words about your sentence, that is, "Chekhov's modesty, his readiness to get on his hands and knees before Tolstoy, his consciousness of his own insignificance before the great

is precisely these thousand stupid ones that suffocate literature." (From Chekhov's notebook.)[2]

Chekhov also was "suffocated" for a long time. Before the "The Peasants" was published, a story that was far from being among his best things, large segments of the public read him with pleasure; but for these readers, he was only an engaging storyteller, the author of "The Card Game" and "The Complaint Book."[3]

Generally speaking, people who liked "ideas" showed little interest in Chekhov. They acknowledged his talent, but they did not take him seriously. I remember how some of them genuinely laughed at me when, as a youth, I dared to compare Chekhov with Garshin and Korolenko. Among them were people who said that they would never read a writer who began his career with the name "Chekhonte."[4] "One simply cannot imagine," they said, "that Tolstoy or Turgenev would use such a vulgar nickname."

Genuine fame came to Chekhov only when his plays were staged at the [Moscow] Art Theater. Most likely, such a state of affairs hurt him no less deeply than what people had begun to say about him after the publication of "The Peasants." After all, his plays were far from being among his best writings. Chekhov became famous because the theater repeated his name a thousand times, and the public remembered such phrases as "twenty-two misfortunes," "dearly esteemed wardrobe," and "they have forgotten the servant."[5]

For a long time, the critics saw Chekhov only as a "gloomy" writer, "the singer of twilight moods," a "sick talent," and as an individual who looked at everything in a hopeless and indifferent way.

Today the critics say quite different things about him. They note "Chekhov's tenderness, sadness, and warmth," his "love for human beings." I can well imagine how he himself would feel, reading about his "tenderness"! Indeed, he would find his "sadness" and "warmth" even more repulsive!

Even when talented people speak about him, they adopt a wrong tone. For example, Elpatievsky writes, "In Chekhov one meets people who are gentle and kind, humble and unassuming. . . . In fact he was always attracted

---

writer, such things are completely lacking in Gorky." Good Lord, such a savage thought about Chekhov is beyond words! With my own hands, I myself would impale you on a stake! (Quoted in N. Vinokur, "Novoe o Buninykh," *Minuvshee,* no. 8 [1992]: 322)

2. Chekhov, *Sochineniia,* 17:57 (see introduction, n. 4).

3. Chekhov wrote both "The Card Game" ("Vint") and "The Complaint Book" ("Zhalobnaia kniga") in 1884.

4. It was a grade-school teacher, a waggish and much-admired priest by the name of Feodor Pokrovsky, who was the first individual to discern Chekhov's talent and who, when calling on the writer in the classroom, gave him the nickname of "Chekhonte."

5. Bunin is quoting from *The Cherry Orchard.*

to such types. . . . He was always drawn to the quiet valleys with their shadows, their hazy dreams, and their quiet tears."

What nonsense! Chekhov was attracted to strong and intelligent people, Suvorin, for example. Chekhov was never so open as with him. He loved Suvorin's company and never wrote to anyone so frankly and frequently as him![6]

Korolenko characterizes Chekhov's talent with such pitiful words as "simple" and "sincere." He claims that the writer has a "grief for ghosts."[7]

In 1948 when I was giving a public reading of my literary memoirs,[8] I stated that I believed Chekhov to be one of the most remarkable Russian writers. But I also said that I did not like his plays, that they were all very poor, and that Chekhov should not have written plays about gentry life, since he did not know anything about it.

My statement called forth a great deal of indignation. For instance, E. D. Kuskova wrote two lengthy feuilletons in *New Russian Word*. "In Geneva," she wrote, "both young and old were offended by what Bunin said about Chekhov, Balmont, and Gorky. . . . These writers are loved even now, and Chekhov is being read despite the fact that old, mournful Russia with its moaners and groaners is long a thing of the past."[9]

That Kuskova dismisses Chekhov as a portrayer of "old, mournful Russia" is really an insult to the writer. In truth, Kuskova is the one who deserves to be insulted, and the "old boys" in Geneva should recall what Gorky, with loathsome coarseness, once called them as members of the Russian intelligentsia: "the pantry with rotten food."

---

6. Alexei Suvorin was the editor of *New Times* (*Novoe vremia*), the largest-circulation newspaper in St. Petersburg. Also the grandson of a serf, Suvorin was twenty-six years older than Chekhov and a self-made magnate, owning besides *New Times* a large publishing firm, five bookshops, and eventually his own theater. It was Suvorin who, early in Chekhov's career, sensed that he was dealing with a man of genius and who, as a mentor and father figure, steered the writer from humorous and "hack" writing to serious literature. Chekhov responded in kind, writing to Suvorin with a freedom, openness, and confidence he rarely showed to others in expressing his views on literature and life.

7. In the 1914 version of Bunin's memoirs on Chekhov, Bunin notes Korolenko's comment on his 1903 stories "Dreams" ("Sny") and "The Golden Bottom" ("Zolotoe dno"): "Chekhov very much likes these stories by Bunin. . . . And we can understand why. After all, they are replete with the same grief for ghosts that we find in Chekhov's last drama [*The Cherry Orchard*]." See L. Kotov, *Chekhov v vospominaniiakh sovremennikov* (Moscow: Gosudarstevennoe izdatel'stvo khudozhestvennoi literatury, 1954), 487.

8. Bunin read his memoirs in Paris on the occasion of his seventy-eighth birthday on October 23, 1948. They were published in *Novoe russkoe slovo* on December 27 and 30, 1948.

9. E. Kuskova, "Do i posle (Iz vospominanii)," *Novoe russkoe slovo*, February 4 and 7, 1949.

One should also take offense at the famous actress Ermolova. Among her published letters there is one to her friend, a Doctor Sredin, in Yalta. She writes, "You asked why I do not like Chekhov's story, 'In the Ravine'? Because all this *Chekhovshchina* is a symbol of impenetrable darkness, of all imaginable diseases and sorrow." But Ermolova so regarded Gorky as a "dear, enlightened soul" that she implored Sredin, "You are close to Gorky. Do not let him turn his back on the bright notes which sound so forcefully in his works."[10]

Reading this, one cannot believe one's eyes! "In the Ravine" is, in every respect, one of the most splendid creations of Russian literature. . . . And Gorky wrote a great many things that were purposely dirty, vile, and gloomy even as they seemed to resound "forcefully" with "bright notes"!

One of the best articles about Chekhov is a 1908 piece written by Shestov in Petersburg, entitled "Creation from the Void."[11] In it Shestov calls Chekhov a "merciless talent."

A broken man usually has everything taken from him, except the ability to recognize and feel his situation. Simply put, his intellectual capabilities become more sharpened and sophisticated; they take on colossal proportions.

Chekhov was the singer of hopelessness. Throughout his almost twenty-five years as a writer, he—monotonously, stubbornly, and grimly—did only one and the same thing: either in one way or another, he killed human hopes. In my opinion, this is the essence of his creative work. . . .

Take a look at Chekhov's work. It is as though he seems to be lying in constant ambush, watching for his chance to dash human hopes. . . . Art, science, love, inspiration, ideals, the future—look at all these notions as Chekhov did, and they immediately dim, droop, and die. Right before our eyes, Chekhov also dims, droops, and dies. The only thing that lives on with him is his remarkable art. . . . As an artist, Chekhov becomes more and more perfect in his craft. Indeed, he attains a virtuosity unmatched by any of his rivals in European literature.

Chekhov dug for hidden treasure. He was a magician, a sorcerer, a snake charmer. Such stances explain his unusual, exceptional attraction for death, corruption, decay—and hopelessness.

10. Bunin is quoting from letters of Maria Ermolova to Leonid Sredin written on September 16, 1899, and on February 22, March 5, and April 12, 1900. See M. Ermolova, *Pis'ma: Iz literaturnogo naslediia; Vospominaniia sovremennikov* (Moscow: Iskusstvo,1955), 154, 171–74.

11. L. Shestov, "Tvorchestvo iz nichego," *Nachala i kontsy* (St. Petersburg: Tipografiia M. M. Stasiulevicha, 1908).

The only philosophy which Chekhov considered seriously, and just as earnestly opposed, was positivist materialism.

The hopeless individual is the only genuine hero in Chekhov's works.

Chekhov has nothing; he has created everything himself. Hence his "creation from the void."

Shestov says that Chekhov, in his writings, is influenced by Tolstoy. . . . [He claims] that without *Ivan Ilyich*,[12] there would be no "A Boring Story."

I am not so sure about that.

M. Kurdyumov also had a new approach to Chekhov. In his 1934 book, entitled *A Troubled Heart*,[13] he noted the religious nature of Chekhov's consciousness.

Kurdyumov writes:

Not only in our country but also in the West, there has long been an established tradition for people to see only Dostoevsky as the key to understanding the Russian temperament. For Westerners interested in complex Russian questions, Dostoevsky and *âme slave* are synonyms.[14]

[Such a view implies that] Chekhov, in his work, seemingly did not raise any issues either for himself or his readers.

Chekhov has simply never been read to the end.

What Kurdyumov says here is remarkable and true:

The worldview of Chekhov-the-man was closely tied to his epoch, with its triumph of rationalism and positivism. But he did not fully accept either belief, nor could he find comfort in them.

Chekhov, by virtue of his personality, as well as by the spiritual condition of his heroes from the Russian intelligentsia, noted the crisis of Russian rationalism as the predominant trend of the time. He took note of its loss of popularity long before such an event became patently obvious to a significant majority of people. Chekhov was able to feel the first cracks in its dikes. In fact, there are all kinds of evidence to assert that Chekhov was carrying these

12. Tolstoy wrote *The Death of Ivan Ilyich* (*Smert' Ivana Il'icha*) in 1886.

13. Mikhail Kurdyumov published *A Troubled Heart: About the Work of A. P. Chekhov, 1904–1934* (*Serdtse smiatennoe: O tvorchestve A. P. Chekhove, 1904–1934*) in Paris in 1934.

14. Kurdyumov's assertion about Dostoevsky is true. Many émigré writers and reviewers saw the writer as a "sick genius" whom they condemned for his morbid introspection, his political conservatism, his "unhealthy" probing into human psychology, and his long and short works which, in their opinion, were difficult, turgid, and artless. Many exiles also feared that since Dostoevsky personified for the West the somber and inscrutable Russian "soul," they too would be seen as irrational and deranged.

fissures within himself . . . and that they manifested themselves in his creative intuition . . . and frank conversations.

Kurdyumov is also correct when he writes: "Chekhov never concealed the fact that for him, human grief was incomparably more important and dearer than 'civil grief.'"

What Kurdyumov wrote further is also true:

Not only the younger generation, but also we ourselves find it difficult to imagine to what extent a Russian writer of Chekhov's time was constrained and repressed by our intelligentsia which imposed on him its tastes, values, and what it considered to be the evils of the day. The more talented a writer was, the more persistently everyone pressured him, the more decisively they demanded that he proclaim predetermined slogans.

At a time when Chekhov's contemporary, Maxim Gorky, was at the height of his noisy fame and proclaiming with a victorious air, "Oh, the human being . . . How this entity arouses such pride!"—Chekhov, with this creative spirit, was saying: "Oh, the human being! . . . How this entity calls forth a tragedy so terrible and pathetic that it brings one to tears."

[Chekhov said,] "Tragic is the life of anyone who has not drowned in vulgar self-contentment."

"It is enough merely to look into any soul to respond with overwhelming pity for it."

"To empathize with tragedy, one does not have to create tragic characters in the spirit of Shakespeare, since human life, in and of itself, is a tragedy. The loneliness of the human soul is especially calamitous."

Such a sentiment was also felt by Chekhov's father, Pavel Egorovich, who ordered for himself a pendant with the inscription, "The lonely person sees a desert everywhere."

I should also add here that Chekhov wore this signet for many years and with it even sealed his letters to Avilova.

[Kurdyumov continues,] "The sadness of Chekhov and his characters is the sorrow of Ecclesiastes in the Bible—the most sorrowful book in the world.[15] 'What good does one gain from all his labors, from his toil under the sun?' . . . 'The individual cannot express everything; the eye cannot be satiated with sight; the ear cannot be sated with hearing. What was, will also be; what has

---

15. Ecclesiastes is a book of the Old Testament purporting to be the work of King Solomon but probably written in the late third century B.C. It focuses on the purpose of life.

been done, will be done again; and there is nothing new under the sun. . . .' There is no memory of the past, nor will there be any memory of the future, or for those who come after."[16]

[Kurdyumov continues,] "Lipa and her mother Praskovia ('In the Ravine'), Olga ('The Peasants') . . . the old priest, Father Christopher ('The Steppe'), the young deacon ('The Duel'), and the student of the theological academy ('The Student'),[17]—and other people with a religious frame of mind—do not see anything senseless in what seems to be absolutely absurd; they do not see anything hopeless and horrible in the most terrible things."

In my view, "In the Ravine" is one of the most remarkable works not only in Chekhov's writing but in all of world literature.

Kurdyumov thinks that *Three Sisters, Uncle Vanya,* and *The Cherry Orchard* are Chekhov's best plays. I do not agree: his single best play is *The Seagull.* . . . Kurdyumov is correct, though, when he says that the "key unseen character in Chekhov's plays, as well as in many of his other works, is the merciless passage of time."

Kurdyumov is also correct when he writes, "Chekhov brings both the human mind and heart into the gloomy realm of things that cannot be resolved. For him the problem of 'unresolved things' is much more important than anything else in the world. It is more important than 'progress,' than the 'welfare of humankind and all other achievements.'"

In the second half of March 1891, Chekhov and Suvorin were in Venice. There they met Merezhkovsky.

Z. N. Gippius describes this meeting:

> We had already been in Venice for two weeks, when Merezhkovsky caught sight of the stooped back of a tall old man in a brown carriage standing in the colorful twilight of Saint Mark's. He said to me, "Why, it is Suvorin! And with him is Chekhov who will introduce me to him. I will not extend my hand to Burenin,[18] but I will to Suvorin. He may be a pea out of the same pod, but he tastes different. In any case, he is an interesting man."
>
> We both considered Chekhov to be the most talented among young writers. Merezhkovsky had even recently written an article about him in *Northern*

---

16. Kurdymov is quoting Ecclesiastes 1:3.

17. Chekhov wrote "The Duel" ("Duel'") in 1891.

18. At this time, the vitriolic Viktor Burenin was being ostracized by the Russian literary world for his articles against the dying poet Semyon Nadson, who was held aloft by the public for his condemnation of political despotism and social injustice. In his diatribe, Burenin

Herald.[19] But Chekhov interested me but little. . . . His writings seemed somehow weak and thin.[20]

Chekhov's being was rooted in a staticlike quality. . . . His genius was one of immobility, not dead ossification. No, he was a lively individual who was also exceptionally gifted. . . . And one of these gifts was not to move ahead in time.

Oh, God, what some people will not write![21]

Speaking philosophically . . . the person who is in movement encounters borders that are unstable and exciting, pliable and resilient. But with Chekhov, these borders are forever solid and determined. What is inside these borders is inside, and what is not in them will never be there. Chekhov treats and understands any movement as superficial. For him to do otherwise would be to allow movement within his borders, his very self. . . . Chekhov never became old. He truly was alien to "age." He was born a forty-year-old man [?—I.B.], and he died a forty-year-old man, seemingly in the very heyday of his life.[22]

Dear God, how some people lack even the slightest spontaneous feeling for life! To say that Chekhov was born as a forty-year-old man! To say that he never advanced with the years?

---

charged that the desperately ill Nadson was a parasite who feigned sickness to live off friends and the public. The result was not only public outrage at Burenin's claim but also the widespread conviction that he had hastened Nadson's death. (The poet had suffered a fatal hemorrhage after the publication of Burenin's pieces.)

19. *Northern Herald* (*Severnyi vestnik*) was published in St. Petersburg between 1885 and 1898.

20. See Chekhov to Maria Chekhova, March 26, 1891, *Pis'ma*, 4:181 (see introduction, n. 2). Like many snobs in St. Petersburg, the literary lioness Zinaida Gippius felt compelled to remind provincial upstarts of their lack of sophistication and experience. For instance, she willfully misinformed Anton that rates for hotels in Venice were by the week, not the day. In her diary, also, she noted that Chekhov was a "a provincial doctor . . . who, within his limits, had fine powers of observation but also displayed typically coarse manners in his dealings with people" (Rayfield, *Chekhov: A Life*, 243; see introduction, n. 230).

21. Bunin had just cause for his remark if only because he was the frequent recipient of Gippius's damning of his work with faint praise. For instance, Gippius wrote, "Bunin is a splendid writer, a sober individual. But what can you do with him?" (Z. Gippius, "Taina zerkala: Ivan Bunin," *Obshchee delo*, May 16, 1921, 3).

Five years later, she wrote, "In Bunin's work, 'art as mirror' takes precedence over thought and imagination. . . . Bunin gives us only the sea, the sky, and his emotions about them, but his picture is so universal and complete that it is difficult to want anything else. . . . I have often thought, 'Are we not making a mistake when we demand something else from Bunin? Would that not destroy the "harmony" of his world?'" (Z. Gippius, "Sovremennye zapiski: Kniga XXIX," *Poslednie novosti*, November 11, 1926, 3).

22. Bunin is quoting from Z. Gippius, *Zhivye litsa* (Prague: Plamia, 1925), 132–34.

Chekhov was a schoolboy, he was a student and a contributor to humorous journals, he was a doctor in the mid-1880s. In the first half of the 1890s, Chekhov spent a year on Sakhalin Island. He lived through the second half of this decade and finally into the beginning of the twentieth century. That is six different Chekhovs!

One need only to look at his portraits.

What a very fine poet Chekhov was!

At the hotel Oreanda, people sat on a bench not far from the church and looked quietly out onto the sea. White clouds stood still on the mountaintops. The foliage in the village did not stir, the cicadas were shrill, and the monotonous sound of the sea wafting from below spoke of the peace and the eternal sleep that awaits us. As the sea resounded in a muffle and indifferent way, so it will resound after we are gone. This expanse, this indifference to life and death, is concealed in each of us. Perhaps such things are also a sign of our eternal salvation, of continual perfection, and of the constant movement of life on this earth. Gurkov sat alongside a young woman who seemed so reassuring, beautiful, and enchanting in the daybreak, in this fantasy-like setting—the sea, the mountains, the clouds, and the wide expanse of the sky. He kept thinking that, truly, if one truly takes stock of existence, everything in this world is splendid, everything except that which we ourselves think and do when we forget about the higher goals of life, about our own human dignity and worth.

A man came by—perhaps it was the watchman. He looked at the couple and left. But this detail also seemed mysterious and beautiful. Apparently, the ship from Feodosia[23] had arrived, a vessel that was lit only by daybreak, not with any other type of light.

"There's dew on the grass," Anna Sergeevna said, after some silence.

"Yes, it is time to go home."

They returned to the city.

—"A Lady with a Dog"[24]

In the distance, the cemetery looked like a dark stripe, as if it were a huge garden or forest. There appeared first a fence made out of white stone, and then some gates. . . . On these gates in the moonlight was a sign that said, THE TIME IS FAST APPROACHING. . . . Startsev made his way through the wicket-gate. The first thing he saw was the white crosses and tombstones on

---

23. Feodosia is in Ukraine, roughly 760 miles south of Moscow and approximately 65 miles northeast of Yalta.

24. Chekhov wrote "A Lady with a Dog" ("Dama s sobachkoi") in 1899.

both sides of a wide alley, together with the dark shadows that emerged both from them and from the poplars there. All around one could see black and white, and how the sleepy trees bent their branches to this whiteness that surrounded them.

It seemed that it was lighter here than in the field. Pawlike maple trees stood out sharply in the yellow sand of the pathways and on the gravestones; the inscriptions on the tombs were clear. Initially, Startsev was struck by the things that he was seeing for the first time in his life and that most likely he would never see again: a world that was unlike anything else, a world in which the moonlight was like a cradle, soft and good, a world where there was no life, no life at all, but also where every dark poplar, every grave exuded the presence of a mystery which promised a life that was splendid, eternal, and quiet. The tombs and the fading leaves, together with the autumnal smell of leaves, gave forth a scent of melancholy, forgiveness, and peace.

All around was silence: the stars looked down from the sky in deep humility, and Startsev's steps sounded sharply out of place. Only when the clock in the church began to strike did he imagine that . . . someone was looking at him. And for a moment, he thought that what he was experiencing was not silence and peace but the dull angst of nonbeing, of repressed despair.
—"Ionych"[25]

The garden was quiet and cool, with dark, restful shadows lying on the ground. Somewhere far away, most likely in the country, one could hear the call of frogs. One could feel May, lovely, sweet May! One could also breathe deeply and find it pleasant to think that it was not here, but somewhere under the sky, in the forest and the fields, and above the trees far away from the city, there now had come to life a special type of spring, mysterious, beautiful, splendid, sacred, and rich, and beyond the understanding of a weak and sinful man. And sensing this, one felt like crying.
—"The Bride"[26]

How wrong Gippius was!

[Gippius writes,] "The word 'normal' was created as if it were just for Chekhov. His appearance was 'normal,' one that suited him and the norms of his time. He was a normal provincial doctor with a normal degree of education who lived, loved, and wrote in accord with his own splendid talent. He confined his precise observation to his own borders; his somewhat rude manners were also normal."

25. Chekhov wrote "Ionych" between 1893 and 1895.
26. Chekhov's "The Bride" ("Nevesta") appeared in 1903.

I never observed Chekhov's rudeness. I never knew him to act in such a way, so he must have changed in this respect.

"Even Chekhov's sickness was somehow 'normal,'" Gippius writes. "After all, no one could imagine him a Dostoevsky or a Prince Myshkin,[27] who collapsed before his bride in a fit of 'sacred' epilepsy, breaking an expensive vase to boot. Nor could anyone imagine that Chekhov could be like Gogol, that is, to fast for ten days at a stretch, burn the manuscripts for *The Seagull, The Cherry Orchard,* and *The Three Sisters,* and then immediately depart from this world."[28]

But Chekhov was not the only one who did not take a match to his writings. Pushkin did not burn his works; neither did many other writers, including Gippius herself. And to indict Chekhov for not having epilepsy or a mental illness is, to put it mildly, rather strange.

Given the state of his health, was it truly normal for Chekhov to travel to Sakhalin? Was it also normal for him to regard his blood spitting in such a frivolous way, in much the same way he had looked upon it in 1884 and again in 1897 when, despite his illness, he traveled to Moscow to see L. A. Avilova?

Gippius asserts that Chekhov courted any woman who caught his fancy in a "normal" way.

She also thinks that his marriage was normal. But I believe that his union with Knipper was a slow suicide. His life with her was marked by his own illness, frequent separations, and endless worry for the both of them— Olga Leonardovna almost died twice in the three years[29] that they were married—and finally, his endless attempts to go off somewhere when he was so sick. Even during the Russo-Japanese War, he wanted to go to the Far East as a doctor, not as a correspondent![30]

[Gippius writes,] "By his integrity alone, Chekhov was a great man. Of course, he was close to and needed by souls who tended to be 'normal': static but wordless."

27. Prince Myshkin is the hero in Dostoevsky's 1868 novel *The Idiot (Idiot).*

28. Gogol burned versions of *Dead Souls (Mertvye dushi)* in 1845 and 1852.

29. Olga Knipper suffered a miscarriage in March 1901 and an attack of acute peritonitis three months later.

30. Bunin's remark is true. Like his fellow citizens, Chekhov pounced on news of the war, grieved over Russia's defeats, and hoped for an end to the hostilities. It is also of interest to note that Chekhov had wanted to go off to war earlier. After hearing about the possibility of a conflict between Russia and England over the Near East, he wrote to Suvorin in December 1896, "If there is a war . . . I shall go. . . . Like Vronsky—not to fight, of course, but to tend the wounded" (Chekhov to Suvorin, December 1896, *Pis'ma,* 6:246). Also, in a letter written to Gorky on July 12, 1900, Chekhov confessed a desire to serve as a doctor in the Boxer Rebellion (Chekhov to Gorky, July 12, 1900, *Pis'ma,* 9:93).

With surprise, Gippius continues, "I do not know where these souls are now: life, movement, and events have all been turned upside down. God knows, how these souls understood the concept of 'normal.'"

Gippius is completely ignorant of Chekhov not only as a writer but also as an individual. For instance, in her view, Chekhov did not like Italy. I will not dwell on this point, since he has written a great deal about his visit there to both relatives and friends. Apparently, [in Italy] Chekhov was reserved with the Merezhkovskys on purpose.[31] He talked of trifles in their presence; he was also irritated by their ecstasies over everything, especially those of "Madame Merezhkovskaya," whom he apparently did not like. As a result, Gippius never forgave him for his indifference to Italy or to herself.

In truth, it was the Merezhkovskys who, in literature and in life, changed a great deal less than Chekhov. It was they who were "ageless," since they were the same from the day they were born to the day they died!

---

31. Truth be told, while both Chekhov and Merezhkovsky were enraptured by the art and architecture of Venice, Chekhov was attuned to the same minutiae-prosaics of the city that had attracted Bunin on his visits there.

As Merezhkovsky recalled, "Chekhov was walking beside me, tall, slightly bent, as usual smiling quietly. . . . He was occupied by unexpected trifles and, as it seems to me, even uninteresting: a guide with a very bald head, the voice of a girl selling flowers on St. Mark's Square, the uninterrupted bells at the Italian stations" (D. Merezhkovskii, "Brat chelovecheskii," *Chekhovskii iubileinyi sbornik*, 204).

Such differences, of course, spoke to the heart of the conflicting worldviews between the two men. "The enthusiastic and pure-minded Merezhkovsky," Chekhov wrote to Suvorin, "would do well to exchange his quasi-Goethe regime, his wife, and his 'eternal verities' for a bottle of good wine, a sportsman's gun, and a pretty girl. His heart would beat better" (Chekhov to Suvorin, March 7, 1892, *Pis'ma*, 5:8).

Chapter Six

WAS THERE AT LEAST ONE great love in Chekhov's life? I don't believe there was.

"Love," he once wrote in his notebook, "is either the remains of something that had once been great and huge but that is now deteriorating; or, it is a part of something that is going to develop into something great and huge in the future but that at present does not satisfy individuals and gives them much less than what they had expected."[1]

Avilova wrote her memoirs with great flair, emotion, rare talent, and unusual tact; they were a great discovery for me.

I knew Lydia Alexeevna well. She was exceptionally honest, intelligent, talented, and shy. She also displayed a rare sense of humor, even toward herself.

Having read her memoirs, I saw a different Chekhov, one that I did not know before.

I never suspected that there had existed a relationship between them.

Even now many people think that Chekhov never experienced any great feeling.

Even I thought such a thing at one time.

Now I firmly declare: he did! And it was toward Lydia Alexeevna Avilova.

I sense that some people will ask: Can we trust Avilova's recollections completely?

Lydia Alexeevna was an unusually honest individual. She never con-

---

1. Chekhov, *Sochineniia*, 17:175 (see introduction, n. 4).

cealed even the negative comments that Chekhov made about her work or about herself. She was a rare kind of woman!

But she kept silent for many years. Throughout her life, even when I knew her, she did not utter a single word about her love [for Chekhov].

I read the foreword to these memoirs, written by some Kotov, and I was amazed at his stupidity. He writes: "In this book, one cannot help but notice the extreme subjectivity and narrowness of the author in bringing to light material on Chekhov. [He is talking about Avilova!—I.B.] For instance, one cannot accept as totally true Avilova's statement that Chekhov based his story 'About Love' on their relationship. What is true about their time together was that Chekhov was interested in Avilova as a writer who could address an extremely engaging topic: the dependent situation of a woman, and the abnormal organization of her family."[2]

Everything about Avilova was charming: her voice, her certain shyness, the look of her wonderful blue-gray eyes.

How beautiful she looked in mourning, at the untimely passing of her arrogant husband, who always ridiculed her writing in such a cruel way.

"Hey there, old lady," he often told her. "Time to go to bed. Enough of your so-called 'creative work'!"

Avilova's maiden name was Strakhova. She was a sister of one of Tolstoy's followers.[3] She was also one of those women whom Chekhov loved so much that he used a somewhat disagreeable adjective to describe them: "sumptuous." Such women are usually called "Russian beauties" or "genuine blood-and-milk types"—an expression which I have always found intolerable, for could there be any worse combination than "blood and milk"? Furthermore, when people say that "so-and-so is a Russian beauty," they are usually referring to a woman from the merchant class. But Avilova had nothing of the merchant class about her. She was tall, well built, and beautifully feminine, with a splendid plait of light brown hair. Such qualities pointed to a noble pedigree, not to anything mercantile. I knew her when she was still a young woman (though

---

2. Vera Bunina comments, "[In the original manuscript] Ivan Alexeevich marked these lines in Kotov's article with two exclamation points and several 'Note Well.' With blue and red pencils, he underlined those places that particularly repulsed him; and with a blue pencil, he wrote in the margins: 'What a shameful . . . (expletive deleted in the text) to have written such a thing!'" Quoted in Bunin, *O Chekhove*, 136 (see preface, n. 4).

3. The person in question is the writer and publicist Fyodor Strakhov.

she already had three children), and I always admired her (though, speaking personally, I prefer another type: dark-complected, thin, and Asiatic).

I loved being with Avilova if only because she was a unique woman with a great sense of humor even when she talked about herself. Her observations were sound; she was a good judge of people. But despite such qualities, she was also very shy, prone to blushing, and often at a loss for words.

For instance, with indescribable humor, she relished telling about her first visit to the editorial offices of the journal *Herald of Europe:*[4]

> Finally, after wavering for quite some time, I gathered up my courage and brought my story to the editor, Stasyulevich. It was just my luck that he was the one who answered the door. I was so seized by shyness that without even saying hello, I began to mumble: "Er . . . I . . . I . . . Matvei . . . Stasyulei Mat-veevi . . . Mikhail Styasyulevich . . . I, you see . . . want to offer myself to you."
>
> At this point I became so confused that without even giving him my manuscript, I ran out into the street as if someone were chasing me. . . . He must have thought that I was crazy.

Avilova first met Chekhov on January 24, 1889.
Lydia Alexeevna writes:

> I received a note from my sister in which she wrote, "Come right away, without fail. Chekhov is going to visit us." My sister was married to the editor and publisher of a widely circulating newspaper, *The Petersburg Gazette.*[5] She was a great deal older than I. Small, fair-haired, with huge dreamy eyes and tiny hands, she provoked in me feelings of both tenderness and envy. Next to her, I seemed tall, full-figured, and ruddy-cheeked. Even worse, I was a Muscovite who had been living in Petersburg for only two years.
>
> My sister was host to many famous people: actors, artists, singers, poets, and writers. But I was married to a student who had just finished his studies and who had taken a position as a junior clerk in the department of public education. What can I say about my past? Only that my dreams never came true.
>
> But I did have one dream—to become a writer. From childhood on, I had written poetry and prose. There was nothing in my life that I loved to do more than to write. For me, the artistic word was power, magic. I read a great deal, and among my favorite authors, "Chekhonte" was far from last

---

4. *Herald of Europe* (*Vestnik Evropy*) was a journal published in St. Petersburg from 1866 to 1918.

5. The *Petersburg Gazette* (*Peterburgskaia gazeta*) was a political and literary newspaper published in St. Petersburg from 1867 to 1917.

place on my list. At that time, incidentally, he was publishing his stories in a newspaper that was being put out by my brother-in-law; and every one of his stories sent me into ecstasy. How I cried over Iona, who shared his grief with his old horse because no one wanted to listen to his troubles anymore.[6] . . . Why was it precisely now, when Chekhov decided to write about such a thing, that everyone started to find him interesting, began reading everything he wrote, and not without a few tears to boot?

[On that evening] Misha (my husband) happened to be busy. As he was not interested in meeting Chekhov, I went alone.

"Ah, if it isn't the lovely Flora," my brother-in-law, Sergei Nikolaevich, greeted me in a loud voice.

Chekhov made several quick steps toward me and, with a sweet smile, took my hand into his. As we looked at each other, it seemed to me that he was surprised by something. Perhaps it was the name "Flora." Sergei Nikolaevich called me that because of my vivid complexion and plentiful hair which I sometimes wound into two long, thick braids.

"She knows all your stories by heart," Sergei Nikolaevich continued. "She probably has even written letters to you but has hidden them somewhere. But even if she did, she certainly will not admit such a thing."

I noticed that [upon hearing this] Chekhov screwed up his eyes slightly. I also saw that his tie was ugly, and his starched collar looked like that of a horse.

At that moment, my sister, Nadya, came in and invited everyone to dinner. . . . I stood to the side, by the wall. Anton Pavlovich, with a plate in his hand, came over to me and grasped one of my braids.

"I have never seen such braids as these," he said. I thought that he was treating me with such familiarity because I was indeed some kind of a Flora, a student. But if he had known about Misha and that I had a son who was almost a year old, then . . .

"Lydia also writes a bit," Sergei Nikolaevich informed Chekhov condescendingly.

Chekhov turned to me and smiled.

"At last I can tell you that I am not a maiden, or a Flora, or a student of Sergei Nikolaevich. He calls me that as a joke. I am Nadezhda Alexeevna's sister. Also, you might as well know that I am married and the mother of a family. And since I have to feed my child, I have to hurry home."

Sergei Nikolaevich heard what I said and yelled loudly over to me, "Maiden Flora, your family will come for you when they need you." "We live so close by," he explained to Anton Pavlovich [and then continued to me], "Sit down. That crybaby of yours is still asleep. Anton Pavlovich, do not let her go."

6. Avilova is referring to Chekhov's 1886 story "Heartache" ("Toska").

Anton Pavlovich bent over and looked into my eyes. He said, "So you have a son? That is very good."

Sometimes it is very difficult to explain or even to make sense of an event. In truth, nothing really happened. We simply gazed into each other's eyes. That was more than enough. It was as if a rocket had burst forth in my soul: bright, joyous, exultant, and ecstatic. I did not doubt for a minute that Anton Pavlovich experienced the same feelings, since we looked at each other with joy and surprise.

"I will come again," Anton Pavlovich said. "We will meet here. Give me everything that you have written or published. I want to read all of it with the utmost attention. Agreed?"

When I returned home, the nurse was swaddling Lyovushka, and he was whimpering and wrinkling his face, as if he were getting ready to cry.

Misha followed me into the nursery. "Take a look at yourself in the mirror," he said angrily. "Your face is all red, your hair is a mess. And what kind of style is this—wearing your hair in braids? You wanted to impress Chekhov. Lyovushka is crying, and you, a mother, are out flirting with a writer."

I knew that, for Misha, the word "writer" was synonymous with "windbag."

"Is Chekhov a writer?" I asked dryly.

I felt the light going out within me and that the unaccountable joy which had lit up my entire world so festively had humbly folded its wings. Everything was finished, everything was as previously. Why must life be light and beautiful? Who promised such a thing?

Chekhov talked openly about his work and his lonely life in a letter to Suvorin on May 4, 1889: "I have something of the psychopath in me. After all, it has already been two years running that I, for no reason whatsoever, have begun to dislike seeing my works in print. I have become indifferent to gossip, critical reviews, success and failure. I am also bored by conversations about literature and about big royalties and fees. In a word, I have become a complete jackass. My soul is somehow stagnant. The reason for this is my personal life."[7]

Three years passed since the time Chekhov first met Avilova.

"I often recalled him," Lydia Alexeevna writes, "and always with sadness that was melancholic and dreamy. By this time I already had three children: Lyova, Lodya, and my baby, Ninochka."

On January 1, 1892, Khudyakov celebrated the twentieth anniversary of the founding of his newspaper. [Avilova provides the following account of her interaction with Chekhov that day.]

---

7. Chekhov to Suvorin, May 4, 1889, *Pis'ma*, 5:203.

People were moving from the living room to the dining room along a stair-case coming from a foyer. . . . Suddenly I saw in the mirror two figures going up the stairs. I see them as clearly as if it happened yesterday: the unattractive head of Suvorin and, next to him, the young, sweet face of Chekhov. Chekhov had raised his right hand to throw back a lock of hair. His eyes were slightly skewed. . . . I recalled my first meeting with Anton Pavlovich, that unexplainable and unreal something that had suddenly brought us together. Would he recognize me? Would he recall our meeting? Would there again arise between us that closeness which had lit up my soul three years ago?

In the crowd we came across each other quite by accident and immediately extended our hands.

"I did not expect to see you," I said.

"But I did," he answered. "Let us sit together like we did the last time we met. Is that all right with you?"

Together we went into the living room.

"Shall I find us two seats?" he asked

"I do not think that we will be able to," I answered. "After all, you will be seated with all the important people, with the crème de la crème, in other words, close to the honoree."

"But it would be nice to sit here—in the corner, by the window. Don't you think so?"

"It would be nice, but I don't think that we will be allowed to do so."

"But I can be very stubborn," Chekhov said, laughing. "I won't let them have their way."

We sat down, laughing and daring each other to start a commotion.

"See how good things can be?" Anton Pavlovich said. "After all, when we met three years ago, we really did not get acquainted, but now, after a long separation, we have found each other again."

"Yes," I said with hesitation. "Our separation has been long. But does it not seem to you that our first meeting took place not in real life but in some far-off forgotten one?"

"But what were we to each other [in that forgotten life]?" Chekhov asked.

"Surely not husband and wife," I quickly answered.

We both burst out laughing.

"But [in that far-off life] we loved each other. What do you think? We were young. . . . And we both perished . . . in a shipwreck, perhaps?" Chekhov continued to fantasize.

"Yes, I seem to recall that it was something like that," I said, laughing.

"That's it. For a long time, we fought the waves. You were holding onto my neck."

"That is because I was completely beside myself. I did not know how to swim. It was my fault that you drowned."

79

"I am also not that good a swimmer. In all likelihood, I sank to the bottom and took you down with me."

"But now we again meet as friends."

"And will you still continue to trust me?"

"But how can I trust you?" I said in surprise. "After all, you did not save me. You were the reason why I drowned. . . ."

"How I once waited for you," I suddenly recalled [to Chekhov]. "When I was still living in Moscow . . . I was not married then."

"Why did you wait for me?" Anton Pavlovich asked in surprise.

"Because I wanted to meet you desperately, and my brother's friend, Popov, told me that he often saw you, that you were very nice, and that you would not refuse his request to visit us. But you never came."

"Tell this Popov of yours that I do not know him at all but that I consider him my worst enemy," Chekhov said in a serious tone of voice.

People began coming up to clink glasses. . . . Each time Anton Pavlovich got up, threw back his hair, and, having lowered his eyes, listened to the congratulations and well-wishing of the guests. Then he sat down with a sigh of relief.

"How old are you?" he asked suddenly.

"Twenty-eight."

"I am thirty-two. . . . What a pity."

"My husband keeps reminding me that I am no longer young. He always keeps adding the years. And so do I."

"So twenty-eight is no longer young?"

I saw [my husband] Misha heading toward me, and I immediately knew that he was not in a good mood.

"I am heading home," he said. "What about you?"

I said that I was staying.

"I understand," he said, but it seemed to me that I had to introduce him to Chekhov.

"This is my husband, Mikhail Fyodorovich," I began.

They shook hands. I was not surprised by the dry, almost hostile expression that appeared on Misha's face, but I was surprised by the way Chekhov was acting. He seemingly tried to smile, but a smile never appeared on his face.

When I got home, a storm was brewing. Misha did not care at all for my lively conversation with Chekhov at the dining table. He also did not like the fact that I was not sitting where I was supposed to be.

Avilova received letters from Anton Pavlovich secretly, at the post office, poste restante. She did so because she was afraid that a letter would arrive home when she was not there and that her husband would get hold of it at an inopportune time. But just the same, her husband knew of her correspondence with the writer, since Avilova sometimes gave him several of Chekhov's letters to read.

> "You see," I often told him, "'how useful these letters are to me. I follow his advice. . . .'"
> "I can well imagine what nonsense you must be writing to him. That is why I would like to read some of it. Let me take a look some time, won't you?"
> But I never did.

Chekhov's biographers will have to take Avilova's memoirs quite seriously.

[Avilova's account continues:]

> "Tell me something about your children," Chekhov said to me. "You come from good stock. It must be nice to have children of your own . . . to have a family."
> "You should get married."
> "Yes, I should get married. But I am not yet a free man. I am not married, but I do have a family. I have responsibilities."
> "Are you happy?" he asked me suddenly.
> Such a question caught me so unawares that it frightened me. I stopped and leaned my back against the piano, but he stood right in front of me.
> "Are you happy?" he repeated.
> "But what is happiness?" I replied in a perplexed type of way. "I have a good husband and good children. I have a family that I love. But if one does love—does that also mean that this person is happy?"

Suddenly someone said to her, "Lydia Alexeevna, you are being called home."

> "What has happened?" I cried out with a shudder.
> "It seems that Lyovushka has fallen ill. Anyuta has just come running over here."
> "Anton Nikolaevich, my dear. . . . I will not be coming back to say good-bye to you. Tell Nadya what has happened. Good-bye."
> I was shivering all over.
> He took my hand.
> "You should not get so upset. Perhaps it is nothing. These things always happen to children. . . . Calm down, I beg of you."
> He accompanied me down the staircase.
> [When I got home] Misha himself opened the door.
> "It is nothing, nothing at all," he began saying in an embarrassed type of way. "He is already asleep and it seems that he is not running a fever. But I

got worried without you being here. I don't know what to do when you are
not around. He kept asking for you. 'Where's Mama?' he kept saying. So you
see, Mother, we are all orphans without you."

He went with me into the nursery. My son did not have a fever.

"Do you have any idea how much you frightened me?" I asked him.

"Forgive me. Are you angry with me? . . . After all, I cannot live without
you. But do forgive me. Let's talk a bit. . . . After all, I spent the entire evening
without you."

But I knew right then and there that for the first time, absolutely, clearly,
and beyond a shadow of a doubt—I knew that I loved Anton Pavlovich.

It was Shrovetide, one of those rare Shrovetides in Petersburg where there
was neither thaw nor rain nor fog; the air was mild and white.

Avilova's husband had left for the Caucasus, and their home was quiet,
peaceful, and calm.

On Friday the Leikins were having guests, and she also had been invited. [Avilova writes:]

"I was afraid that you would not come," Praskovia Nikiforovna [Leikina] said
in a loud voice, "and that would have been a pity, a very great pity." She then
whispered, "People have been waiting for you," but still in such a loud way so
as to change the sound of her voice, not its intensity. . . .

Anton Pavlovich was in a very cheerful mood. He did not roar with laughter (he never did so); he did not raise his voice, but his unexpected remarks
made me laugh. He suddenly began envying the thick epaulets of some military officer, insisting that if he had such epaulets, he would be the happiest
man in the world.

"Oh how the women would love me then. There would be no end to those
who would fall in love with me. This I know for sure."

When people began getting up from the table, he said, "I would like to
take you home. Is that all right with you?"

We followed the crowd out onto the porch. . . . Fearing that all the cabbies
would be taken, I told Chekhov to hurry along. He quickly approached one
of the sleighs, sat down in it, and yelled over to me, "We're all ready to go."

I approached, but since Anton Pavlovich was sitting in the sleigh on the
side next to the sidewalk, I had to go around to get to the other side. I was
wearing a long cloak, and my hands were not free . . . since I was carrying my
purse, my opera glasses, and the train of my dress. My feet were getting stuck
in the snow, and I found it very difficult to move without help.

"Some cavalier you got there," Potapenko said, as he was leaving the affair.

"What was Potapenko yelling about a cavalier?" Chekhov asked. "Was he
talking about me? What kind of cavalier am I? I am a doctor after all. But how
am I at fault as a cavalier?"

"If you were a cavalier, would you have done what you did? You should first seat the lady and make sure she is comfortable; only then should you find a place for yourself."

"I really do not care for your condescending tone," Anton Pavlovich replied. "You are like an old woman when you grumble. Now if had I those epaulets . . ."

"What? Again those epaulets?"

"Here we go again. You are angry and grumbling anew. All because I did not carry the train of your dress."

"Listen here, Doctor. . . . I can barely find enough room as it is, and if you don't stop shoving your elbow into me, I am certainly going to fall out."

"You also have a nasty temper. If only I was wearing some thick epaulets."

"Will you be staying in town for long?" I asked.

"I plan to be here for a week. I think that we should see each other a bit more often, say, every day, perhaps? Is that all right with you?"

"Come by tomorrow evening," I blurted out without thinking. Anton Pavlovich was surprised.

"You mean, to your home?"

For some reason we were both silent for some time.

"Will there be a lot of people there?" Chekhov asked.

"On the contrary, there will be no one. Misha is in the Caucasus, and when he is gone, nobody visits me. . . . It will be just the two of us, so we can talk and talk."

"I will come without fail," Chekhov said in his wonderful bass voice which somehow sounded especially resonant in the vast and quiet expanse of the mild winter air. "I would like to persuade you to write a novel about how you were once in love with an officer."

"Who told you such a thing?"

"You yourself. A long time ago. Don't you remember? Are you going to argue with me about this, too?"

"Well, see you tomorrow."

"Yes. But you are not going to get angry at me again. You will be a bit kinder than the way you were today. A woman must be gentle and kind."

I had no idea what was in store for me.

Finally the evening arrived.[8]

I had begun to wait from nine o'clock on.

I had prepared a little cold dinner, along with vodka, wine, beer, and fruit. In the dining room, the table had been set for tea. I had intended first to drag Chekhov off to the nursery. "He will be jealous," I thought. "The children will not be asleep, but they will be on their way to bed and be especially charm-

---

8. Chekhov met Avilova at her home on February 13, 1895.

ing. That is their best time. Then we will go to tea. After that, we will head for the study where it will be much more comfortable than in the dining room. How many things do we have to tell each other there."

Soon after nine, the bell rang. Having put my hand to my heart, I waited a bit until [my servant] Masha opened the door and said something in reply to a question from my guest. Then I also went out into the vestibule and immediately froze in horror. Two people, a man and a woman, were taking off their coats. That meant that they were planning to stay for the entire evening. Even worse, they were the Sh.'s, acquaintances of Misha, whom he always had to force me to visit, since I disliked them so much. I positively could not stand their being here. Both of them were mathematicians who taught somewhere.

"Yes, yes, it's us, it's us!" Vera U. cried out. "Mikhail Fyodorovich is in the Caucasus, isn't he?"

"Why, this is quite a feast you have here," Vera U. exclaimed behind my back. "Were you expecting someone? Petya, [what a shame that] you and I had such an early dinner."

I played the hostess and kept putting food before them.

"This sauce is very tasty. Did you cook this? What? You did it yourself? But Mikhail Fyodorovich says that you do not like being a housewife, but that your talents lie more in the sphere of fantasy, of poetry."

The big clock in our dining room showed half past ten. It was clear that Anton Pavlovich was not coming. At this point, I was very glad for his absence.

Suddenly I heard the bell in the foyer and the voice of Anton Pavlovich. He was asking Masha about something.

"Are you all right?" Vera U. cried out to me. "Petya! Hurry up and get some water. . . . Lydia Alexeevna has taken ill."

"No, it is nothing," I said feebly. "Why do you think that I am sick?"

"You turned as white as chalk."

Anton Pavlovich entered and I introduced him to my guests.

The place suddenly became filled with laughter.

"What? You are Anton Pavlovich Chekhov?" Vera U. asked. "But Lydia Alexeevna did not warn us that she was expecting such a guest. . . . Well, now that you are here, Anton Pavlovich, you can answer all my questions which keep coming up every time I read your works. I really would like to know your opinions about things."

She fell on Chekhov like a lynx on a helpless deer. She got her claws into him, dragged him about, tore him to pieces, all the time laughing and exclaiming as she did. She accused him of wasting his talent on trifles, of beating around the bush, of not solving problems, and of not presenting ideals in his works. Everything he wrote, she continued, was vague, diffused, without mathematical precision.

[Vera said,] "No, there is nothing of the mathematician in your works. Ha, ha, ha."

Anton Pavlovich occasionally looked at me in a lost kind of way. . . . Unwillingly, he put up a weak defense, speaking only in monosyllables. He sat there next to his glass of tea, his eyes lowered.

But suddenly Sh. got up and said to his wife, "Vera, it's time we go home."

"Home?" she exclaimed. "But, Petya, when will I have another chance to tell Chekhov everything that he should hear? After all, he needs to understand his duty as a writer."

The door slammed shut, and Anton Pavlovich and I, exhausted, headed for the study.

"You are tired," Anton Pavlovich said. "I will leave. Your guests have worn you out."

What was going on inside of me? I could hardly speak.

"No, I beg you to stay."

"By the way . . . could you please give me what you promised? Your manuscript, together with the newspapers with your stories in them."

I had prepared everything beforehand and handed him a packet.

"I am so ashamed and embarrassed. Here I invited you as a guest, and I have nothing to say."

"You should go to bed," Chekhov said. "Your guests have tired you out. You are not quite yourself today, certainly not like before. . . . You will be glad when I leave. . . . Do you remember our first meetings? You want to know something? . . . I was genuinely attracted to you. It was really serious. I loved you. It seemed that there was no other woman in the entire world whom I could love as I did you. You were beautiful and touching; your youthfulness was so fresh and bright and charming. I loved and thought only of you. And, when I saw you again after a long separation, it seemed that you had become even more beautiful, and that you were different, someone new. I knew that I had to meet you again, to love you in a still greater and new way. I also knew that it would be even more difficult to be separated from you."

He was sitting on a couch with his head thrown back. I was sitting on an armchair directly across from him. He spoke quietly, as if giving full vent to his wonderful bass voice. But his face was severe, and his eyes were cold and demanding.

"Did you know all this?" he asked.

It was as though he was angry with me and reproaching me for having deceived him.

He took my hand but immediately let go of it. . . .

"Oh, what a cold hand," he said.

He then got up and looked at the clock.

"It is half past one."

My ears were ringing, and my mind was awhirl with thoughts, but I could not stop or seize or understand any of them. What was going on in my head? How tormenting it all was.

I got up with difficulty and went to see him off.

"So we will not see each other again," he repeated. I was silent and barely shook his hand.

We were living on the fourth floor. . . . I stood on the landing and watched him run down the stairs. When he reached the first landing, I called out to him, "Anton Pavlovich."

He stopped and raised his head. He waited for a while and then again took off.

I said nothing.

On the next day a delivery man presented me with a packet of my manuscripts, together with a letter and a book. The book was a newly published edition of Chekhov's stories, replete with this dry inscription: "To L. A. Avilova, from the author."[9]

After two tormenting days, I made a decision. At a jewelry store, I ordered a locket for a watch fob that I wanted to look like a book. On one side, I wrote, "Short novels and stories by An. Chekhov," and on the other, "Page 267, lines 6 and 7."

If he looked up these lines, he would read, "If you ever need my life, come and take it."[10]

When the fob was ready, I packed it up and sent it to my brother in Moscow. But before I did so, I grabbed hold of the packing and tore off the printed address of the store where I had purchased the locket in Petersburg. I then asked my brother to deliver it to the editorial offices of *Russian Thought*.[11]

My brother gave the package to [the editor] Gol'tsev and asked that it be forwarded to Anton Pavlovich.

All of the above I did with a sense of gloom and despair. I had torn off

---

9. As scholars point out, Avilova is mistaken about both the time and the nature of the deliveries. The facts are these. On the day after their meeting, Avilova received from Chekhov a letter, the contents of which were quite at variance with the avowals of love he had purportedly made the evening before.

"You are wrong to say that I was bored with you in an unconscionable way," Chekhov wrote to Avilova. "I was not bored, but I was a bit depressed at seeing how tired your face was because of your visitors" (Chekhov to Avilova, February 14, 1895, *Pis'ma*, 6:23).

10. Avilova is quoting a line from Chekhov's 1892 story "The Neighbors" ("Sosedi"). Interestingly, Chekhov did not like the story.

11. *Russian Thought* (*Russkaia mysl'*) was a moderate liberal and populist journal that was published in Moscow between 1880 and 1918.

the address of the store because I did not want to make an outright confession of my love. I also removed the address of the store because I thought that if Chekhov still had some lingering doubts about our relationship, I could made a hasty retreat. After all, how could I surrender my life to him! Such a decision would have immediately affected four lives: mine and those of my children. But would [my husband] Misha give them to me? And could Anton Pavlovich really take them?

There was not the slightest doubt that Anton Pavlovich received my gift. Worried and anxious, I awaited the consequences of my action. First it seemed to me that he would come. Then I thought that I would receive a letter from him, imagining what he would say in advance, even if it be a cold rebuke.

But time passed, and there came neither Chekhov nor a letter from him. There was simply nothing at all.[12]

How sick and tired I got of trying to sort out my thoughts.

But for me one thing was clear: there was nothing more obvious, natural, and even inevitable than my love for Chekhov.

Chekhov once said to me: "Your sense of right and wrong is both genuine and innate. That is a lot." He said such a thing apropos of our conversation as to whether it was fair or just that the wrong choice of a husband or a wife should ruin one's life. Some people said that justice and fairness had nothing to do with the issue and that since the church had blessed the union, it had to be strong and indissoluble. Others hotly countered such a view with all kinds of reasons to the contrary.

Chekhov was silent, but then he suddenly asked in a low voice: "And what is your view on the subject?"

I replied, "What does one need to know if it is worth it or not?"

"I do not understand," he replied, "If what is worth it? If the new feeling is worth all the sacrifice? . . . After all, there would have to be some sacrifice. First of all, there are the children. One need not feel sorry for oneself, but think about the victims. Only then does it become clear, if it is worth it or not."

Later, much later, I recalled this conversation and understood its

---

12. Chekhov never acknowledged receipt of the watch fob personally. In fact, he apparently thought so little of Avilova's gift that at one of the rehearsals for the premiere of *The Seagull* in 1896, he gave the thing to Vera Kommissarzhevskaya, who played the role of Nina. (In the play, Nina gives a similar object to Trigorin.)

When a year later Kommissarzhevskaya asked him what she should do with the item, Chekhov replied that when she tired of the watch fob, she should send it back to him at Melikhovo.

great significance for me; for it was then that Anton Pavlovich said to me, "Your sense of right and wrong is genuine. That is a lot."

But was it really enough for him to love someone? He, his very self!

Chekhov never mentioned my gift. Our correspondence came to an end. I had to go on living without him.

Avilova accompanied her brother, Alexei, to a masquerade[13] which she later described so wonderfully that it would do justice to any great writer. As I see it, Alexei knew that Chekhov would be at this affair but concealed it from his sister.

"I am so glad to see you," Avilova said in an altered voice as she approached Chekhov.

"You do not know who I am. After all, I am wearing a mask," he answered, looking at her attentively.

She trembled with excitement and surprise. Without saying a word, Chekhov took her by the arm and led her around the ballroom. Fearful that Nemirovich-Danchenko and others would recognize her, he suggested that they move to a side room.

"And do you know who I am? Who? Tell me!" she said.

She tore her hand from his and stopped. He smiled.

"Do you know that my play will soon be performed onstage?" he replied, not answering her question.

"I know. It is *The Seagull*."

"Yes, *The Seagull*. Will you be there on opening night?"

"Absolutely."

"Once you are there, you must be very attentive, since I will answer your question from the stage. Pay strict attention. Do not forget."

He again took her hand and pressed it to himself.

"How will you answer me?"

"In many ways. But follow the play and remember everything that will be going on."

"I do not understand," Avilova said. "Are you laughing at me? How can you tell me something from the stage? How will I understand which words are meant precisely for me? After all, you do not know who I am."

"You will understand."

"It is hot in here!" She went up to the mirror. "I want to powder my nose. I will turn around and take off my mask."

Chekhov sat down with his back to Avilova.

---

13. The masquerade took place on January 27, 1896, almost a year after the supper at Avilova's home.

She followed his movements in the mirror. He did not move and she did not take off her mask.

They then sat down side by side, drinking as they did so.

Everything in Avilova's memoirs is written so charmingly. . . . Her head was spinning slightly. Her heart was first beating hard; then it stopped altogether. She looked into Chekhov's face and said, "I love you. You, you. . . . It seems that not a single hour goes by without my thinking of you. When I saw you, I could not take my eyes off of you. My happiness was so great that it was almost unbearable. Do you believe me? My darling one!"

"But I do not know who you are. You are wearing a mask."

The Soviet biographer, Kotov, after having read Avilova's confession (everything that I have cited here), states in his introduction that the relationship between Chekhov and Avilova arose primarily because he was interested in her as a writer who focused on the dependent situation of women. Émigré literary scholars, God love them, simply have never paid any attention to Avilova's memoirs.

So what did Lydia Alexeevna hear when she went to the opening night of *The Seagull*?

"It is very difficult," she writes, "to describe the feeling that I had when I saw and listened to everything that was happening onstage."

[At one point in the play] Nina comes out to bid farewell to Trigorin. She hands him a pendant, explaining, "I had this engraved with your initials on one side and, on the other, the title of your book."

"What a splendid gift," Trigorin says, kissing the pendant.

Nina leaves . . . and Trigorin, looking at it, turns the pendant over and reads, "page 121, lines 11 and 12." He repeats these numbers twice; then he asks Arkadin, who has just come in, "Are there any of my books in this house?"

The book already in his hands, Trigorin repeats, "page 121, lines 11 and 12." When he finds the lines, he reads them quietly, but attentively, "If you ever need my life, come and take it."

From the very moment when Nina gave the pendant to Trigorin onstage, something strange happened to Avilova. At first, she froze. Barely breathing, she lowered her head because it seemed to her that everyone in the auditorium had turned to her as one person and was now looking at her straight in the face. There was a ringing in her ears; her heart was pounding like crazy. But she did not miss the reference, nor did she forget it later: "page 121,

lines 11 and 12." The numbers were different from the ones that she had ordered to be inscribed on the locket for Chekhov. "Without a doubt, he had
answered me from the stage," Avilova writes, "and that answer was meant
only for me."

Since Chekhov's book was in the bookcase in her home, it was easy for her to
find it and read it. But she had to take tea, eat some ham, listen to Misha, and
answer him whenever he spoke to her. But what was there in the book? On
page 121, lines 11 and 12! Oh, if she could only get to it as soon as possible!

She went into the study with a candle in her hands. She hurriedly
found the book, turned to page 121, and counted down the lines. She read:
"What phenomena are there in life! But why are you looking at me with such
ecstasy? Do you like me?"

Totally puzzled, she reread the lines.

"To go to bed," Avilova writes, "this was something I simply could
not do.

"But it was as if my consciousness was struck by lightning. I had chosen lines from his book. Was it possible that he had chosen lines from mine?

"Misha had long been asleep. I jumped up and ran back into the study.
I found my little book, *The Happy Man*,[14] and there on page 121, lines 11
and 12, I read: 'Young girls should not go to masquerades.'[15]

"So this was his answer! He had guessed at everything, he knew
everything."

Suvorin's theater was performing a play in translation.

During the intermission . . . Avilova caught sight of Anton Pavlovich. . . .
When he saw her, he quickly stepped forward to meet her and took her by the
arm.

"The play is boring," he said hurriedly. "Don't you think so? It is not
worth watching it until the end. I could take you home. You are alone, aren't
you?"

"Please do not do anything on my account," she answered. "If you
leave, you will upset Suvorin."

Anton Pavlovich frowned.

"You are angry with me. But where and when can I talk to you? I have
to do so."

"What would you think about the street as the best possible place?"

"Just tell me: where and when?"

14. Avilova first published *The Happy Man* (*Schastlivets*) in 1893.
15. In other words, Chekhov is telling Avilova that it is improper for a young married woman
to abandon her family and run off with him.

The doors of the box opened and in stepped Suvorin.

"Everyone is looking for you. Go to your seat quickly," she said. She burst out laughing and quickly went down the corridor.

"It seems clear that I have gotten over my illness," she told herself.

She wanted to go into the auditorium but changed her mind. She went to the cloakroom, got her coat, and left. The wind was coming up in gusts and preventing her from walking.

"Everything I said and did just now was so amazingly clever!" she reproached herself. "I have gotten over him all right! . . . Good God, how miserable I am! He wanted to talk to me. About what? 'I have to do so,' he told me. . . . And what did I do? Did I insult him again?"

She thought a bit and decided sadly, "No, he understood everything. He understands everything, he knows everything . . . and he finds it all very difficult."

On March 18, 1897, Chekhov wrote to Avilova, "Dear Lydia Alexeevna, I know that you are angry with me but that, in any case, you also wish me well. Nonetheless, I still would very much like to see you. I will be in Moscow before March 26th."[16]

She sent to him her Moscow address, and on the 23rd, she received a note from a delivery man there: "Saturday, the hotel 'Moscow,' Room No. 5.

"I arrived in Moscow earlier than I had planned. When can we see each other? The weather is foggy and dank. As I am not feeling too well, I will try to stay inside. Can you visit me, without waiting for me to visit you? Wishing you all the best. Yours, Chekhov."

[Avilova writes,] I immediately wrote back that I would be at his place that evening.

Just as I had promised in my letter, I entered the hotel "Moscow" at 8:00 P.M.

The doorman took my coat, and I began walking up the stairs.

Suddenly the doorman called out after me, "Whom are you looking for?"

"Chekhov."

"He is not at home. He has gone out."

"It cannot be! Perhaps he just gave orders that no one visit him? He is not feeling well. He wrote me that."

16. In his letter, Chekhov continued: "Change your anger to mercy and agree to have dinner or supper with me. Really, it would be lovely [if you would come]. I will not fail you no matter what happens. Only ill health could keep me at home." Chekhov to Avilova, March 18, 1897, *Pis'ma*, 6:307.

"I do not know anything about this. Only that he is not in. He took off this morning with Suvorin."

I stood on the staircase, totally confused.

Then a servant came out running.

"No one believes me when I tell them that Anton Pavlovich is not at home," the doorman told him.

"But I have an appointment with him. I wrote to him and . . ."

"Letters and notes have been piling up all morning," the doorman said.

I quickly ran down the stairs. On a glass table lay a pile of mail. I quickly went through it, found my letter, and squeezed it in my hand.

The next day, Avilova's brother, Alyosha, came by and told her that Anton Pavlovich had become so seriously ill that he had been taken to the hospital.

On the morning of the 25th, she received a note.

"Monday. Here is my criminal curriculum vitae. On Friday night I began spitting up blood. The next morning I left for Moscow. At six o'clock Suvorin and I went to the Hermitage restaurant to have dinner. I had barely sat down when my throat began bleeding in a serious way. Suvorin took me to the 'Slavyansky Bazaar.'[17] The doctors there examined me, and I had to stay in bed for more than twenty-four hours. Now I am back at the hotel 'Moscow.' Yours, A. Chekhov."[18]

[Avilova continues:]

About three o'clock on Tuesday, Alyosha and I went to the reception room of the hospital where we were met by a woman in white.

"Excuse me, ma'am . . . my sister would like to see Chekhov," Alyosha said.

The woman's face became filled with horror; she raised her arms and shoulders.

"That is impossible! Absolutely impossible! Anton Pavlovich is extremely weak. Perhaps only Maria Pavlovna will be allowed to see him."

"Maybe we can talk to the doctor?"

"To the doctor? That will not do anything."

17. The "Slavyansky Bazaar" was one of the best hotels in Moscow; it opened in 1872 and closed in 1917.

18. A second hemorrhage had forced Chekhov to a clinic run by Dr. Alexei Ostroumov, a specialist in pulmonary disorders. It should also be noted that for the first time, Chekhov acknowledged his illness in an open and frank way.

"To calm our patients," he told Suvorin, "we usually tell them that their coughing is due to some upset of the stomach and that when they have a discharge of blood, it is of a hemorrhoidal

When the doctor came in, he immediately announced, "No, you cannot see Anton Pavlovich. There is no way I can let you see him."

"In that case, would you please tell him that I received his note today . . . and that I came to see him, but that I was not allowed in."

"You received a note today? But he took sick three days ago."

I took the note out and handed it to him.

"He wrote this yesterday."

The doctor frowned but did not take the letter.

"Wait here," he said, leaving quickly.

"You see? They will let you in . . . ," Alyosha said.

Lydia Alexeevna's younger brother, Alexei Alexeevich Strakhov, a musician, adored his sister. I met him later in emigration, as he visited us at "Belvedere."[19] Unfortunately, I then did not know about the tie between Chekhov and his sister. Equally regrettable, Alyosha is no longer alive.

[Avilova continues:]

When the doctor returned, he first looked at me in an attentive way; then he shook his head and spread his hands in a gesture of hopelessness.

"What can I do?" he said. "Anton Pavlovich is demanding to see you. Are you in Moscow for a visit? . . . Does that mean that even though he was sick, he came here from the village in such weather just to see you?"

"Suvorin was also coming here," I started to say.

"Oh, that makes a lot of sense. You mean to tell me that he risked his life to see Suvorin? The fact of the matter is, madam, that Anton Pavlovich is dangerously ill, and that any kind of excitement would be a disaster for him. I bear no responsibility for what may happen. That is the way it will be."

I was completely at a loss.

"What should I do? Leave?"

---

origin. But no cough is ever caused by a condition of the stomach, and a discharge of blood is always from the lungs. My blood is coming from my right lung as it did with my brother and another relative of mine who also died of consumption." See Suvorin's diary entry dated March 24, 1897, in A. Suvorin, *Dnevnik Alekseia Sergeevicha Suvorina,* 286 (see introduction, n. 42).

Sister Masha was also under no illusions as to her brother's illness. "At the clinic I was taken to a special ward," she recalled in her memoirs. "Anton lay on his back. He was forbidden to talk. After exchanging greetings with him, I went up to the table to conceal my agitation. On it was a drawing of lungs. They were drawn with a blue pencil, except for the upper parts which were colored in red. I knew what it meant." Maria Chekhova, *Iz dalekogo proshlogo,* 164–65 (see chap. 3, n. 16).

19. "Belvedere" was the name of Bunin's summer villa in Grasse in southwestern France.

"You cannot do that now. He is waiting for you and all excited. So what can we do? Let us go see him."

We began climbing the stairs.

"No matter what he says—you are not to say a word! It would be harmful for him if you do so. Remember: any kind of conversation, any kind of excitement will cause him to start bleeding again. I am giving you three minutes, that is all."[20]

"Come this way," he added softly. "Do not worry, it will be all right. . . . You, too, have to remain calm. I will be back in three minutes."

Chekhov was lying there alone. He was on his back with his head turned to the door.

"How kind of you to come," he said quietly.

"Oh, you must not talk!" I interrupted him, my voice filled with fear. "Are you suffering? Are you in pain anywhere?"

He smiled and showed me a chair alongside his bed.

"I only have three minutes," I said and took the clock from his table. He took it from me but also held my hand.

"Tell me, would you have come to visit me in the hotel, if I had been well?"

"To visit you? But I already did so, my dear."

"You were there?!"

"Please do not talk! You really must not."

"I am weak," he whispered.

"What should I talk to you about so that you will keep quiet?"

"Are you leaving today?"

"No, tomorrow."

"So that means you can come again tomorrow without fail. I will be waiting for you. Will you come?"

"Of course I will come."

The doctor came in and smiled kindly at Chekhov.

"It is time, Anton Pavlovich. We do not want to tire you."

"One more minute. . . . Lydia Alexeevna! I have a request."

The doctor held up a warning finger as if to silence him. He then gave Chekhov a piece of paper and a pencil. Anton Pavlovich wrote, "Get my proofs[21] for me from Gol'tsev at *Russian Thought*. Also, bring me something of yours to read and something else besides."

When I read what he had written, he took his note back and added, "I very much lov . . . am grateful to you." He had crossed out "lov" and smiled.

---

20. It should be noted that only Chekhov's sister Maria was allowed to come and go as she pleased. The other exception was Tolstoy, who harangued Chekhov with lectures on literature and life for more than thirty minutes but whom no one dared ask to leave.

21. The proofs were for Chekhov's story "The Peasants."

I said good-bye and went to the door.

Suddenly Anton Pavlovich called out to me.

"Lydia Alexeevna! You look just like an actress on tour!" he said loudly.

"It's the dress. It's something from 'The Seagull,'" I said, laughing.

The doctor was getting upset.

"Anton Pavlovich! You yourself are a doctor. . . . If you are worse tomorrow, I will not let anyone in to see you. No one!"

As Alyosha and I were walking back, I constantly wiped the tears that were pouring down my face.

When I got home, two telegrams were waiting for me. One said: "I hope to see you on the 27th. We miss you very much." The other: "Leave right away. We await you with kisses."

On the next morning there was a third missive: "Send me a telegram, telling me when you are leaving Moscow. I await your return."

I headed for the editorial office of *Russian Thought* to get the proofs from Gol'tsev.

When he found out that I had been at the hospital, he began asking about Chekhov's health. Then he called in two or three other people.

"Here is some new news about Anton Pavlovich."

"It's too bad that it is spring," someone said. "Yesterday the ice broke on the river. This is the most dangerous time for sick people."[22]

"I heard that he is in a very bad way, that his illness is dangerous," someone else added.

"Does that mean that visitors are allowed to see him?"

"No, no," Gol'tsev said. "Lydia Alexeevna will give him our regards and best wishes. Tell him that there is no rush with the proofs. He should not tire himself out."

I left the editorial office in great distress. Anton Pavlovich seemed to me to be a dying man, and here everyone was bringing up the river and saying that this was the "most dangerous time to be ill" and that he was in a very bad way. . . . I felt that everyone saw him as already gone.

---

22. In his diary, Suvorin also makes mention of the breaking ice. When he visited Chekhov in the clinic, the writer was, as usual, denying the gravity of his illness, "laughing and jesting . . . while spitting blood into a large vessel." When Suvorin, hoping to take Chekhov's mind off his illness, mentioned that ice floes had begun to break up on the Moscow River, Chekhov's face clouded immediately. He responded, "When a peasant has consumption, he says, 'There is nothing I can do. I will go off in the spring with the melting of the snows.'" See Suvorin's diary excerpt, written on March 26, 1897, in Suvorin, *Dnevnik Alekseia Sergeevicha Suvorina*, 288.

Chekhov continued to believe, though, that despite his lungs, he still had years to live. "I shall buy a dressing gown," he told Suvorin on April 1, 1897, "and bask in the sun. I will eat and eat." Chekhov to Suvorin, April 1, 1897, *Pis'ma*, 6:320.

It was too early to go to the hospital. The people there would not have let me in before two, and so I went to the river.

When I reached the bridge, I went up to the railing and looked down. The ice was spotty. In some places, it had covered the river completely; but in others, it was gone almost altogether. The day was sunny, somehow particularly blue and sparkling; but at the same time, I saw it as menacing, not unlike the turbulent, restless river which was rushing under the bridge. Huge blocks of ice rushed by, spun around, and were carried off into the distance. To me it seemed that the river was running faster and faster, making me slightly dizzy.

The picture was one of things being sharpened, broken, and carried away. Life, too, was rushing by like a river; it, too, was being cut sharp, broken, torn from its roots, and carried away. "This is the most dangerous time. . . . Anton Pavlovich is doing poorly, very poorly!"

I suddenly recalled the seal which he had been using on his letters recently. The small red circle of the sealing wax was inscribed with these words: "The lonely one sees a desert everywhere he goes."

"I lived happily until I reached thirty," Chekhov once told me.

After thirty, did life overpower him? Did it break him?

Life! Could it satisfy an individual like Chekhov? Could it but not poison his soul with bitterness and hurt?

No sooner did he look around him with a serious and demanding air than he began to feel as though he were in a desert, that he had indeed become a lonely man.

I went to buy flowers. Anton Pavlovich had written: ". . . and something else besides." So I thought that flowers would be this "something else."

I got to the hospital in the nick of time. A nurse met me.

"No, Anton Pavlovich is not getting any better," she replied in answer to my question. "He hardly slept at all last night. In fact, he keeps spitting up more and more blood."

"Does that mean that I will not be allowed to see him?"

"I asked the doctor and he said that it was all right to let you in."

The nurse obviously found my presence annoying, since she kept looking at me with disapproving looks.

I tore off the thin paper wrapping from the bouquet of flowers.

"Oh, no!" the nurse exclaimed. "You cannot bring them with you! Surely you must understand that such sweet-smelling flowers in the ward of such a sick patient will . . ."

I became frightened.

"Well, if I cannot bring them with me, I will leave them here with you."

She smiled.

"On second thought, as long as you have brought them, you might as well show them to him."

When I entered the ward, I saw those same gentle, summoning eyes.

He took the bouquet in both of his hands and hid his face in them.

"These are my favorite flowers," he whispered. "How nice the roses and lilies of the valley look."

The nurse said, "But, Anton Pavlovich, there is no way that you can have such things in here. The doctor will not allow it."

"I myself am a doctor," Chekhov said. "And I say that I can have them! Put them in some water, please."

The nurse again threw a hostile glance at me and left.

"You are late," Anton Pavlovich said and weakly squeezed my hand.

"No, I was here. But they would not let me in until two o'clock. It is two now."

"It is now seven minutes past two, my dear. Seven minutes! And I was waiting and waiting."

"You should not be talking!" I interrupted him.

"When are you leaving?"

"Today."

"Oh, no! Stay one more day. Come and visit me tomorrow, I am begging you!"

I got out all three telegrams and gave them to him to read. He read them and reread them for a long time.

"I still think that you can stay one more day."

"This 'come home soon' distresses me. Perhaps my children have taken ill?"

"I am sure that they are fine. Stay one more day for me. For me," he repeated.

I said quietly, "Anton Pavlovich! I cannot."

Thoughts were racing through my head in a chaotic way.

"Well, if you cannot, you cannot," Anton Pavlovich said.

But I was certain that he again knew and understood everything. [He knew] about Mitya's jealousy and my fear that my husband would find out.

That night on the train home, she did not sleep. She could not get over how she was feeling.

On the 29th she received a letter from Anton Pavlovich:

"Your flowers are not dead but keep getting prettier and prettier. My colleague-doctors here have allowed me to keep them on the table. Generally speaking, you are kind, very kind, and I do not know how to thank you.

"I have to stay here until Easter. So that means that I will not be in Petersburg any time soon. But I am feeling better and spitting up less and less blood."

"I often remember one of Chekhov's stories," Avilova recalled. "The one he called 'A Little Joke.'"[23]

The story goes like this: It is a wintry day. A young man and young woman are sledding on an icy hill. Every time they race downward with the wind in their ears, the woman hears, "I love you, Nadya."

But perhaps she only thought she heard such a thing?

They again climb up the hill and get on the sleigh. But the sleigh rushes off the edge and flies into the air. . . . Again she hears, "I love you."

But the brief moment [between Chekhov and Avilova] passed. Everything became usual, routine; Anton Pavlovich's letters were indifferent and cold.

She awaited the August 1898 issue of *Russian Thought* with great anticipation. With Chekhov's letters, Avilova had grown accustomed to reading things between the lines. Now it seemed to her that he had especially sought her attention to the August issue and that he wanted her to read it as soon as possible.

So as soon as the issue came out, I bought it but did not take it to the library as I usually did.

The title alone—"About Love"—excited me greatly. I ran home with the issue in my hands, guessing about its contents all along the way. I had no doubt that "About Love" had something to do with me, but what could Chekhov have written?

Sitting at the desk in Misha's study, I cut the pages of the book and began reading it.

In this story, a character named Luganovich invites another character, Alexin, to his home. Luganovich's wife, Anna Alexeevna, makes an appearance. She has recently given birth to a son. Beautiful and young, she is introduced to Alexin as "Anna Alexeevna Luganovich" and makes a striking impression on him. I also had a little boy when I first met Anton Pavlovich.

I suddenly recalled [Chekhov saying], "Doesn't it seem to you that when we first met, we did not become acquainted, but that we found each other after a long separation?"

This is what Anton Pavlovich had asked me at his jubilee dinner.

I continued reading, greedy and impatient for more.

23. Chekhov's "A Little Joke" ("Shutochka") appeared in 1886.

[Alexin says,] "I never felt that I had the time to even think about the city [I visited], but the memory of that slender, fair-haired woman has stayed with me to this day. I keep thinking about her as if a light shadow had fallen on my soul."

A page later, after a second meeting, Alexin continues, "I was unhappy. Whether I was at home, in a field, or in a shed, I kept thinking of her."

Heavy tears began to fall on the paper, and I quickly kept wiping my eyes so that I could continue to read.

[Alexin continues,] "We talked for a long time, then we fell silent. But we never admitted our love for each other; shy and jealous, we kept our feelings a secret. We were afraid of anything that could reveal this secret even to our very selves. I loved tenderly, deeply, but I was also thinking and asking myself where could our love lead, and if we had enough strength to fight our feelings for each other. To me it seemed unlikely that my sad and burdensome love would, suddenly and rudely, interrupt the happy flow of life that had enveloped her husband, children, and household. . . . Would it even be honest to do such a thing? . . . What would happen to her if I became sick and died?

"She, apparently, was having similar thoughts. She was thinking of her husband and children."

I was no longer crying but sobbing, almost choking as I did so. So he did not blame me; he even justified my actions, understanding and grieving along with me.

[Alexin continues,] "I felt that she was close to me, that she was mine, and that we could not be without each other."

"In her final years," Avilova continued to read, "Anna Alexeevna showed a different side to her character. She was strangely irritated with me; no matter what I said, she never agreed with me. Whenever I dropped something, she would say coldly, 'Congratulations.'"

Of course, I remembered that I had "congratulated" him when he had dropped his hat into the mud. Most likely, he had wanted to push back a strand of his hair with his hand, but he had pushed his hat off instead.

[Alexin continues,] "I understood then when one loves another, one's musings about this love must proceed from the sublime, from something more important than the mundane notions of happiness or unhappiness, virtue or vice; otherwise, one should not muse about love at all."

Reading the book to the end, I lay my head on it.

The notion that musings about love had to proceed from some "sublime" and that they were more important than virtue or vice, happiness or unhappiness, was something that I did not understand. I knew and understood only one thing: life had me in its clutches, and I could not break free of its vicelike hold. If my family had prevented me from being happy with Anton Pavlovich, Anton Pavlovich had prevented me from being happy with my family.

The excerpt from the story "About Love" did not render the piece in its entirety, but it sheds light on Avilova's relationship with Chekhov. [Avilova writes:]

[Alexin continues,] "I was unhappy. Whether I was at home, in the fields, in a shed, I was thinking about her. I tried to understand why a young, clever, and beautiful woman had married a boring man . . . and borne his children. I also tried to comprehend the hold that this boring man had on her. . . . [I tried to figure out] why she had met him, not me, and why this terrible mistake had happened to us.

"Arriving in town, I kept seeing in her eyes that she had been waiting for me. Indeed, she herself had confessed to me that from that morning on, she had had a special feeling and had guessed that I would come."

[Avilova continues:] I grabbed a piece of paper and wrote a letter to Anton Pavlovich. I did not think about what I was writing. So as not to change my mind, I immediately went out and dropped the letter in a mailbox. But on the way back, I immediately regretted what I had done. My letter to him was not kind.

After several days, I received an answer.

Dated August 30 and written at Melikhovo, Chekhov wrote:

I am going first to the Crimea, then to the Caucasus. When it gets cold there, I will go somewhere abroad. That means I will be coming to St. Petersburg.

I really hate to leave here. Indeed, the mere thought of departing from my home makes my hands fall to my side and kills any desire I have for work. It seems to me that if I could spend this winter either in Moscow or in St. Petersburg and live in a nice warm apartment, I would be cured completely.

This wandering life, especially in wintertime—winter abroad is particularly repulsive—has really thrown me for a loop.

You are unfair in your judgments of the bee. A bee first sees bright and beautiful flowers; only later does it make honey.[24]

As regards everything else—the indifference, the boredom, the fact that talented people live and love only their own images and fantasies in the world—I can say only this: the soul of another is a mystery.

24. Furious that she had been cast as a heroine in one of Chekhov's stories, Avilova had compared Chekhov to a bee gathering honey, heedless of the damage it may be doing to the flower.

The weather is ghastly: damp and cold.
I grasp your hand firmly. Wishing you health and happiness.

Yours,
Chekhov[25]

Yes, his loneliness was great. He knew everything about his disease; he loved
Avilova and feared for her. He wanted to protect her, but he did not want to
destroy her family, for he knew what kind of mother she was.

In mid-April 1899, Chekhov arrived in Moscow. Avilova wrote to him that
she would be traveling through there on May 1.
"I will still be in Moscow on May 1st," he answered her. "Will you
come from the station and drink some coffee with me? If your children are
with you, bring them along. . . ."
But it was not easy for her to visit Chekhov with her family. She only
had about two hours between trains. She also had to feed her children and
to arrange a separate compartment on the train for them. It simply was not
worth her going anywhere for only a quarter of an hour. This is exactly what
she wrote to Anton Pavlovich. But no sooner had Avilova and her children
finished breakfast at the station than they caught sight of Anton Pavlovich,
who was walking all around, trying to find them. He had a package with him.
"Look at the caramels that I have brought you," he said, after he had greeted
them. "They are called 'writers' candies.' Do you think that you and I will
ever be accorded such an honor?"
[Avilova replied, sifting through the candies,] "The wrapping around
each candy has a picture of Turgenev, Tolstoy, Dostoevsky . . .
"Your picture is not here," she said. "That's strange. But do not worry.
It will be."
Anton Pavlovich called the children over to himself and sat Ninochka
on his knee.
"Why does this one remind me of a schoolteacher?" he asked.
"Why a schoolteacher?"
[Avilova recalled in her memoir,] "But he kept running his fingers

25. More ironic, perhaps, is Chekhov's letter to Avilova on April 29, 1892, in which he com-
plains of just such a situation. "Can you imagine it?" he wrote. "An acquaintance of mine, a
woman of forty-two, recognized herself as the twenty-two-year-old heroine of my story 'The
Grasshopper,' and everyone in Moscow is accusing me of libel" (Chekhov to Avilova, April 29,
1892, Pis'ma, 5:58).
    It is of further interest to note that critics have seen Avilova also a prototype for Anna
Sergeevna in "A Lady with a Dog" ("Dama s sobachkoi") and Masha in Three Sisters (Tri sestry). See A. Rachmanova, Ein Kurzer Tag: das Leben des Arztes und Schriftstellers Anton
Pawlowitsch Tschechow, trans. A. Von Hoyer (Frauenfield: Huber, 1961), 304, 336.

through her fair curls and looking into her big gray eyes so affectionately that I was filled with motherly pride. Ninochka laid her little head on his shoulder and smiled."

"Children like me," he said.

A porter came by and announced that Avilova and her children could take their seats.

"We were about to begin walking," Avilova writes, "when I noticed that his coat was open. As his hands were full, I stopped him and began buttoning up his coat." [She continues:]

"That is how people get colds," I said.

"And that is how people always remind me that I am sick and good-for-nothing. Can anyone ever let me forget such a thing? Under any circumstances, whatsoever?"

"And here I am in good health, but I barely managed to convince you to write to Maria Pavlovna to send you some warm clothes. You can worry that I do not catch cold, but I cannot?"

"Why are we arguing, my dear?" Anton Pavlovich asked, smiling.

"You are not in a good mood today," I answered; and, laughing, I added, "but I see you are wearing new shoes."

"They are not new at all," Anton Pavlovich objected in a very angry type of way.

We were walking along the platform.

"You know, we have known each other ten years already," Chekhov said. "Yes, ten years. We were young then."

"And are we really so old now?"

"You—no. But I am worse than an old man. Old men go on living, where they want to, how they want to. They live to enjoy themselves. But I am tied down by disease in everything I do."

"But you are feeling better."

"You yourself know how I am improving."

Then, in a sudden burst of animation, he said, "You know, it often seems to me that I can get well and recover completely. Do you think that such a thing is possible? Can it really be that my life is over?"

From the window of the compartment I saw the faces of my three small children, nodding and laughing.

"Let's get into the train car," Anton Pavlovich suggested. "It is not enough that you have a difficult temper, but you are also careless and flighty. Your clothes really upset me. How could you go horseback riding, dressed like that? How far could you go in that getup?"

The children were so happy that we were together, it was as though we had not seen each other in a long time.

Anton Pavlovich again called Ninochka over to him and set her on his knee. My son handed a book to Anton Pavlovich.

"I bought this here at the kiosk. Have you read it?"

Anton Pavlovich took the book and began leafing through it.

"I have read it," Anton Pavlovich told my son in a very serious way. "It is an edition of Pushkin. It is a very good book."

Lodya's face was shining.

"It is poetry. Do you like poetry, Anton Pavlovich?"

"Yes, I like Pushkin's poetry very much."

We heard the bell ringing. Anton Pavlovich rose to his feet.

I suddenly remembered the way Alekhin said good-bye to Luganovich right before the train departed: "I embraced her, she snuggled up to my chest." . . . I suddenly felt my heart beating; it was as though something had hit me on the head.

I saw how Anton Pavlovich said good-bye to the children. But he did not say good-bye to me at all. He merely walked out into the corridor. I went out after him. He turned around suddenly, and, looking at me in a severe, cold, and almost angry type of way, he said, "Even if you get sick, I will not come and see you. I am a good doctor, but my fees are very high. . . . You could not afford me. So it seems that we will not be seeing each other again."

He quickly shook my hand and left.

"Mama, Mama," my children were shouting. "Hurry up, hurry up."

The train had already started to move slowly. I saw the figure of Anton Pavlovich float past the window, but he did not look back.

How could I know that this would be the last time I would see him . . .

On that cold, spring, moonlit night, nightingales were singing in our garden. There were several of them. When the one closest to our home fell silent, the others who were farther away could be heard in the distance. The crystal sound of their chirping and the transparent purity of their modulations made the air seem more fresh and streamlike. I was standing on the open step of our balcony, covered with a shawl and looking into the distance where the stars sparkled over the tops of the bare trees.

Even in this warm shawl I was cold. There was no wind at all, but the air kept moving in waves, making the warbles of nightingales sound like crystal icy springs.

It would be difficult to describe nighttime any better than this. What restraint—to write about her feelings without saying a word about herself!

Chapter Seven

AFTER WE LEFT MOSCOW, we could not get any information on the fate of Lydia Alexeevna Avilova. In mid-November 1922, when we were living in Paris, we received a letter from Czechoslovakia. Having glanced at the last page, I saw the signature: L. Avilova. I found it strange that the letter had been directed to the address used by our relatives who wrote to us from Russia. In those years, we lived almost exclusively for what was going on in our homeland, in concern and fear for the fate of our relatives and loved ones. With trepidation, we read Avilova's letter.

A great many years have passed since Lydia Alexeevna departed from this earth. Now, after having read her memoirs, I decided to publish excerpts from her letters to me.

Lydia Alexeevna went to Czechoslovakia to be with her ill daughter, the very same Ninochka who had charmed me in Moscow and who had sat on the lap of Anton Pavlovich when he last saw Avilova at the train station.

I publish these letters of Lydia Alexeevna Avilova with considerable abbreviations.

November 10, 1922

Dear Ivan Alexeevich and Vera Nikolaevna,

Since I left Russia exactly one month ago,[1] I have had this terrible urge to contact you. But perhaps the feeling is not mutual. Right before I left, I

1. Although rules of entry and exit had been fashioned by the new Soviet state in late December 1917, the political and economic situation there allowed considerable leeway for Russians on both sides of the border.

   Mass emigration from the USSR became possible only from 1920, when the Bolsheviks fashioned agreements with other countries both on options for citizenship and on exchanges of prisoners of war, refugees, hostages, internees, and the like. The Bolsheviks refused to recognize that individuals wished to leave the homeland for political reasons; so the only way people

visited [Vera's mother] Lydia Fyodorovna [Muromtseva]. She is doing very well and has changed but little. . . . It happened that I arrived there just when people were celebrating the [seventieth] birthday of [Vera's father] Nikolai Andreevich [Muromtsev]. There were many guests, and I did not want to go in. But everyone there literally dragged me in for a piece of the birthday cake. Perhaps because I refused and ran off, I must have seemed awkward and impolite. I cannot talk to people whom I do not know very well. I particularly fear anyone who is cheerful and lively. Lydia Fyodorovna made me feel very ashamed for the way I was acting. She thought that my spirits were down. Perhaps so, but I did not have the slightest idea of what lay ahead of me.

I . . . so missed [my daughter] Ninochka that I could no longer live without her. When I first saw her [in Czechoslovakia] I was horrified: she has a new, terrible, and very rare disease. Although this illness is typically accompanied by periods of insanity, Ninochka's mind has remained clear. But it has so affected her motor skills that she can no longer get about. Her face is like an inert mask; her movements are robotlike. People say that she is now more lively and better than what she had been previously. I simply cannot imagine what she was like earlier.

Ninochka has a three-year-old child. I can hardly begin to think what she has had to suffer! A refugee with a child, enduring the most unbearable poverty to boot. But at least we are now together.

Forgive me for taking up your time with family matters. Most likely, you do not even remember Ninochka. But somehow it seems to me that both of you are as close to me as before, and that as I was going abroad, I continued to think of you as friends. How much water has flowed under the bridge since we last saw each other.

Of course, if we could meet, we would have so much to talk about. But I really do not know what to write to you, because I do not know if you have changed like everyone and everything else about me.

I have not read anything for a long time. I cannot afford to buy any books.

---

could emigrate legally was to opt for citizenship from another state, either through a genuine claim or the pretense of legal rights. Passports to leave the country had to be approved not only by the People's Commissariat but also by the Special Department of the Cheka. Such policies worked best in theory, though. The overall instability of the young government—in particular, its inability to seal borders—virtually guaranteed illegal emigration until 1923, when the Bolsheviks established a special section of the secret police for that purpose.

It should also be noted that Russian émigrés in Paris and Kharbin could and did pay large sums of money to free relatives from Soviet confines as late as 1932.

For more on the emigration from the Soviet Union in this period, see Y. Felshtinsky, "The Legal Foundations of the Immigration and Emigration Policy of the USSR, 1917–1927," *Soviet Studies* 34, no. 3 (1982): 336–43.

I was also robbed on the way here.[2]

I will wait for you to write back to me. I am so lonely. You have always been very kind to me; and, it is a pleasure for me to write to you.

Wishing you all the very best,

Devotedly,
L. Avilova

December 20, 1922

Dear Ivan Alexeevich and Vera Nikolaevna,

Your letter [asking me about my life in Russia] triggered in me a strange pain, one that took the place of any joy that I had in hearing from you. But it is a pleasant pain nonetheless, since I am so endlessly grateful to you [for responding to my letter].

I have already become accustomed to need, to being without money. I also have grown quite used to enduring all kinds of other hardships. So I beg you not to do anything which may cause any trouble on your part. If you could only know how happy I am that I can now correspond with you . . .

No one has survived the revolution with greater adventures than I. [After 1917] I continued to live in Moscow, in the same small apartment [as previously]. I spent four years within the same four walls. Of course, I often got out—so what I just told you is not quite accurate—but I never went any farther than Smolensky Market[3] and the alleys and lanes near my home. Since my boys and I had absolutely nothing to live on, we were on the verge of starving. So, at the first opportunity, I headed to the market every day to sell anything of my old belongings, things that I had kept other people from stealing. As my rags were very much in demand, I hung all my skirts and blouses about myself and took my place in line along with the other individuals who were selling their things. In this way, I could make enough money to feed my sons and myself.

What a dream it was merely to have a whole loaf of black bread! But it was difficult to get hold of such a thing, and dangerous, too. How many times did I have to run from the commissars, to hide from roundups [by the police]. But standing in the market was interesting, especially in the summer, when I

---

2. In Sofia, Bulgaria, on their way to France, the Bunins also were robbed of their belongings. Besides money and Vera's diamonds, Bunin lost his academic gold medal. Stolen documents, though, were returned to him by mail.

3. Smolensky Market (Smolenskii Rynok), located roughly a mile west of the Kremlin and known from the seventeenth century, was destroyed in the Soviet urban planning of the mid-1920s.

did not have to suffer from the cold. Our lines were called "bourgeois" or "noblemen's" queues, since the men and women who were selling things in them were not commissars but former proprietors, in other words, "high" society. One can say that we were the cream of Moscow, since, when we were together, we found it pleasant to practice speaking French. In summer, the sun beat down on us mercilessly, and you can well imagine how difficult such a situation was for me. I knit ties, handbags, and tobacco pouches. For the most part, business was good, if only because my customers were soldiers and people from the villages who went crazy every time they got hold of some money. In particular, the villagers who grew vegetables and who lived not far from the city eagerly bought up everything that caught their eye: clothes, jewelry, silverware, and especially curtains.

After a year, though, this market underwent a drastic change. We no longer had the right to stand or walk about with goods. We now had to pay for licenses. Old things were not as easy to sell as previously, since "novelty" shops had opened up to benefit speculators. Also, the villagers were no longer buying things. For almost two years, we were on the verge of starvation. I now know well what it means to be hungry!

Do you think that hunger is such a simple thing? It has a mentality all its own; and if I did not jot down, faithfully and in detail, all the things that I had to go through, I most likely would not have believed everything that I had to endure. The cold made my hunger even more difficult to bear. The thermometer never got above four degrees [Celsius]; and in the morning, it often registered zero degrees, and sometimes even lower than that. There was absolutely no way we could get warm. Wood was scarce; there was no coffee or tea. We had to drink an absolutely repulsive mush of fried carrots!

I became sick and finally went to see the doctor. I had this fantasy that he would prescribe quinine to end my constant fever. I also thought that I could go right away to the drugstore and buy huge quantities of everything I needed so as not to go there twice a day and to beg for more medicine. But the doctor did not prescribe quinine. Rather, he told me that I had tuberculosis, that I needed nourishment, and that I had to stay in bed because I had acute anemia and an enlarged heart. By this time, though, my sons had come up with several ways of earning money so that I could quit selling things. Besides, I had run out of "goods" and was selling items that I needed for myself.

Imagine all the official and periodic entertainments that we were privy to—searches, arrests, and attempts to have other people live in our apartment. (When my older son was arrested, I nearly went out of my mind.) But these big troubles were not as distressing as the little ones, perhaps because they happened more rarely and charged you with energy. In a word, they were not bug bites, but blows, from which one had no defense. The little troubles occurred so frequently that it would be difficult to count them all. Pipes exploded with the freezing weather; portable stoves constantly gave off smoke! Filth everywhere! Dampness and soot! There were mice on the table, in the beds, even in the pockets of my dress. There were also the bedbugs that we had brought in from offices and buildings, since these places had been made into apartments, after they had been requisitioned and turned into pigsties.

But as I look back, I now think that the entire situation was tolerable. Good God, the best thing was all the things that I kept thinking about as I sat alone in my apartment for days and nights on end. My sons came and went; sometimes they were gone for days before they returned. They had their own lives and work. But I had nothing but my thoughts. Even when I stood in line for hours, I kept dreaming that I would write in the evening and "sort out" the mess that was my soul. At the very least, I could still feel that!

But then I wound up in a sanatorium where the people got me back on my feet, since I was no longer hungry or forced to live in the dampness and cold. . . . This was just at the time when the powers that be had introduced the New Economic Policy (NEP).[4] There was a great deal of discussion and excitement . . . if only because people were replacing the burned-out fences, putting glass in the windows, and, most important, opening up the stores.

One time I went to the English store on Kuznetsky Street[5] to realize a long-held dream: I wanted to buy a mousetrap. (I had been catching mice with my hands.) I could not believe my eyes! What was once dead had come back to life . . . and it made for a very strange impression. But at that time, the stores were almost empty inside. For example, in the English store, there was not a single bowl without a crack or a chipped rim or a cover. But I did buy three mousetraps!

At that time also, I began to dream about being with Ninochka. I had heard nothing from her for a year and a half. I did not know if she was alive or dead. An acquaintance who was going abroad gave me his word that he would look for her. He found Ninochka and even arranged for a correspondence between my daughter and me. My son-in-law also wrote to me to say that my presence was necessary. So I made up my mind to be with them no matter what. At that time, my son-in-law and daughter were living in Serbia, and it seemed impossible for me to move there. Fortunately, when they had

4. The New Economic Policy (*Novaia ekonomicheskaia politika,* or NEP) was an economic system, part capitalist, part state-controlled, that Soviet officials introduced in Russia in 1922 and which sought to revive the economy. It was discontinued in 1928.

5. The "English store" (*Angliiskii magazin*) on Kuznetsky Street was one of many (prerevolutionary) foreign luxury shops, located roughly a half mile north of the Kremlin.

to move to Czechoslovakia, things became easier for me. I went there with my sister.

I have plenty to do here. I look after poor Nina and my three-year-old grandson. Only at night am I free for an hour or two. If we do not have visitors, I feel like reading or writing. I wish for newspapers and books desperately.

As you can see, my life [in Russia] was not interesting, but I wrote a great deal from the beginning of the revolution on. It also seems to me that I have thought about things more in my loneliness there than I did at anytime else in my rather long life. But such thoughts do not come without a price. Do you know what the immediate result of such thinking is? To my surprise, I have become a stranger anywhere I go. I meet many émigrés here, people of my own rank and station, but I have nothing in common with them.

But I have already written about so many things in this letter that I had better not take up a new topic.

[When I was in Moscow] I often saw [Bunin's brother] Yuly Alexeevich.[6] He is very thin and old. We sometimes took a walk together and talked about you.

Yours,
L. Avilova

February 17, 1923

Dear Ivan Alexeevich and Vera Nikolaevna,

Did you receive my last letter? Perhaps I am too impatient to wait for a reply. In the remote place where I live, a letter is such a joy!

In March I hope to send Ninochka to Budapest for a cure. The doctors say that there she can recover completely. My sister is well situated [as a teacher] in Budapest. For a one-hour lesson, she gets a room; for another hour lesson, dinner and so forth. So she can have Ninochka stay with her. Travel [for my daughter] there will not be expensive. But I will remain here with my grandson.

My sister writes that in Budapest spring has come and that the people there go out without coats; but here we have blizzards, muds, slush, and constant wind. Also, there was a period of time here when I had completely fallen apart. Something was wrong with my lungs, and my heart was so enlarged that I could barely walk. I had to see a doctor. . . .

"Perhaps, someone needs my help here? Is the patient a man or a woman?" the doctor said, entering into our two rooms and wearing a hat and coat. "Would you like me to help you?"

---

6. Yuly Bunin died in Moscow in July 1921.

When I said yes, he declared, "Well, in that case, I will take off my coat."
When I handed him some paper money, he even gave me back change.

March 5, 1923

Dear Vera Nikolaevna,

I have just received your letter. Thank you very much for your reply. Right
now I am totally consumed with my dream to send my daughter for a cure in
Budapest. There is somebody there who specializes in the new disease [that
my daughter has]; he even has his own clinic. . . . I heard about him when I
was still in Moscow. Of course, my main concern is money . . . and the fact
that we do not have any.

Furthermore, there is no way we can count on help from Russia. My son
writes that prices are way up again and that it is very difficult to live. My
three-year-old ties my hands. I cannot leave him. Also, there is no possibility
of my earning any money here. The city in which I live is very small, and no
one needs lessons. My sister could not earn anything while she was here with
me; but she seems to be doing more or less all right in Budapest. . . . That is
why I want to send Ninochka to her.

The doctors here keep giving injections to Ninochka, but I do not see any
results. The same cramps, the same awful mask, and the same silence all
drive me to despair. This is no way to live! Before I arrived here, Ninochka
did not believe that I was coming; she said that she simply wanted to die.
How terribly difficult life has become for her! Just imagine, she appears absolutely normal and has the same inner life as before. But she is condemned
to immobility and silence. It is as though she does not think or even exist.
How horrible and tormenting it is to see her!

She has a child whom she adores, but he runs away from her, for he seems
to be afraid of the expression on her face.

Ninochka's illness is like a fairy tale in which a sorcerer turns a princess
into a frog, but only on the outside. My sister writes that she has spoken with
a doctor and that Ninochka's illness is not serious and can be cured in a short
time. . . . I have sold, pawned, or lost anything of value that I once had. All I
have left are two inexpensive rings; but if I sell them now, I will be left without anything at all. Such a situation would be terrible, living as I do in a foreign land. After all, anything can happen!

Also, my health is not very good, and I always have a lot of work to do. I
often think, "What if I cannot go on anymore and take to my bed? What if I
would need treatment or be kept in a completely helpless situation?" Thank
God that I do not have the time to think of such things! My grandson takes up
my day; and in the evening, I have to sew, darn, and mend things. My son-in-
law sometimes gives me proofs to read. By the end of the day, I fall asleep like
a dead person, but I have to get up two or three times during the night.

Can you really send a parcel to my son [in Moscow]? Famine is starting there again.

You gave me so much joy when you told me about how a French critic wrote that Ivan Alexeevich has "founded a [literary] school." If this Ivan Alexeevich would recall my words to him, perhaps he would have to admit that, for all practical purposes, I was the first person who ever told him such a thing. But then this Ivan Alexeevich would probably burst out laughing.

P.S. Nina's illness is called "acute encephalitis."[7]

In March at a meeting of former Muscovites, [my wife] Vera Nikolaevna asked that a "Hoover package"[8] be sent to Avilova's son [in Moscow]. At this meeting I. A. Kistyakovsky, hearing Lydia Alexeevna's name, asked: "Which Avilovs are they?" When he learned about Ninochka's illness, he told Vera Nikolaevna that an insurance company with a division in Paris was holding stock that had belonged to Avilova's dead husband and that it was worth ten thousand francs.[9] Kistyakovsky promised to inform Lydia Aleexevna about these shares.

April 3, 1923

Dear Ivan Alexeevich and Vera Nikolaevna,

On your advice I wrote to Igor Alexandrovich [Kistyakovsky]; and, he answered me so quickly and with such sympathy that I was convinced of his willingness to help me.

When I think of you, I become quiet, warmhearted, and a bit sad. One cannot send one's emotions through the mail, and I do not know how even to begin to express my feelings for you. Could I do so, though, simply by saying, "thank you"?

I sent Nina off to Budapest by pawning off my "last mill." Do you remember that the poet K. was always pawning off his "last mill" in his verse? The revolution has greatly affected my memory. But since I do not have a mill, I pawned my last ring, getting for it more than I had anticipated: 300

---

7. Encephalitis is inflammation of the brain brought about by viruses, bacteria, and other microorganisms. Symptoms of the disease include headache, nausea, vomiting, blackouts, and convulsions.

8. Bunin is referring to the parcels of food, medicine, clothes, and other staples that the American Relief Administration (of which Herbert Hoover was chair from 1919 to 1923) delivered to Soviet Russia for the children and sickly there. A typical food package consisted of 49 pounds of flour, 25 pounds of rice, 10 pounds of fats, 10 pounds of sugar, and 3 pounds of tea. In the years between 1921 and 1923, more than 75,000 tons of foodstuffs found their way into the cities and provinces of the starving Soviet state. For more on the efforts of the American Relief Administration in Russia, see H. Fisher, *The Famine in Soviet Russia (1919–1923): The Operations of the American Relief Administration* (New York: Macmillan, 1927).

9. Since in 1923 the franc was worth US $.0678, the amount here was roughly $700.

crowns.[10] I have such a strange pawnbroker here! For a good diamond I received 150 crowns, but for a couple of small and inexpensive sapphires, I received almost twice as much. Whenever I try to get a loan, I always drag my grandson with me, and together, we apparently get sympathy for our plight. What a sweet grandson I have! Everywhere people spoil him and give him treats and affection. What's more, he is so very funny.

Ivan Alexeevich, have you read *Under the Two-Headed Eagle*?[11] Almost everyone here is raving about it. They raise their hands and say, "Oh! Oh!" It is only Nina who, with forced gentleness, says, "There is a great deal of vulgarity in it, and all the characters are fools. But parts of it are not bad." Who is right?

I send you my fondest regards. I very much want to say, "I love you both." I cannot help but do so. Forgive me.

Yours,
L. Avilova

P.S. Happy holiday! Christ Has Risen!

In April, at a gathering to benefit journalists and writers, we succeeded (after much trouble) in obtaining 300 francs for Avilova.

April 23, 1923

Dear Ivan Alexeevich and Vera Nikolaevna,

I do not know how to thank you! I am so very happy! Tomorrow I will send the money to Nina [in Budapest]. She is already undergoing treatment, and my sister writes me letters full of faith and hope. Nina herself has written to me, and I am surprised to see how her handwriting has changed. Instead of completely unreadable scribbles, she now writes almost even letters. That means that her hands are firmer and do not tremble or twitch.

Who else, besides you, must I or can I try to thank? Will you help me here and tell me what to do? My excessive gratitude must seem funny to you, but I assure you that it is very genuine.

Part of the money that I received I used for my own personal (and great) pleasure. Before I even returned home, I immediately bought myself a pair of shoes. My son-in-law suggested that I keep my old shoes to exhibit in "a museum of social paradise." [In them] every step was a torment, and to my misfortune, I had to walk a great deal. But now I will thank you with every step I take.

---

10. Given the exchange rate at the time, Avilova received about $80.

11. Avilova has the title wrong. Pyotr Krasnov's runaway best seller, *From the Double-Headed Eagle to the Red Banner, 1894–1921* (*Ot dvuglavago orla k krasnomu znameni, 1894–1921*), was published in Berlin in 1921.

But, my dear friends, if you only knew how tired I am! After all, I am an old woman, but I still have to work like a young and healthy one. I sometimes feel like crying simply because I do not have the strength anymore. I wish that people would take pity on me and let me rest. This is why I have become so silly and confused. Forgive me for telling you all these things, but know that my soul is still alive, and that with all my heart, I am grateful for your concern and kind thoughts.

Love,

L. Avilova

In May the Committee of Writers and Scholars[12] sent Lydia Alexeevna 500 francs.

May 16, 1923

Dear Ivan Alexeevich and Vera Nikolaevna,

Never did I expect anything like this! Nina was going to return here [to Czechoslovakia], but now she has to stay and continue her treatment in Budapest! She has begun to write me long letters—something she could not do earlier—and her handwriting has become more legible and assured. I do not know if she has begun talking yet, but maybe now that she is writing, she can express her thoughts.

My sons write that they will soon be able to help me financially, since their salaries have increased significantly, and they are not at all in need. I have truly come alive.

How you have helped me! In my most dire hour, you extended your hand to me.

Forgive me for writing on a scrap of paper. But my job as a nanny does not give me a free moment to write a letter or even read a bit.

June 4, 1923

Dear Ivan Alexeevich and Vera Nikolaevna,

Nina is undergoing treatment in Budapest, and I am completely alone with [my grandson] Mishka. My Mishka is a wonderful child, naughty but sensitive, tender, and gentle. He is only three and a half, but all day long we talk about horses, foxes, cats, and wolves and the like. Mishka keeps me on my feet. The minute I lose track of him, he is off doing something naughty. There is no time to read or even think.

12. The Committee to Assist Russian Writers and Scholars in France (Komitet Pomoshchi Russkim Pisateliam i Uchenym vo Frantsii) existed from 1921 to 1939 in Paris and claimed as its members almost all of Russia's émigré intellectuals and writers living in the country at that time.

My sister wrote to say that Nina was getting better and that the doctor hopes to send her back to me as an absolutely new person.

At long last, Nina came back to me.

The first few days she talked a great deal. She not only answered my questions, but she also gave me great joy by keeping up her side of the conversation. But because everyone here had grown accustomed to not talking to her, no one supported Ninochka but me. So with each day, her vivacity began to disappear, and she again became a shadow among the living. She also has begun to sleep less. She does not take a nap in the afternoon but paces about quickly and even runs through the apartment. She reads books nonstop. These are great achievements in themselves, but she has become so very thin. She saves on food and eats very poorly. . . . Moreover, she has begun losing her eyesight, and her vision is blurred—a consequence of the atropine[13] she has been taking. But she is also suffering less from cramps.

These improvements sometimes disappear, though, and the overall effect is terrible. . . . Furthermore, [when Ninochka returned home] two very unpleasant bits of news were waiting for her. The first was a new law about foreigners, the result being that support for my daughter is being cut by 60 percent. The second was that no sooner did Ninochka step out of the train than she was informed that we had to vacate the nice room we had been renting.

But the very next day, I received a letter from Igor Alexandrovich Kistyakovsky, who told me that I could either sell or mortgage the shares of stock that had belonged to Misha. (If I sell them, I will receive 120,000 francs.) In the meantime, he offered to lend me 100 Swedish crowns (400 francs) until I see better times.

You can imagine how delighted I was to hear such a thing! It was as though I had acquired wings! I was not afraid of anything anymore. I wrote to my sister, telling her that Nina, Misha, and I were coming to Budapest in the fall and for her to find a room for us there. (Most likely, we will have to leave here.) I counted the days, waiting to sign the papers from Kistyakovsky. But all the deadlines have long since passed, and I have not received anything from him. When I think that Kistyakovsky may have made a mistake and that I will not receive anything, I get shivers down my spine and feel like vanishing from this earth.

As I said before, we will probably have to leave here. But Nina does not know, nor do I hope that she even suspects such a thing. But it is a sad and most likely, unavoidable consequence of her illness. Her husband is young and quite flighty. . . . It also seems that he is ready to abandon his son and to

---

13. Atropine is an alkaloid used to treat both spasms and dysfunctions of the heart. Side effects of the drug include dilated pupils, blurred vision, constipation, and dry mouth.

leave him in my care. In any case, he told me that he will solve the problem in a "mature" way and let me know what he has decided. But the fact of the matter is not the "maturity" of such a decision, but that if Nina remains here and comes to know and see what everyone else knows and sees, her health will not improve.

I am on good terms with my son-in-law. We talk frankly but gently and even affectionately. I cannot condemn him too harshly. I want only that he spare Nina and hide everything from her for the time being.

But imagine my plight if Kistyakovsky has indeed made a mistake. I will have no money and we will all be at the mercy of my son-in-law.

You know, everyone here has gone crazy—bachelors and married men alike! On Falconry Day,[14] my son-in-law made himself a hunter's outfit with all kinds of hussar's pelisse and other paraphernalia so that he could parade on horseback in front of his lady friend. . . . A former assistant prosecutor is looking for a wife or a mistress, and as soon as he meets a woman or a girl, he proposes to her right away. When his "intended" turns him down, he goes about, angry and grim, complaining that he has no luck with women. Another one, a hale and hearty type, does nothing but complain of his health. He throws temper tantrums and deserves a name that I used to hear in Moscow: "Sour Spleen." But this "spleen" is also proud and grand, if only because he is always "the last one to leave somewhere, the last one to do something." Of course, he is also the first one to threaten, kill, and execute anyone who gets in his way. He is proud and grand because he has preserved his "soul," that is, he never wavers in his convictions or uses any part of his brain.

The men here think only about getting drunk. Indeed, they drink whatever they can get their hands on. They never subscribe to a newspaper, buy a book, or talk about something other than their own affairs. Since they all think that they have "'complished" something in life, they now rest content. Their one indisputable characteristic is their intransigence. Like a hawk, they watch for anyone who shows signs of compromise, who does "not burn with hatred." One should burn, they say! And this "burning" should be the only thing in life.

All the married men here are on their second or third wife. The more fortunate of them have two at the same time. But they are also for the sacrament of marriage, for the *Domostroi*,[15] for religious traditions and ceremonies, and

14. The Society of the Falcon was founded by two Czech patriots in 1862, their goal being to liberate and renew the Slavic peoples through physical, spiritual, and moral well-being. See T. Andreeva and M. Guseva, *Sport nashikh dedov: Stranitsy istorii rossiiskogo sporta v fotografiiakh kontsa XIX-nachala XX veka* (St. Petersburg: Liki Rossii, 2002), 38–40.

15. The *Domostroi* or *The Foundation of a Home* was a sixteenth-century codex, authored or edited by a monk named Sylvester who served as chaplain to Ivan the Terrible and who fashioned a codex of rules and regulations which stressed unquestioning respect and obedience

most important, for the moral formation of their children. The child, these men say, must respect and cherish his parents. He must pray and "kiss his father's hand"! When my son-in-law is here, he makes [his son] Misha say before the little one goes to bed, "Lord, have mercy on Papa and Mama. . . . My goose does not have a head, and my horse is still and dead."

When someone yells at Misha, "You have been naughty again!"—I hear spanking and Misha crying out, "I am being beaten. Someone save me!" He is such a good-natured boy, though, that he does not get upset or offended.

But then it starts all over again: "Have mercy, Lord" on a long list of unknown grandmothers, aunts, and uncles. Again it is "Kiss your father's hand" and such edifying conversations as: "Do you want to be a soldier? Do you want to go off to war?"

After my son-in-law fulfills his fatherly duty, he disappears for the entire evening and returns home drunk. "I demand that Mishka be brought up this way," he tells me, "for my son must not think but act. We [Russians] think way too much."

Sometimes I lose total control of myself. Something rips through me, and I raise such a scandal in the presence of these men, this honorable public, that later I feel ashamed. But are they so high and mighty? Can they admit even for a second that they are lost and good-for-nothing, that they are people who are stuffy, dried-up, and afraid of light and air? They know only one thing, that "I joined the Bolsheviks" and even closer to the truth, that "I was a Social Revolutionary,"[16] one of those that they "will thrash." They also think that no matter what I was then, I am crazy now. And an old woman, to boot! . . . Also, they ask what can one expect from an old woman, other than the fact that she is amusing? . . . So they treat me like a funny crank. After all, besides me, they have no one to make fun of.

But all my outbursts cost me dearly. What a desperate situation I am in! Many Russians are arriving here. They all come and talk to me because I have, relatively speaking, also recently come "from there." I have poured out my soul to two or three of them. But it seemed to me that they were just humoring me. Here one must have a point of view, no matter what. One

---

both for the tsar and for the father of the Russian Orthodox home. (For instance, the section on domestic life is entitled "Instruction on How to Teach, Save, and Inspire a Wife, Children, and Servants by Fear and Terror.")

The *Domostroi* was the modus vivendi for conservative Russian gentry and merchants well into the nineteenth century. It also served as a creative impulse for the fictional families of the novels of Sergei Aksakov, for the plays of Alexander Ostrovsky, and, most notably, for Maxim Gorky's autobiographical novel, *Childhood* (*Detstvo*), written in 1912 and 1913.

16. The Social Revolutionaries, a political party founded in 1901, represented the older populist tradition of Russian radicalism. The party's program was to transform Russia's agricultural life along socialist lines.

must also be affiliated with a group. But I have no point of view. I hate one thing here, another thing there. I keep searching and sighing. You can well imagine how desperately I love my homeland, my Russians, my "type of people" who have now disappeared somewhere and without whom I cannot live. . . . I remember this coachman in Russia, his old, kind, and wrinkled face. He once asked me, "Shall we run off together?" I burst out laughing. He let out a loud grunt and, waving his hands, he said, "Oh, the times we live in!"

In Russia there were several people who understood a thing or two, but I found it terrible to live there. Here, though, I am disgusted and bored, and I am afraid that I will die without ever seeing my country again.

Fortunately, one of my acquaintances from Czechoslovakia owns a great many Russian books. He lent me all of Herzen, Merezhkovsky (his trilogy, *Resurrected Gods*),[17] and several books by L. Tolstoy, Gorky, Leskov, and Saltykov-Shchedrin. I simply cannot read Gorky's tales. I tried many times but always gave up. I also never liked Tolstoy's *The Power of Darkness*,[18] but I now have read it so many times that I almost know it by heart. How I want to read Bunin's *The Peasants*.[19] I wanted to order a copy from Prague, but it was not in the catalog of books there.

August 15, 1923

Oh, my dear friends,

Since I last wrote to you, events have been moving at an incredible speed. Nina has divorced her husband. Kistyakovsky has informed me that the money [from my husband's stocks] has been sent from Paris to Prague. We are also planning to return to Russia.[20] When one considers the facts, it all seems quite simple. Perhaps they truly are simple, but you can well imagine that I do not understand a thing. Indeed, it still seems to me that I am seeing all this craziness in a dream and that when I wake up, I will be amazed that I could ever dream such a thing.

---

17. Merezhkovsky's trilogy is actually entitled *Christ and Antichrist* (*Kristos i Antikrist*) and features *Death of the Gods: Julian the Apostate* (*Smert' bogov: Iulian Otstupnik*), written in 1896; *Resurrection of the Gods: Leonardo da Vinci* (*Voskreshie bogi: Leonardo da Vinci*), written in 1901; and *Antichrist: Peter and Alexis* (*Antikrist: Pyotr i Alexei*), written in 1905.

18. Tolstoy wrote *The Power of Darkness* (*Vlast' t'my*) in 1886.

19. Bunin never wrote a work entitled *The Peasants*. Most likely, Avilova means his novel *The Village* (*Derevnia*, 1909–10).

20. The Soviet government, fearful that émigrés abroad would be recruited by anti-Bolshevik organizations to bring down the new Communist state, allowed Russians to return to the homeland but only if they could join family and relatives there. See Felshtinsky, "Legal Foundations," 332–36.

My son-in-law, after a two-week acquaintance with a divorced woman—and despite all my requests to the contrary—announced to Nina that he wanted to marry this individual. He was in a great hurry to get a divorce; but he promised Nina that if he got one unexpectedly soon, he would not remarry while Nina was in Czechoslovakia. He is also surrendering his son to her, on these conditions: Mishka will be raised loving his father; he will visit my son-in-law's mother in Moscow; and Nina will report to him about Mishka once a month.

My son-in-law's rejection of his son, his frank confession of a new love to his sick wife, and other things of this type so raised himself in his own eyes that he experienced inexpressible joy, a splendid condition of the soul. So instead of a drama, we got such a vaudeville that we did not even know what to be surprised at. But no one sees what I see: that state of Nina's soul. It does not belong in a vaudeville. Good Lord!

Vera Nikolaevna wrote to me, saying that Ivan Alexeevich liked Nina greatly. Why? After all, Nina was never pretty; she was also always much too modest and restrained. She had low self-esteem and always tried to pass unnoticed. Only Nina's closest friends knew what she was really like, who she really was. Ivan Alexeevich was right in his conjectures about her. Most likely, he discerned in my daughter something higher than beauty: her "sweetness," a quality akin to one of his heroines in his stories. Nina is thoughtful, humble, and gentle; but she also has a powerful will and an unconquerable persistence. She has a secret corner in her soul in which she works, tirelessly and imperceptibly; she wishes to put everything in order and to make all things pure, light, and clear. Nina is very easygoing and always ready to retire into the background; but, if that corner of her soul is touched or under siege, she is capable of the most energetic resistance. Her illness has sapped this energy and has made it completely imperceptible to the undiscerning eye, but she keeps on working just the same. I now have to convince myself of Nina's inner strength. She was stunned when her husband told her that he wanted to hurry with a divorce and to marry another woman. She did not sleep the entire night; she also kept watch over her son, never taking her eyes off of him. I had such a need to talk, blame, rebuke, and condemn my son-in-law that I did not pay any attention as to whether Nina was listening to me or not. I did not stop talking; I never ran short of accusations or memories. Only when I grew tried did Nina say to me, "Remember, it is all my fault because I was sick. I bear no malice toward him. This is the way I can and want to deal with the situation. Help me, but do not torment me." So because this is what Nina wanted, that is why we are living the way we do now.

My son-in-law believes that he is the one who has arranged things so marvelously. Taken with his own sense of genius, he becomes quite familiar with anyone he meets. But with Nina, he is tender, condescending, and playful.

"Well, how are we today?" he says. "All dressed up? Looking your best? Well, then smile! Give me your hand!" But after he kisses her hand, he goes off to his "fiancée" and stays with her until late at night. When he finally does return home, he cries out from the corridor where he sleeps, "Ninochka, get me some matches! Do you have any clean socks for me? Get a move on, for God's sake!"

Sometimes I ask my daughter, "Nina, let me be the one to throw the matches at him!" But resigned to her situation, she merely kisses my hand. "Mamochka," she says, "he is giving Mishka to me." But my son-in-law is giving him up only because he is flighty and because the boy would be a burden who would get in his way.

On the day that Nina and her husband were divorced, Kistyakovsky sent me 1,000 francs. That evening [my son-in-law] Vladimir Vladimirovich told Nina about his upcoming marriage; and, on the following day, I received the money. A miracle! From that morning on, it became my responsibility to support Nina and Misha and to refuse help from my son-in-law. If I had not done such a thing, I do not know what would have happened to me.

Nina does not want to undergo any more treatment [for her illness]. She even refuses to take her medicine. . . . My sons [in Moscow] write that we should return to Russia as soon as possible. I miss them terribly, and Nina and Mishka will be warm and comfortable there. Nina's brothers adore her.

I cannot help but return to Russia. How long will my money last with a sick woman and a little child in my care? What if I myself fall ill? After all, I have tuberculosis and a heart condition, so I am not in the best of shape. I have to make sure my rejected ones are protected and taken care of. I have already begun to arrange for Nina's repatriation [to Russia]. The process is very difficult and I do not know what one has to do; but people here have promised to help me.

Why is it that people with differing outlooks on life can give such disparate meanings to the words they use? Why is it that a person with a different worldview [than I have] can have such a blank, inscrutable face? How is it possible to be any more alien to people and places than we are here?

The majority of the people that I know are extremely amiable, but that is all. I, too, am amiable. But that is decisively everything. Words must be superficial.

October 25, 1923

My dear friends,

You are probably already in Paris; and I have not written to you there for such a long time. Actually, that is not quite correct. I have written to you often, but I never could finish my letters and send them off to you. I either keep getting interrupted; or the following day brings news that makes what I have just written to you not worth sending. My life is amazingly monotonous on the surface but, with my emotions and moods, also quite colorful. I was as poor as a church mouse, but then I became rich. I was subordinate to someone else, but then I became my own person. I never imagined that my time here in Czechoslovakia would come to an end and that now we are on the verge of going home, to our loved ones. An entire series of magical changes has brought about excitement, misgivings, hope, and despair. But I am amazed at one thing. How is it that with all this nervous pressure, with all the tiring and unending work, I have not only kept myself going but also have regained my health and even gotten younger?

Vera Nikolaevna is right. Fantastic things have happened to me. It was one miracle that I received some money (10,000 francs). It was a second miracle that I got my daughter back and a little grandson to boot. Now I am waiting for a third one: Nina's recovery. It seems as if people have discovered a new way to fight encephalitis, an approach that is meeting with remarkable success. Nina is undergoing this treatment.

Can you imagine how I worry about Nina? As of late, her health has declined significantly, and there are new complications: she has acute pain in her back and hand. Since her movements are slow and her distress intolerable, she can barely walk. I have to bathe and dress her. (To tell you the truth, I am also having a difficult time of it. I get so very tired with my two invalids that in the evening I drop off to sleep.)

Nina's neuralgia must be a result of her encephalitis, but so far there is no cure for this second illness. But her voice has returned, giving me great cause for joy. Sometimes, though not often enough, she livens up, laughs, and makes jokes. But is this improvement or mere happenstance? There was one amazing day when she said that she felt splendidly and that she was doing a great deal better. But that moment passed, and she was the same as before.

We have already received permission to return to Russia.[21] Now I am doing everything I can to get a visa for Poland. If it does not come through, I will be the unhappiest person in the world. I am scared to death to go around the world, getting on different trains, and sailing across the sea. I do not think that I will be able to manage it all! And it will be my fault if my daughter and grandson catch colds.

As I write to you, I can barely hold up a pen because I am so tired. My head has this ringing sound; I am searching for the simplest words. Mishka has a cough, and I do not get enough rest even at night. But what a funny boy my Mishka is! We are teaching him to speak French, and he is picking it up

21. Avilova, along with her daughter and grandson, returned to Russia in 1924. Nina died in 1930.

rather easily. He also mixes Czech and Hungarian words into his French. "They are also foreign," he tells me. I make up all kinds of fairy tales for him. I also have a copy of Afansiev's fairy tales[22] to tell him when I run out of stories of my own.

Please continue to write me at this address. Perhaps I can write to you from Russia? I will send you a letter right before we leave. May God grant you all the best.

Yours,
L. Avilova

I know nothing about Avilova's fate after she returned to Russia. We lost contact with each other.

In the footnotes to a collection of memoirs by Chekhov's contemporaries, one reads:

Avilova, Lydia Alexeevna (1865–1942)[23]

22. Alexander Afanasiev's popular *Russian Folk Stories* (*Russkie narodnye skazki*) came out in a variety of editions and years, including 1899, 1913, and 1922.

23. The date of Avilova's death is not correct. She died at the home of her son Vsevelod on September 23, 1943. Toward the end of her life, Avilova wrote, "Everything about me is now gray and old. I find it burdensome, tiresome, and repulsive to live. Indeed, I am no longer living. . . . More and more I wish for solitude, quiet, and peace. And a dream that Anton Pavlovich and I are both young and together. And in this note, I have tried to untangle a tangled skein of silk, to decide a single question: Did both of us love? Did he? Did I? . . . But I still cannot do so" (quoted in Vatsuro et al., *Perepiska,* 1:556–57; see introduction, n. 197).

Chapter Eight

IN LATE SEPTEMBER to October 18, 1905, I visited— for what would be the final time—the deserted, extremely somber house of Anton Chekhov in Yalta. I lived there with Maria Pavlovna and "Mamasha," Evgenia Yakovlevna. The days were sleepy and gray, and our life there went on quietly, if monotonously. My time with Chekhov's mother and sister was very difficult, if only because everything—the garden, the house, his study— was exactly as it was when he was alive. Only now he was no longer among us! I also found it difficult to decide when to leave and tear myself away from this life. It was overwhelming to abandon and leave in complete isolation two women whose Chekhovian self-restraint and spiritual remoteness only exacerbated their deep unhappiness. I often saw their tears, but I also saw how they quickly got hold of themselves.

The only thing that Chekhov's mother and sister allowed themselves was to ask that I remain with them a bit longer. "Remember how Antosha loved it when you visited us," they often said. And in truth, it was very difficult to leave the house which had almost become like a family home to me. But I also felt that I could never return there again. I could never reenter that study where everything had been preserved as when he had worked there in life. I could never again approach that desk with its great many trinkets, dear and elegant things that he had bought on the way from Sakhalin to Colombo. Indeed, it always surprised me how Chekhov could write there, since I could never read even a line amid the clutter. I also could not bare to see that niche with its sofa which was situated behind the armchair at his desk and on which he sometimes loved to sit and read. On it there still lay a copy of Tolstoy's *Resurrection*.[1]

There always have been a great many screamers in the world, and these days their numbers are legion. But Chekhov was one of those people about whom Sa'di said, "The one who has a bottle of musk in his pocket does not cry

---

1. Tolstoy wrote *Resurrection* (*Voskresenie*) in 1899.

about it at a crossroads. The aroma of the musk speaks for him."[2] I once ventured the opinion that Chekhov had never been friendly or on close terms with anyone. Now I know that it is a fact.

If it happened that a talentless person started to poke fun or to imitate someone, Chekhov, in shame, did not know where to hide his eyes. What did he not feel when he read about his own "gentleness"! When one speaks of Chekhov, though, one should use the word "gentleness" only with the greatest caution. He was even more repulsed by such expressions as "sadness and warmth." The critics went even further when they sometimes compared Chekhov, the embodiment of firmness, clarity, and restraint, to Komissarzhevskaya!

Perhaps Chekhov disliked poetry because he hated "high-flown" expressions, the so-called poetic beauties, not to mention the way that so many poets, especially now, used such words so carelessly. With what admiration did he speak of Lermontov's "The Sail"![3]

"Such a piece is worth more than all those Bryusovs, Ureniuses, and their ilk," he once said.

"What Urenius?" I asked.

"Isn't there such a poet?"

"No, there is not."

"Well, then it must be Uprudius,"[4] he said seriously. "I think he lives in Odessa. People in Odessa think that they live in the most poetic place in the world. After all, there is Nikolaevsky Boulevard.[5] There is also the sea, the cafés, the music, and all the conveniences of home. Why, one can have his shoes shined every minute there."

With great pleasure I recall that Chekhov could not stand such words as "beautifully," "colorfully," and "succulently."

I once remarked, "Polonsky said it well when he said that 'beautifully' is not 'beauty.'"

"I could not have said it better myself," he agreed. "After all, people do not know that 'colorfully' is a word which painters use as a curse."

---

2. Bunin is quoting from Sa'di's 1258 work, *Gulistan* (also known as *The Rose Garden*), specifically from chapter 8, entitled "On the Art of Addressing People."

3. Lermontov wrote the poem "A Lonely Sail Blazes Whitely" ("Beleet parus odinokii") in 1832.

4. The poets Urenius and Uprudius either are extremely obscure or did not exist. There is also the possibility that Chekhov might be referring to the poet Ivan Oreus (better known under his pseudonym, Konevskoi).

5. With its wide shady vistas, Nikolaevsky Boulevard (now Primorsky Boulevard) was the most picturesque of Odessa's streets.

Sometimes Chekhov laughingly insisted that one of the best poems at the beginning of the twentieth century was written on the walls of Gilyarovsky's home in Yalta:

> Friends, we have a lovely place,
> Have a ball, relax, enjoy.
> There's Sharik and Tuzik with his slanted snout.
> There's also a fellow named Bakakoi.

The representatives of the new art which Tolstoy so accurately called "stupid, overdone caricatures"[6] Chekhov found both amusing and repulsive. How could he do but otherwise? After all, he personified nobility and measure. A man of the highest simplicity and artistic virtue, he could not but become indignant over "stupid, overdone caricatures," their exceedingly great artificiality, shamelessness, and invariable deceit!

Chekhov died at the wrong time. If he had lived, Russian literature perhaps would not have given way to such banality and decline. It would not have become the province of tongue-tied poets who proclaim their genius in every tavern.[7]

It was perhaps the way Chekhov and I came up with images and ideas for stories that brought us closest together. He was unusually hungry for such

---

6. "This new art," Tolstoy told Mikhail Stakhovich on January 29, 1908, "this new poetry, the things that Balmont writes—these are stupid, overdone caricatures. I don't understand anything about them." Quoted in N. Gusev, *Dva goda s L. N. Tolstym* (Moscow: Posrednik, 1912), 70.

7. Bunin is referring to gatherings at such restaurants and nightclubs as the Bear (Medved') and the Stray Dog (Brodiachaia sobaka) in Petersburg where, in the years immediately prior to the revolution, writers and artists met to share their ideas and works.

Bunin had little use for either place. About the Stray Dog he wrote in his *Memoirs* in 1950:

The Stray Dog in Petersburg, where Akhmatova said, "We are all sinners here, we are all whores," was also the setting for *The Flight of the Virgin Mary with the Child into Egypt.* It was some kind of "liturgical thing" for which Kuzmin wrote the words, Sats composed the music, and Sudeikin thought up decorations and costumes.

As regards the "action" of the piece, the poet Potyomkin had a donkey that was severely swaybacked and walked along on two crutches. On its back, it carried Sudeikin's spouse who played the Mother of God.

Among the frequenters of the Stray Dog were quite a few future Bolsheviks: Alexei Tolstoy, then still a young and strapping individual with a huge fat face, and hair cut in a peasant style, and looking like an important *barin* in his raccoon coat and top hat; Blok, who had the impenetrable, stonelike face of a handsome poet; Mayakovsky, who, dressed in a yellow jacket, had lips that were crooked, pursed, and toadlike, and eyes that were extremely dark and provocative in a bold and gloomy way. (I. Bunin, *Vospominaniia* [Paris: Vozrozhdenie, 1950], 46)

things. With delight, he repeated some successful turn of phrase two or three days in a row. For this alone, I will never forget him and will always feel pain that he is no longer here.

Chekhov once bought a little book that contained some of my stories, together with pieces by Andreev, and that bore the pompous title *Rising Stars*,[8] with our portraits on the cover. He had gone for a drive along the embankment and had come back tired. His face was greenish gray, his lips were smiling but ashen-colored. His eyes, though, shone with an inner light, with an excitement which could sparkle within him for the most insignificant reason and which lasted for a very long time. Indeed, insignificant reasons and things were often the catalysts for Chekhov's playful, creative thinking. They even inspired the youthful fervor with which he once asked Korolenko, "Do you want me to write a story about this ashtray?"

On that day, Chekhov roared with youthful laughter when he imagined how people in Mariupol, Berdyansk,[9] and other provincial places would revere a book like *Rising Stars*. Looking first at my portrait—I looked like a dark-haired dandy—and then at Andreev's, he said, "This one is the French deputy Bouquichon, and that one is the Cossack Ashinov."

"When I started to write, oh, what rubbish I wrote. Good God, what rubbish," he said.

But even if he had written nothing else besides "Sudden Death of a Horse" or "A Love Affair with a Double Bass,"[10] one could say that into Russian literature a wonderful mind had blazed forth momentarily, if only because very few people "with intelligence in every cell of their brain" could think up and relate such wonderful absurdities and amusing stories as these. Chekhov himself esteemed both his talent for jokes and those who understood them quickly.

"Yes, it is a most telling sign," he often said, "for if someone does not understand a joke, he is a lost cause."

"Most often," I once added, "it is women who have such a problem. No matter how intelligent they may seem, they never understand jokes."

8. Bunin forgets that in *Rising Stars: A Collection of Stories and Verse* (*Voskhodiashchie zvezdy: Sbornik rasskazov i stikhotvoreni* [Odessa: S. Poliatus, 1903]), he published two of his works: his poem "I Pity Youth" ("Zhal' mne iunosti") and his story "Above the City" ("Nad gorodom").

9. Both Mariupol and Berdyansk are located on the Black Sea in Ukraine, approximately six hundred miles south of Moscow.

10. Chekhov wrote "A Love Affair with a Double Bass" ("Roman s kontrabasom") in 1886 and "The Sudden Death of a Horse" ("Skoropostizhnaia konskaia smert'"), also known as "A Forced Declaration" ("Vynuzhdennoe zaiavlenie"), in 1889.

125

"Oh, yes," he replied. "You know, one does not have to be a brain to know what is going on."

"Everything is simple in life," Chekhov often said, rejecting in literature all that was artificial, skillfully arranged, and calculated to amaze the reader.

Chekhov did not like his success. He was afraid of his fame, of becoming a "fashionable writer."

[Chekhov said]: "One does not need plots [for stories], for in reality, such things do not exist. Everything is mixed up in life, the profound and the trifling, the great and the insignificant, the tragic and the comic. You, ladies and gentlemen, are simply robots and slaves to routines from which you cannot part."
    I agree.

Chekhov once wrote to the actor Svobodin, "Unhappiness with self is a key feature of any genuine talent."

In everything that concerned work, Chekhov was both strict and uncompromising. How mercilessly did he rebuke Lika Mizinova when she, having started a translation, never completed the task: "You have no absolutely no desire for long-standing work. . . . Next time do not anger me with your laziness. Also, please do not even think of justifying yourself. When the matter concerns urgent work and the promise to do it, I accept no excuses. I do not understand such things."

[Chekhov said,] "Talent is work. Talent is responsibility. Talent is conscience."

Chekhov wrote to Gilyarovsky about Pleshcheev: "Pleshcheev senses beauty in the works of others. He knows that, first and foremost, the charm of any story is its simplicity and sincerity. But Pleshcheev himself cannot be sincere and simple in his works. He lacks courage to do so."

[Chekhov said,] "Talent is the knowledge of life. Talent is also courage!"

He wrote: "Talent is freedom, including the freedom from passion." He said that an "artist must always do a great deal of thinking; otherwise he cannot live."

V. Tikhonov noted about Chekhov: "He was thinking constantly, every minute, every second. Also, whether he heard a cheerful story, told something himself, sat at a friendly gathering, talked with a woman, or played with a dog—Chekhov always listened. That is why he sometimes cut you off in midword or, seemingly distracted, asked you the most inappropriate question. In the middle of a conversation, also, Chekhov would sit down at a table and start writing things on sheets of paper."[11]

I also noticed that he was always thinking about something.

"Genuine talents," Chekhov wrote to his brother Nikolai, "always sit in the dark or take their place in a crowd far away from an exhibit. . . . Even Krylov said that an empty barrel is easier to hear than a full one."

He had a remarkable sense for what went on in a woman's heart; he understood what it meant to be feminine in a powerful and precise way. Among the images [of women] in his dreams were many who were captivating and loved him. Chekhov was one of those rare people who knew how to talk to women, to touch them, and to enter into spiritual closeness with them.

God gave him very sharp eyes!

[When I was a child] my parents took me from Voronezh [where I was born] to their estate in Oryol.[12] It was from that time on that I begin to recall my life, for it was [at this estate] that I spent my childhood and adolescence.

It was also during this time that there occurred the famous "impoverishment" of the gentry,[13] as the now-forgotten writer Terpigorev-Atava entitled his well-known book.[14] After he departed the literary scene, I was the one who, people said, "sang hymns" to fading gentlemen's nests. Then came Chekhov, who also "sang hymns" to the fading glory of "cherry orchards."

Although Chekhov had only the barest understanding of gentry landowners, their orchards and estates, he, even to this day, enchants almost everyone with the sham beauty of his *Cherry Orchard*.[15] Having given us

---

11. See V. Tikhonov, "Vospominaniia i pis'ma," *Mir Bozhii,* no. 8 (1905): 8.

12. Voronezh is approximately three hundred miles southeast of Moscow, and Oryol is about two hundred miles southwest of Russia's capital.

13. After the emancipation, gentry landowners faced not only the loss of their serfs but also undeveloped markets, primitive modes of transportation, and inadequate capital for modern (read: "capitalist") methods of farming. Further, rather than exploit economies of scale by farming the estate as a single unit, most nobles rented numerous small strips of their land to the peasants. As a result, the land possessed by gentrymen in Russia fell by nearly a third between 1877 and 1905.

14. Bunin is referring to Sergei Terpigorev-Atava's work, *Impoverishment: Essays of Gentry Ruin (Oskudenie: Ocherki pomeshchichego razoreniia),* published in 1881.

15. Bunin's criticism of *The Cherry Orchard* knew no restraint. For instance, in a diary excerpt dated October 20, 1922, he wrote, "Why don't people realize that this *Orchard* is the poorest thing that Chekhov has done, that it is like an oil painting." Quoted in Grin, *Ustami Buninykh,* 2:88 (see introduction, n. 191).

many truly splendid things, Chekhov is for me one of the most outstanding of our Russian writers. But I do not like his plays.[16] In fact, I am even somewhat embarrassed by them. I find it unpleasant to recall many of his dramatic characters; for example, Uncle Vanya; or Doctor Astrov, who drones on that he is out of place and worries about planting forests; or Gaev, this supposedly terrible aristocrat who, in Stanislavsky's interpretation, shows his gentry ways with such repulsive refinement, that is, he keeps cleaning his nails with a cambric handkerchief. I will not even bother to note another gentry character, Simeonov-Pishchik, whose name is straight out of Gogol.

I grew up in precisely such an "impoverished" gentry nest. It was a manor situated in the remote steppe, complete with a big orchard, though not a cherry one. Notwithstanding Chekhov, there were never any such cherry orchards in Russia.[17] Gentry orchards often had sometimes spacious places where cherries grew; but again, despite what Chekhov says, never alongside the manor house. Furthermore, there is nothing wondrous about cherry trees. Everyone knows that they are extremely ugly things with gnarled branches and small flowers and leaves. They are not at all like the huge, luxurious blossoms that grew under the windows of the manor house on the stage of the Moscow Art Theater. It is also absolutely unlikely that Lopakhin would be in such a hurry to cut down these profitable trees, before Ranevskaya would have the chance to leave her home. Most likely, he did so only so that Chekhov could have the audience at the Moscow Art Theater hear the sounds of axes and, at the same time, see the demise of gentry life and hear Firs say offstage, "They have forgotten the servant." Incidentally, this Firs is a rather credible figure but only because this type of a gentry servant has been written about a hundred times before Chekhov. Everything else about this drama, I repeat, is insufferable. For instance, Gaev, like other personages in Chekhov's plays, constantly interrupts his conversations by muttering nonsense. As if playing billiards, he repeats, "Yellow ball in the middle. . . . Doublet in the corner."

Ranevskaya, supposedly playing the part of both a gentry woman and a Parisian, laughs and cries hysterically, "Oh, my wonderful orchard! Such masses of white flowers! Such a blue sky! My nursery! My dear splendid lit-

---

16. On July 31 or August 1, 1947, Bunin had written to Mark Aldanov, "I have always looked upon Chekhov's plays almost as repulsive." Quoted in Zweers, "Perepiska," 176 (see chap. 1, n. 38).

17. Bunin obviously did not know that Chekhov had a cherry orchard of some fifty trees at his estate at Melikhovo and that when Chekhov informed his sister, Maria, in 1902 that the title of his new play would be *The Cherry Orchard,* he had just been informed that the grove at Melikhovo had been cut down by Mikhail Konshin, the new owner of the estate. (There were also cherry trees in Chekhov's youth in Taganrog.)

tle room!" (She cries.) "My sweet little bookshelf!" (She kisses the thing.) "My darling little table! Oh, my childhood, my innocence!" (She laughs from joy.) "My white, my totally white orchard!"[18]

Later there is a scene that is straight out of *Uncle Vanya*. Anna, in hysterics, says, "Mama, Mama, why are you crying? My dear, good, kind mama, my wonderful, splendid mother, I love you. . . . I bless you! The cherry orchard has been sold, but do not cry, Mama! We will plant a new orchard, one that will be more luxurious than this one. And, a joy, a deep, quiet joy will flood your soul like the sun in early evening, and you will smile, Mama, you will smile!" Next the student, Trofimov, acting like something from "The Stormy Petrel," exclaims, "Forward! Resolutely we go to that bright star which burns there in the distance! Forward! Do not lag behind, friends!"

Ranevskaya, Nina Zarechnaya.[19] . . . Even their names sound like those of provincial actresses.

Incidentally, why did Stanislavsky and Nemirovich[-Danchenko] name their theater the Moscow "Art" Theater? Surely must not art be the province of any theater, just as it is in any form of creative activity? Surely has not every actor in every theater claimed to be an artist? Surely does not such an individual continue to claim to do so today? Or have there have been so few actors, both in Russia as well as in all the other countries of the world, who have not been artists as well?

Equally annoying, the Moscow Art Theater is now known as the "Gorky" Moscow Art Theater.[20] First and foremost, it was Chekhov who made this theater so famous.[21] Even now an image of a seagull is on the curtain there.[22] But then an order came down from above to rename it after Gorky, the author of that pulplike and thoroughly artificial *The Lower Depths*. Humbly, Stanislavsky and Nemirovich[-Danchenko] agreed to the change, though Nemirovich[-Danchenko] once announced to Chekhov in a solemn and public way and for everyone to hear: "This is your theater, Anton."

---

18. In his notebooks in June 1914, Bunin also wrote about Ranevskaya, "The heroine in *The Cherry Orchard* . . . had nothing in common with the gentry. . . . Her sole reason for being in the play was so that Knipper could have a part." Quoted in Grin, *Ustami Buninykh,* 1:202.

19. Nina Zarechnaya is a character in *The Seagull.*

20. The Central Committee of the Communist Party ordered that the Moscow Art Theater be renamed the "Gorky Moscow Art Theater" on September 17, 1932.

21. Compare Stanislavsky's remark to Olga Knipper in August 1903: "No matter how one looks at it, our theater is Chekhov's theater. Without him, we would be in dire straits." Stanislavsky, *Sobranie sochinenii,* 263 (see chap. 3, n. 86).

22. The image of the seagull still remains on the curtain of the Moscow Art Theater.

How the Kremlin can frighten people! For instance, before me lies a book, published in Moscow in 1947 and entitled *Chekhov as Recalled by His Contemporaries*. In it are the recollections of [Chekhov's sister] M. P. Chekhova, who writes, "Anton Pavlovich was surrounded by people from science, art, literature, and politics. Such people as Alexei Maximovich Gorky, L. N. Tolstoy, V. Korolenko, Kuprin, and Levitan were all visitors in our home."

During the last years of Chekhov's life, I , too, was a guest in his home. Every time I was in Yalta, I not only visited him on a daily basis but often stayed with him for weeks on end. I was almost like a brother to M. P. Chekhova, who, now as a very old woman, did not have the courage to mention me [in her memories of her brother]. Coward that she is, though, she recalls other people with their full names and patronymics, for example, "Alexei Maximovich [Gorky] and Vyacheslav Mikhailovich Molotov." About the latter, she writes in a servile way, "It is obvious that Vyacheslav Mikhailovich Molotov spoke not only for himself but for the entire Soviet intelligentsia when he wrote to me in 1936, 'The little home of A. P. Chekhov is like the writer, part and parcel of our homeland. It is my belief that everyone should visit it. A Chekhov admirer, V. Molotov.'"

What wise and gracious words!

"The Gorky Art Theater." How do you like such a thing! But that is only a drop in the sea. All of Russia has been renamed the USSR; and, with resignation, the people there have acquiesced to the most outrageous and idiotic insults to Russian historical life. The city of Peter the Great now bears the name of Lenin. Ancient Nizhnyi Novgorod has been recast as Gorky.[23] Tver', the equally ancient capital of the appanage principality of the same name, is now called Kalinin, after a most insignificant typesetter;[24] and Königsberg, the city of Kant,[25] is now called Kaliningrad.[26] Even the entire Russian emigration responded to these changes with the utmost indifference. The diaspora also turned their back on other equally disturbing things. For instance, they applauded a curly-haired drunk who enchanted them with hacklike, heart-tweaking lyrics, sung to the music of an accordion and a harmonica. They did not pay attention to Blok, who justly said about this individual, "Esenin is a vulgar and blasphemous talent." Russian émigrés also closed

23. Nizhnyi Novgorod is situated approximately 270 miles east of Moscow and was called Gorky from 1932 to 1991.

24. Tver', located ninety miles northwest of Moscow, has also been known as Kalinin since 1931. In his pre-Party life, Mikhail Kalinin (president of the Soviet Union from 1923 to 1946) worked as a lathe operator, a steamfitter, and a patternmaker for cannons, but never as a typesetter.

25. Kant lived his entire life in Königsberg.

26. Königsberg has borne the name Kaliningrad since 1946.

their eyes and turned a deaf ear when Esenin promised to turn the Russia of Kitezh[27] into some "Inoniia,"[28] crying out as he tore open his accordion:

> I promise you Inoniia!
> The breath of Kitezh I hate!
> I will pray to God in obscenities!
> And pluck out his beard before it's too late!

I began to publish my works at the end of the 1890s. The so-called decadents and symbolists who appeared several years later kept insisting that Russian literature was "at a dead end." It had begun to wither and turn gray; it knew nothing except realism, the protocol-like description of life. But was it all that long ago that such works as *The Brothers Karamazov,* "Klara Milich," and "The Song of Triumphant Love"[29] appeared in print? Was the verse that was published at this time, for example, Fet's *Evening Fires*[30] and the poetry of V. Solovyov, so realistic? Could one ever call "gray" the best things of Leskov, not to mention the later pieces of Tolstoy, his incomparably splendid "folk" tales, *The Death of Ivan Ilyich,* and *The Kreutzer Sonata*?[31] Were the first pieces of Garshin and Chekhov also not new in spirit and form?

At that time, the titles of books were also trite: *The Snow Mask, A Goblet of Snowstorms,* and *Serpentine Flowers.*[32] Even worse, those who came up with these titles invariably placed them in the top left corner of the book

27. Esenin published "Inoniia" in 1918. In Russian lore, Kitezh is one of two places: a town that escapes destruction by the Tatars by sinking into Lake Svetoloyar near Voskresensk; or a village near Suzdal', approximately 125 miles northeast of the Russian capital, which was, in fact, laid waste by the Tatars but which, in calm weather, makes its presence known by rending the air with the sound of church bells and revealing its ruined buildings at the bottom of a lake. Beyond the appeal of Kitezh to Esenin and other Russian writers, Rimsky-Korsakov used the legends of the city as the basis for his 1907 opera *The Tale of the Invisible Town of Kitezh and the Maid Frevonia* (*Skazanie o nevidimom grade Kitezhe i deve Fevronii*).

28. According to the memoirist V. Chernyavsky, Esenin conceived of "Inoniia" as "another land" (*inoniia strana*), as an entity that actually existed in the real world. See S. Esenin, *Sobranie sochinenii v piati tomakh,* vol. 2 (Moscow: Gosudarstennoe izdatel'stvo khudozhest-vennoi literatury, 1961), 266.

29. Dostoevsky published *The Brothers Karamazov* (*Brat'ia Karamazovy*) in 1879 and 1880. Turgenev published "The Song of Triumphant Love" ("Pesn' torzhestvuiushchei liubvi") in 1881 and "Klara Milich" in 1883.

30. Fet wrote *Evening Fires* (*Vechernye ogni*) in 1883.

31. Tolstoy's *The Kreutzer Sonata* (*Kreitserova sonata*) appeared in 1889.

32. Alexander Blok published *The Snow Mask* (*Snezhnaia maska*) in 1907; Andrei Bely, *A Goblet of Snowstorms* (*Kubok metelei*) in 1908; and Konstantin Balmont, *Serpentine Flowers* (*Zmeinye tsvety*) in 1910.

cover. I recall how once Chekhov, having looked at such a thing, suddenly burst out laughing and said, "But this is for people who are cross-eyed!"

Chekhov told me that the "decadents" were more than just hoodlums.

"What kind of decadents are they!" he exclaimed. "They are the most hale and hearty peasants. They should be arrested and forced to serve in the army."

Truly, almost all the "decadents" of the time were "hoodlums" and the "most hale and hearty peasants," but in no way could one call them healthy or normal. The faculties (not to mention the literary talents) of the "decadents" of Chekhov's time, as well as of those who swelled their ranks and later became famous, were indeed great, but they were akin to those of God's fools,[33] the insane, or people prone to hysterics. Indeed, could any one of them be regarded as healthy in the conventional sense of this word? They were no longer called decadents and symbolists but futurists, argonauts, and mystical anarchists. Writers such as Gorky and Andreev were followed by the wasted and wan Artsybashev and by Kuzmin with his half-bare skull and deathlike face, made up like the corpse of a prostitute.[34] All of them were cunning and sly, since they possessed the qualities of God's fools and of insane and hysterical people to call attention to themselves.

What a remarkable accumulation of these unhealthy, abnormal types came into existence during Chekhov's time! How they multiplied in the years after his death! There was the consumptive [Zinaida] Gippius who, not for nothing, wrote under a man's name. There was Bryusov, who was consumed with a mania for glory. There was the mute and stonily inert Sologub—a "brick in a suit," Rozanov once called him[35]—the author of "quiet boys" and

33. "God's fools" (*iurodovye*) were "madmen-idiots" who reputedly possessed gifts of prophecy and other spiritual powers.

34. Bunin was not far off the mark in his description of Kuzmin. Georgy Ivanov recalled that Kuzmin accepted guests in a "silk kimono and fan." Alexei Remizov remembered, "At one time Kuzmin had a beard—black as black can be! And went about in a maroon velvet *poddyovka* [heavy coat] . . . [and] a brocaded golden-colored shirt worn outside his trousers" (both citations in A. Remizov, *Kukha: Rozanovy pis'ma* [Berlin: Z. I. Grzhebin, 1923], 106).

Kuzmin's physical appearance was also cause for comment. "His frostlike swarthy face seemed dry and yellowish," a colleague recalled. "His gray hair, combed forward to his forehead, did not conceal his baldness. His huge eyes were lost amid gray eyebrows and a deep net of wrinkles" (N. Bogomolov, *Mikhail Kuzmin: Stat'i i materialy* [Moscow: Novoe literaturnoe obozrenie, 1995], 10–12). To such a "physiognomy," Remizov added, "Kuzmin's eyes looked askance, just like those of a horse! . . . They also had a touch of makeup about them, making Kuzmin look like Pharaoh Tutankhamen or like someone who had escaped from a bonfire in the hermitages beyond the Volga. Kuzmin also used so much rose-smelling perfume that he reeked like a [scented] icon on a holiday" (Remizov, *Kukha*, 106).

35. Bunin is again quoting from Gippius, *Zhivye litsa*, 16 (see chap. 5, n. 22).

The Petty Demon,[36] with its pathological hero, Peredonov, the singer of death and the "father" of his own devil. There was the frenzied Volynsky, the stormy "mystical anarchist" Chulkov, and the stunted and terrible-looking Minsky, with his huge head and stagnant black eyes.

The following may seem strange to many people, but it is the truth: Chekhov did not like actors and actresses. He often said about them:

> Such individuals lag behind the rest of Russian society by some seventy years. They are vulgar people, consumed with pride. For example, I remember that when Solovtsov died, I asked an actor, "Do you remember the telegram that you sent to the theater after Solovtsov's death?"
> "Does it really matter about what one writes in telegrams and letters? Does it really matter about what one sometimes has to say so as not to offend the people in charge?"
> Having fallen silent momentarily, he added, laughing anew, "Like those at the Moscow Art Theater, for example."

In spring 1899, I was walking along the embankment in Yalta when I saw Chekhov and someone else coming toward me. Chekhov's face was buried in a newspaper, in part because of the sun, in part because the individual who was walking alongside him was saying something in a ringing bass and constantly waving his hands high from under his cloak. When I greeted Chekhov, he turned to me and said, "Meet Gorky." Having introduced myself to him, I took a good look and saw that what the people in Poltava had been saying about him was correct, right down to his cloak, cane, and extremely strange-looking hat. Under this cloak, Gorky was wearing a yellow silk shirt, embroidered with silks of various colors around the collar and hem and girded with a long, braided, cream-colored belt.

He was not a big fellow, but rather tall and somewhat stooped. He had reddish hair, greenish eyes, and a ducklike nose with wide nostrils and freckles. He also had a yellow mustache which, when he coughed, he kept moistening with saliva and smoothing down with his huge fingers. As we walked further, he began to smoke, inhaling deeply, and again to drone and wave his hands. Having finished his cigarette, he first spat on his cigarette holder to put out the butt; then he threw it away. He continued to talk, periodically looking at Chekhov to see what kind of impression he was making. Gorky spoke loudly, as if from the depths of his soul. He poured forth a fiery out-

---

36. Bunin is referring to such child characters as Sasha Pylnikov in *The Petty Demon* (*Melkii bes*), written in 1907.

burst rife with graphic images and heroic exclamations that were purposely primitive and coarse. He told an endlessly long and interminably boring story about some rich Volga merchants and the peasants who lived with them. The story was tiresome not only because of its unrestrained pathos and images but also because of its overriding hyperbolic monotony: these rich merchants were all like the giants from Gorky's folktales. Chekhov was hardly listening. But Gorky kept talking and talking.

Almost from that very day on, though, there arose between Gorky and me something akin to a friendly affection, which, from his side, bordered on the sentimental with his shy excitement over me and my writing.

"You are the last writer from the nobility," he told me, "from that culture which gave to the world Pushkin and Tolstoy!"

Also on that day, after Chekhov had hailed a cab to return to his home in Autka, Gorky invited me to drop in at his place, a rented room on Vinogradskaya Street. Once there, he wrinkled up his nose and smiled a happy but comically awkward and stupid smile. He also showed me a picture of his wife with a fat, lively-eyed child in her arms. Also, showing me a piece of light-blue silk, he said, still grinning, "You see, I bought it for a jacket for her . . . this very woman here. . . . I am bringing it to her as a gift."

[In later years] Gorky was a completely different person than the one whom I had met earlier with Chekhov on the embankment in Yalta. Then he had been a dear man, comic in his poses and modest to the point of self-abasement. He spoke in a bass voice, often with heroic coarseness and in the playfully sincere speech of people from the Volga, for whose accent he had kept apologizing. He also performed with singular delight and verve. I later learned that Gorky could carry on monologues from morning to night and do it all so adroitly and deftly as he entered fully into various roles and parts that demanded expression. In fact, when Gorky wanted to be especially convincing, he could easily summon forth tears in his greenish eyes.

In spring 1901, Kuprin and I were in Yalta. (He lived next to Chekhov in Autka.) We had been visiting Varvara Konstantinova Kharkeevich, the directress of the women's high school there and a splendid woman who adored writers.

Kuprin and I had tried to see her at Easter but did not find her at home. So we went into the dining room where we came across her Easter table. We began to make merry, helping ourselves, and eating and drinking.

Kuprin said, "Let's leave a poem on the table." Laughing, we began to compose something. I wrote on her tablecloth (something that she later embroidered on):

> In Varvara's dining room
> Was a table set for a ball,

> Ham, turkey, cheese, sardines,
> But suddenly nothing at all!
> Blaming a crocodile came to naught
> For Ivan Bunin was at fault.[37]

When Chekhov heard the poem, he laughed for several days and even learned the work by heart.

On October 16, 1930, in Grasse, I wrote:

Along the wall at Lubyanka,[38] secondhand booksellers are standing by their shops and stalls. A thick-faced little boy who sells cheap novels and tattered books "at a discount" is looking to buy a collection of Chekhov's works from a serious old bookseller. The man wants twelve kopecks for the collection, the boy offers eight. The bookseller is quiet, the boy insists on his price. The boy keeps on, badgering, but the bookseller pretends that he is not listening and arranges the books in his stall in a nervous way. Suddenly, he exclaims with unusual, unexpected energy: "If Chekhov could rise from his grave, he would give it to you but good! A man writes and writes; he comes up with twenty-three volumes of works. But you, you fat-faced thing . . . want his works for a song!"

---

37. The poem has more than a ring of truth. For instance, in a diary excerpt dated August 8, 1945, Nina Berberova recalled, "It was my birthday. With difficulty I obtained half a pound of sausage. I set the dining room, cut twelve pieces of dark bread, and put the twelve pieces of sausage on them. The guests came at eight and, as was proper, first sat in my room. . . . When I poured the tea, the guests came into the dining room.

"Bunin entered first, took a look at the sandwiches, and, without even hurrying, ate . . . all of the twelve pieces of sausage. So when the others came to the table . . . they found only bread. . . . [It was] spread out on two plates . . . and looking rather strange and pitiful." Quoted in N. Berberova, *Kursiv moi*, vol. 2 (New York: Russica Publishers, 1983), 515.

38. Lubyanka is an area just northeast of the Kremlin in Moscow.

Chapter Nine

HERE IS CHEKHOV'S INSCRIPTION on a book that he gave to me as a gift. The book is in Moscow, but the inscription was published in the twentieth volume of his letters. It reads:

To Ivan Alexeevich Bunin, with admiration and delight. Anton Chekhov.

He had a remarkable genealogy: a talented peasant clan that came from the north.

To Chekhov's cousin, **M. M. Chekhov:** "I love all possible reveling, Russian ones, especially the dances and wine."

From youth on, he always worried about others.

Chekhov's face changed with each passing year.
In a picture taken at his graduation from high school in 1879, his hair is combed straight, and his long upper lip has a mole.
In one taken in 1884, he has a large, independent-looking face. Alongside him is his brother Nikolai, a genuine Mongol.
A portrait drawn by his brother at approximately the same time shows him looking like a thick-lipped youth from Bashkiria.[1]
An 1890 snapshot depicts him as handsome, lively, and bold, with a pointed mustache.
A picture in 1892 renders him as a typical provincial doctor; and one, taken in 1897, shows him in a carriage and looking pointedly at someone.
What a thin face he now has!
The best portrait of Chekhov can be found in *Chekhov as Remembered by His Contemporaries.*

---

1. Bashkiria is located some seven hundred miles southeast of Moscow.

Among the many visions that Chekhov had, there was one of Garshin hurling himself down a dark and dirty staircase. Chekhov loved Garshin.

[Chekhov recalled,] "[Garshin's] life is unbearable! And the staircase is dirty. I see it before me: dark and dirty."

Chekhov often said, "The individual must be a clear thinker, lead a moral life, and be in prime physical condition."

"My God, how many good people does Russia have!" Anton Pavlovich wrote to his sister.

Tolstoy had a tender regard for Chekhov. Smiling affectionately, he once embraced Chekhov by the shoulders and said, "You are Russian! You are very, very Russian!"

"On the Enisei [River]," Chekhov wrote, "life begins with a howl and ends in a boldness, the likes of which could never happen in a dream. On one shore there is Krasnoyarsk, the best and most beautiful of all the Siberian villages. On the other there are mountains that remind me of the Caucasus in that they, too, are hazy and dreamlike. I stood and thought: 'What a full, bold, and intelligent life will someday illumine these shores.'"[2]

He also wrote in a letter to [Leontiev-]Shcheglov, "I can say that I have lived! I have seen it all. From the hell of Sakhalin to the paradise of Ceylon."

Sakhalin—Was it normal for him to go there?

In his youth, he was like his mother (but then there was his father to contend with!).

A description of the Sunday market alongside Chekhov's house on Trubnaya Square[3] in Moscow: "People swarm about like crabs in a net. There are thousands of sheepskin coats, overcoats, fur caps, top hats. One hears the polyphonous songs of birds, recalling the presence of spring."[4]

A wonderful passage.

---

2. Krasnoyarsk, the Enisei River, and the Enisei Ridge are approximately twenty-five hundred miles east of Moscow.

3. Trubnaya Square is approximately two miles north of the Kremlin.

4. Bunin is quoting from Chekhov's 1883 sketch "In Moscow on Trubnaya Square" ("V Moskve na Trubnoi ploshahdi").

Chekhov's "The Murder" is an unusually splendid work.

What did Chekhov die of? Here is what Skitalets wrote:

In Memory of Chekhov

Implacable fate brought him to the grave.
A terrible illness took him by the hand. . . .
It entered his chest, and was with him always:
The ghastly disease of his native land.

Prophets, leaders, rebellious angry souls,
Rush to punish, flog, and chide,
But he loved people with a tender love,
Like a mother, a child at her side.

He drank cups of toxic fiery sadness,
It entered his chest, deep, like springs.
Poisoned with the angst of our life, he suffered
The patience of slaves, the dullness of kings.

The air of vulgarity did not let him breathe,
Cold enmity tormented him to the bone,
Too late, the mob raked him raw with their love,
But wherever he went, he was always alone.

He lived under an evil, mysterious fate
A power that was dark, heartless, and cruel,
And every drop of happiness he drank
An invisible hand turned to gruel.

Understood late, and judged in vain,
He died because life was poor, a joke.
People on earth were unhappy and coarse,
His native land groaned under its yoke.

Leaving his world, he summoned you, freedom!
With his last breath, he called for you to come,
Even as he felt that night was strong, his land was done,
And that distance chilled the rays of the sun.

O homeland mine, raise up prayers
Bless the sacred shadow with your love,
But curse with hate, contempt, and scorn
The traders who sell you from below and above!

Let his death fall on these decrepit reptiles
With worm-eaten hands untouched by balm
Who dealt the final blow and then stood at his grave,
Crying the loudest about friendship and calm.

Shine over the homeland, O powerful light,
Chase away the black shadow, the birds of night
And bring back life over the dark grave,
Come the solemn day, the wished-for right.

These lines were the introduction to an anthology, published by Knowledge[5] and dedicated to Chekhov's memory.[6]

How could Gorky print such a thing!

Even now people do not know Chekhov as they should.

5. Knowledge (Znanie) was a publishing association founded in St. Petersburg in 1898. Joined by Gorky in 1900, it published literary almanacs and works of critical realism.

6. Skitalets's "In Memory of Chekhov" ("Pamiati Chekhova") appeared in *Anthology for the Association Knowledge for 1904* (*Sbornik tovarishchestva Znanie za 1904 god*) in St. Petersburg in 1905.

Appendix: List of Individuals Mentioned in the Text

Adamovich, Georgy (1884–1972), poet and critic
Afanasiev, Alexander Nikolaevich (1826–71), historian and folklorist
Akhmatova, Anna Andreevna (1888–1966), poet
Aksakov, Sergei Timofeevich (1791–1859), novelist
Aldanov, Mark Alexandrovich (1886–1957), writer
Alexander the Great (356–323 B.C.), also known as Alexander III, king of Macedon from 336 to 323 B.C. and conqueror of Asia
Alexander III (1845–94), tsar of Russia from 1881 to 1894
Al'tshuller, Isaak Naumovich (1870–1943), doctor for Anton Chekhov and Leo Tolstoy
Amfiteatrov, Alexander Valentinovich (1862–1938), novelist, playwright, journalist, critic, and short-story writer
Andreev, Leonid Nikolaevich (1871–1919), writer
Artsybashev, Mikhail Petrovich (1878–1927), novelist and short-story writer
Ashinov, Nikolai Ivanovich (1856–?), Cossack mercenary and military leader
Auden, W(ystan) H(ugh) (1907–73), American poet
Aurelius, Marcus (A.D. 121–80), Roman emperor from A.D. 161 to 180 and Stoic philosopher
Avilov, Mikhail Fyodorovich (1863–1916), husband of Lydia Avilova
Avilova, Lydia Alexeevna (1864–1943), writer

Bakhrakh, Alexander Vasilievich (1902–85), writer
Balmont, Konstantin Dmitrievich (1867–1943), poet
Barantsevich, Kazimir Stanislavovich (1851–1927), writer
Batyushkov, Fyodor Dmitrievich (1857–1920), editor
Belinsky, Vissarion Grigorievich (1811–48), thinker, writer, and critic
Bely, Andrei (pseudonym of Bugaev, Boris Nikolaevich) (1880–1934), poet and writer
Berberova, Nina Nikolaevna (1901–93), poet, writer, and memoirist
Bernhardt, Sarah (1844–1923), French actress

Bilibin, Viktor Viktorovich (1859–1908), friend of Anton Chekhov
Blok, Alexander Alexandrovich (1880–1921) poet and playwright
Boborykin, Pyotr Dmitrievich ((1836–1921), novelist and playwright
Bryusov, Valery Yakovlevich (1873–1924), poet, novelist, and critic
Bunin, Alexei Nikolaevich (1824–1906), father of Ivan Bunin
Bunin, Ivan Alexeevich (1870–1953), poet, novelist, and friend of Anton
  Chekhov
Bunin, Nikolai Ivanovich (1900–1905), son of Ivan Bunin
Bunin, Yuly Alexeevich (1857–1921), brother of Ivan Bunin
Bunina, Lyudmilla Alexandrovna (1835?–1910), mother of Ivan Bunin
Burenin, Viktor Petrovich (1841–1926), poet and publicist
Bykov, Pyotr Vasilievich (1843–1930), bibliographer

Catherine the Great (1729–96), also known as Catherine II, empress of
  Russia from 1762 to 1796
Chekhov, Alexander Pavlovich (1855–1913), writer and brother of Anton
  Chekhov
Chekhov, Anton Pavlovich (1860–1904), playwright and writer
Chekhov, Egor Mikhailovich (1798–1879), grandfather of Anton Chekhov
Chekhov, Ivan Pavlovich (1861–1922), brother of Anton Chekhov
Chekhov, Mikhail Alexandrovich (1891–1955), actor, director, son of
  Alexander Chekhov, and nephew of Anton Chekhov
Chekhov, Mikhail Mikhailovich (1851–1909), cousin of Anton Chekhov
Chekhov, Mikhail Pavlovich (1865–1936), brother of Anton Chekhov
Chekhov, Mitrofan Egorovich (1836–94), uncle of Anton Chekhov
Chekhov, Nikolai Pavlovich (1858–89), painter and brother of Anton
  Chekhov
Chekhov, Pavel Egorovich (1825–98), father of Anton Chekhov
Chekhov, Vladimir Ivanovich (1894–1917), son of Ivan Chekhov
Chekhova, Evgenia Yakovlevna (1835–1919), mother of Anton Chekhov
Chekhova, Marfa Ivanovna (1840–1923), aunt of Anton Chekhov
Chekhova, Maria Pavlovna (1863–1957), sister of Anton Chekhov
Chulkov, Georgy Ivanovich (1879–1939), writer, essayist, and critic
Corneille, Pierre (1606–84), French dramatist and poet

Darwin, Charles (1809–82), English naturalist
David (1000?– 960? B.C.), second king of Israel
Davydova, Alexandra Arkadievna (1848–1902), editor and publisher
Delille, Jacques (1783–1813), French poet and translator
Diaghilev, Sergei Pavlovich (1872–1929), ballet producer
Diogenes (412–323 B.C.), Greek philosopher

Dobrolyubov, Nikolai Alexandrovich (1826–61), critic
Dostoevsky, Fyodor Mikhailovich (1821–81), novelist

Elpatievsky, Sergei Iakovlevich (1854–1933), physician and writer
Ermolova, Maria Nikolaevna (1855–1939), actress
Ertel', Alexander Ivanovich (1855–1908), novelist and short-story writer
Esenin, Sergei Alexandrovich (1895–1925), poet

Fet, Afanasy Afanasievich (1820–92), poet
Flaubert, Gustave (1821–80), French writer
Fyodorov, Alexander Mitrofanovich (1868–1949), poet

Gaboriau, Émile (1832–73), French writer
Garshin, Vsevolod Mikhailovich (1855–88), short-story writer
Gilyarovsky, Vladimir Alexeevich (1855–1935), friend of Anton Chekhov
Gippius, Zinaida Nikolaevna (1869–1945), writer
Gnedich, Pyotr Pyotrovich (1855–1935), writer, translator, and art historian
Goethe, Johann Wolfgang von (1749–1832), German poet, dramatist, novelist, and statesman
Gogol, Nikolai Vasilievich (1809–52), novelist and short-story writer
Goldenweiser, Alexander Borisovich (1875–1961), pianist, professor, and friend of Leo Tolstoy
Gol'tsev, Viktor Alexandrovich (1850–1906), editor
Goncharov, Ivan Alexandrovich (1812–91), writer
Gorky, Maxim, pseudonym of Alexei Maximovich Peshkov (1868–1936), writer and critic
Grigorovich, Dmitri Vasilievich (1822–99), writer

Hauptmann, Gerhart (1862–1946), German playwright, poet, and novelist
Hegel, Georg Wilhelm Freidrich (1770–1833), German philosopher
Herzen, Alexander Ivanovich (1812–70), novelist and publicist
Homer (ninth century B.C.), Greek poet
Hoover, Herbert Clark (1874–1964), president of the United States from 1929 to 1933

Ibsen, Henrik (1828–1906), Norwegian dramatist
Iollos, Grigory Borisovich (1859–1907), publicist
Ivan the Terrible (1530–84), also known as Ivan IV Vasileevich, tsar of Russia from 1553 to 1584
Ivanov, Georgy Vladimirovich (1894–1958), poet, prose writer, essayist, memoirist, and critic
Izmailov, Alexander Alekseevich (1873–1921), critic

James, Henry (1843–1916), American novelist and critic

Kalinin, Mikhail Ivanovich (1875–1946), president of the USSR from 1923 to 1946

Kant, Immanuel (1724–1804), German philosopher

Keller, Fyodor Eduardovich (1850–1904), general

Kharkeevich, Varvara Konstantinova (?–1932), headmistress

Khudyakov, Sergei Nikolaevich (1837–1928), editor and publisher

Khudyakova, Nadezhda Alexeevna (1837–1928), wife of Sergei Nikolaevich and sister of Lydia Avilova

Kiselyov, Alexei Sergeevich (?–1900), friend of Anton Chekhov

Kiselyova, Maria Vladimirovna (1859–1921), friend of Anton Chekhov and husband of Alexei Kiselyov

Kistyakovsky, Igor Alexandrovich (1876–1941), lawyer

Klyuchevsky, Vasily Osipovich (1841–1911), historian

Knipper, Anna Ivanovna (1850–1919), mother of Olga Knipper

Knipper, Olga Leonardovna (1868–1959), actress and wife of Anton Chekhov

Knipper-Nardov, Vladimir Leonardovich (1876–1942), opera director, singer, and brother of Olga Knipper

Komissarzhevskaya, Vera Fyodorovna (1864–1910), actress

Kondakov, Nikodim Pavlovich (1844–1925), historian

Konevskoi, pseudonym of Ivan Ivanovich Oreus (1877–1901), poet

Koni, Anatoly Fyodorovich (1844–1927), lawyer

Konshin, Mikhail (n.d.), timber merchant

Korolenko, Vladimir Galaktionovich (1853–1921), writer

Kovalevsky, Maxim Maximovich (1851–1916), sociologist

Krylov, Ivan Andreevich (1769–1844), journalist, playwright, and fabulist

Kuprin, Alexander Ivanovich (1870–1938), writer

Kurkin, Pyotr Ivanovich (1858–1934), doctor and statistician

Kuskova, Ekaterina Dmitrievna (1869–1958), publicist, publisher, memoirist, and political activist

Kuzmin, Mikhail Alexeevich (1875–1936), poet, prose writer, playwright, and critic

Kuznetsova, Galina Nikolaevna (1902–76), poet, prose writer, and memoirist

Lavrov, Pyotr Lavrovich (1823–1900), populist, historian, sociologist, and editor

Lazarev-Gruzinsky, Alexander Semyonovich (1861–1927), writer

Leconte de Lisle, Charles-Marie (1818–94), French poet

Leikin, Nikolai Alexandrovich (1841–1906), editor and publisher

Leikina, Praskovia Nikiforovna (?–circa 1918), wife of Nikolai Leikin

Lenin, Vladimir Ilyich, pseudonym of Vladimir Ilyich Ul'yanov (1870–1924), revolutionary leader and writer

Leoncavallo, Ruggiero (1858–1919), Italian composer

Leontiev-Shcheglov, Ivan Leontievich (1856–1911), friend of Anton Chekhov

Lermontov, Mikhail Iurievich (1814–41), poet and novelist

Leskov, Nikolai Semyonovich (1831–95), journalist, novelist, and short-story writer

Levitan, Isaak Il'ich (1860–1900), painter

Linder, Max, screen name of Gabriel Leuvielle (1883–1925), French motion-picture actor

Lintaryova, Elena Mikhailovna (1859–1922), doctor and friend of Anton Chekhov

Machiavelli, Niccolò (1469–1527), Florentine statesman and writer

Mamin-Sibiryak, Dmitri Markisovich (1853–1912), writer

Marlitt, Eugenie (1825–87), German writer

Maupassant, (Henri-René-Albert-) Guy de (1850–93), French writer

Mayakovsky, Vladimir Vladimirovich (1893–1930), poet

Men'shikov, Mikhail Osipovich (1859–1919), journalist

Merezhkovsky, Dmitri Sergeevich (1865–1941), poet, novelist, critic, and philosopher

Mikhailovsky, Nikolai Konstantinovich (1842–1904), critic

Minsky, Nikolai Maximovich (1855–1937), poet

Mizinova, Lydia (Lika) Stakhievna (1870–1937), friend of Anton Chekhov

Molotov, Vyacheslav Mikhailovich (1890–1986), Soviet statesman

Moskvin, Ivan Mikhailovich (1874–1946), actor

Muromtsev, Nikolai Andreevich (1852–1933), social figure and father of Vera Muromtseva-Bunina

Muromtseva, Lilia Fyodorovna (1855?–1923), mother of Vera Muromtseva-Bunina

Muromtseva-Bunina, Vera Nikolaevna (1881–1961), longtime partner of Ivan Bunin, whom he began living with in 1907 and married in 1922

Nadson, Semyon Yakovlevich (1862–87), poet

Naidyonov, Sergei Alexandrovich (1868–1922), dramatist

Nemirovich-Danchenko, Vladimir Ivanovich (1858–1943), playwright and director

Nicholas II (1868–1918), emperor of Russia from 1894 to 1917

Nilus, Pyotr Alexandrovich (1869–1943), artist

Odoevtseva, Irina Vladimirovna, pseudonym of Iriadna Gustavovna Geinike (1901–90), poet, prose writer, and memoirist

Offenbach, Jacques (1819–1880), French composer
Orlov, Ivan Ivanovich (1851–1917), doctor
Ostroumov, Alexei Alexeevich (1844–1908), doctor
Ostrovsky, Alexander Nikolaevich (1823–86), playwright

Panina, Sofya Vladimirovna (1871–1957), countess
Pashchenko, Varvara Vladimirovna (1870–1918), mate of Ivan Bunin in union (most likely common-law) from 1891 to 1894
Peshkova, Ekaterina Pavlovna (1886–1938), first wife of Maxim Gorky
Peter the Great (1672–1725), also known as Peter I, tsar of Russia from 1682 to 1725
Pleshcheev, Alexei Nikolaevich (1825–93), poet, prose writer, playwright, critic, and journalist
Plevako, Fyodor Nikolaevich (1843–1908), lawyer
Pokrovsky, Feodor Pavlovich (1835–98), priest and grade-school teacher of Chekhov
Polonsky, Yakov Petrovich (1819–98), poet
Potapenko, Ignaty Nikolaevich (1856–1929), playwright and prose writer
Potyomkin, Pyotr Petrovich (1886–1926), poet
Purishkevich, Vladimir Mitrofanovich (1870–1920), politician and accomplice in the assassination of Rasputin
Pusheshnikov, Nikolai Alexeevich (1882–1939), nephew of Ivan Bunin
Pushkin, Alexander Sergeevich (1799–1837), prose writer and poet

Rachmaninoff, Sergei Vasilievich (1873–1943), pianist and composer
Racine, Jean (1639–99), French dramatist
Rasputin, Grigory Efimovich (1871?–1916), wanderer, alleged healer and holy man
Remizov, Alexei Mikhailovich (1877–1957), novelist, dramatist, poet, memoirist, and short-story writer
Repin, Ilya Efimovich (1844–1930), painter
Rimsky-Korsakov, Nikolai Andreevich (1844–1908), composer
Rossolimo, Grigory Ivanovich (1860–1928), friend of Anton Chekhov
Rousseau, Jean-Jacques (1712–78), French philosopher and author
Rozanov, Vasily Vasilievich (1856–1919), writer, critic, philosopher, and journalist
Ryurik (circa 860), semilegendary founder of the first Russian state

Sa'di (1184?–1291), Persian poet
Sagadaichnyi, Pyotr (?–1622), Ukrainian political and military leader
Sakharov, Ivan Nikolaevich (1863–1919), lawyer and political activist
Saltykov-Shchedrin, Mikhail Egorovich (1826–89), writer

Samuel (eleventh century B.C.), Hebrew judge and prophet

Sanin, Alexander Akimovich (1869–1956), theatrical director

Sats, Natalya Il'inchina (1903–63), writer, actor, and director

Schiller, Johann Christoph Friedrich von (1759–1805), German poet and dramatist

Sedykh, Andrei, pseudonym of Yakov Mikhailovich Tsvibak (1902–93), writer, publisher, and editor

Semyonov, Sergei Terentievich (1868–1922), writer and playwright

Serebrov-Tikhonov, Alexander Nikolaevich (1880–1956), writer

Sergeenko, Pyotr Alexeevich (1854–1930), Tolstoyan scholar and writer

Severianin, Igor, pseudonym of Igor Vasilievich Lotaryov (1887–1941), poet

Shakespeare, William (1564–1616), English poet and dramatist

Shavrova-Iust, Elena Mikhailovna (1873–1937), writer

Shchepkina-Kupernik, Tatiana L'vovna (1874–1953), actress

Shchurovsky, Vladimir Andreevich (1852–?), doctor

Shestov, pseudonym of Lev Isaakovich Shvartsman (1866–1938), critic and philosopher

Sinani, Isaak Abramovich (?–1917), shopkeeper

Skabichevsky, Alexander Mikhailovich (1838–1910), literary critic and historian

Skitalets, Stepan Gavrilovich (1861–1941), writer

Smagin, Alexander Ivanovich (n.d.), landowner and suitor of Maria Chekhova

Sobolevsky, Vasily Mikhailovich (1846–1913), editor

Sologub, Fyodor Kuzmich (1863–1927), poet, dramatist, novelist, and short-story writer

Solomon (tenth century B.C.), king of Israel from 961? to 922 B.C.

Solovtsov, Nikolai Nikolaevich (1857–1902), actor, director, and theatrical entrepreneur

Solovyov, Vladimir Sergeivich (1853–1900), philosopher, writer, poet, and teacher

Sredin, Leonid Valentinovich (1860–1909), doctor

Stakhovich, Mikhail Alexandrovich (1861–1923), political figure and member of the Duma

Stalin, Joseph, pseudonym of Iosif Vissarionovich Dzhugashvili (1897–1953), Soviet leader

Stanislavsky, Konstantin Sergeevich (1864–1938), director

Stasyulevich, Mikhail Matveevich (1826–1911), editor

Strakhov, Alexei Alexeivich (1874–?), musician and brother of Lydia Avilova

Strakhov, Fyodor Alexeevich (1861–1923), writer, publicist, Tolstoyan scholar, and brother of Lydia Avilova

Struve, Gleb Petrovich (1898–1985), literary critic and scholar
Sudeikin, Sergei Iurevich (1882–1946), painter and stage designer
Suvorin, Alexei Sergeevich (1834–1912), editor and publisher
Svobodin, Pavel Matveevich (1850–92), actor

Teleshov, Nikolai Dmitrievich (1867–1957), writer
Terpigorev-Atava, Sergei Nikolaevich (1841–95), writer
Tikhonov, Vladimir Alexeevich (1857–1914), writer
Tolstoy, Alexei Nikolaevich (1883–1945), Soviet writer
Tolstoy, Ilya L'vovich (1866–1933), second son of Leo Tolstoy
Tolstoy, Lev (Leo) Nikolaevich (1828–1910), novelist
Tsakni, Anna Nikolaevna (1879–1963), wife of Ivan Bunin from 1898 to
     1899
Turgenev, Ivan Sergeevich (1818–83), novelist, playwright, and short-
     story writer
Tutankhamen (fourteenth century B.C.), pharaoh of Egypt from 1358 to
     1350 B.C.

Vashuk-Neishtadt, Rimma Fyodorovna (1879–1958), friend of Anton
     Chekhov
Vega, Lope de (1562–1635), Spanish dramatist and poet
Veresaev, Vikenty Vikentievich (1867–1945), writer
Veselovsky, Alexander Nikolaevich (1838–1906), professor and academi-
     cian
Vishnevsky, Alexander Leonidovich (1861–1943), friend of Anton
     Chekhov
Voltaire, pseudonym of François-Marie Arouet (1694–1778), French au-
     thor and philosopher
Volynsky, pseudonym of Alexei L'vovich Flekser (1863–1926), critic and
     art historian

Wilson, Edmund (1895–1972), American critic, writer, and dramatist

Yuzhin-Sumbatov, Alexander Ivanovich (1857–1927), actor and playwright

Zaitsev, Boris Konstaninovich (1881–1972), writer and dramatist
Zenzinov, Vladimir Mikhailovich (1880–1953), writer and memoirist
Zhirkevich, Alexander Vladimirovich (1857–1927), lawyer and writer
Zlatovratsky, Nikolai Nikolaevich (1845–1911), writer
Zola, Émile (1840–1902), French writer

Index

Index

Index

Ivan Bunin (1870–1953), a poet and a writer of prose fiction, won the Nobel Prize in Literature in 1933. Three of his works, *Night of Denial: Stories and Novellas*, *The Liberation of Tolstoy: A Tale of Two Writers*, and *The Life of Arseniev: Youth* are also published by Northwestern University Press.

Thomas Gaiton Marullo is the director of the Program in Russian and East European Studies at the University of Notre Dame. He is the author of *If You See the Buddha: Studies in the Fiction of Ivan Bunin* and the editor and translator of five other volumes of Bunin's work: *Ivan Bunin: The Twilight of Émigré Russia, 1934–1953; The Liberation of Tolstoy: A Tale of Two Writers; Cursed Days; Ivan Bunin: From the Other Shore, 1920–1933;* and *Ivan Bunin: Russian Requiem, 1885–1920*.